TRANSACTIONS

OF THE

AMERICAN PHILOSOPHICAL SOCIETY

HELD AT PHILADELPHIA
FOR PROMOTING USEFUL KNOWLEDGE

NEW SERIES—VOLUME 66, PART 5
1976

THE PERSECUTION OF PETER OLIVI

DAVID BURR

Associate Professor of History, Virginia Polytechnic Institute and State University

THE AMERICAN PHILOSOPHICAL SOCIETY
INDEPENDENCE SQUARE
PHILADELPHIA

August, 1976

PUBLICATIONS

OF

The American Philosophical Society

The publications of the American Philosophical Society consist of PROCEEDINGS, TRANSACTIONS, MEMOIRS, and YEAR BOOK.

THE PROCEEDINGS contains papers which have been read before the Society in addition to other papers which have been accepted for publication by the Committee on Publications. In accordance with the present policy one volume is issued each year, consisting of six bimonthly numbers, and the price is $8.00 net per volume.

THE TRANSACTIONS, the oldest scholarly journal in America, was started in 1769 and is quarto size. In accordance with the present policy each annual volume is a collection of monographs, each issued as a part. The current annual subscription price is $20.00 net per volume. Individual copies of the TRANSACTIONS are offered for sale.

Each volume of the MEMOIRS is published as a book. The titles cover the various fields of learning; most of the recent volumes have been historical. The price of each volume is determined by its size and character.

The YEAR BOOK is of considerable interest to scholars because of the reports on grants for research and to libraries for this reason and because of the section dealing with the acquisitions of the Library. In addition it contains the Charter and Laws, and lists of present and former members, and reports of committees and meetings. The YEAR BOOK is published about April 1 for the preceding calendar year. The current price is $5.00.

An author desiring to submit a manuscript for publication should send it to the Editor, George W. Corner, American Philosophical Society, 104 South Fifth Street, Philadelphia, Pa. 19106.

TRANSACTIONS

OF THE

AMERICAN PHILOSOPHICAL SOCIETY

HELD AT PHILADELPHIA
FOR PROMOTING USEFUL KNOWLEDGE

NEW SERIES—VOLUME 66, PART 5
1976

THE PERSECUTION OF PETER OLIVI

DAVID BURR

Associate Professor of History, Virginia Polytechnic Institute and State University

THE AMERICAN PHILOSOPHICAL SOCIETY
INDEPENDENCE SQUARE
PHILADELPHIA

August, 1976

Copyright © 1976 by The American Philosophical Society

Library of Congress Catalog
Card Number 76-24254
International Standard Book Number 0-87169-665-7
US ISSN 0065-9746

PREFACE

Six years ago, when I began research on Petrus Johannis Olivi, I intended to write a book that would tell everything anyone ever wanted to know about him. I eventually came to see that such a book is neither possible nor desirable at this time. Olivi was a prolific writer who produced over sixty works, the precise number depending on how one chooses to divide them up. Only around half of his writings have been published at all, and even fewer have appeared in modern critical editions. Thus a great deal more editorial work will be necessary before anyone can expect to write a definitive study of Olivi.

In the meantime, some value can be derived from a brief, general treatment of Olivi's travails based on what scholars have accomplished to date. The present work attempts to fill this need. It combines analysis of Olivi's thought with a narrative and examination of the various attacks on that thought in his own lifetime and during the first three decades following his death. Presumably such a work will offer an adequate overview for those who are too busy to track down the Olivi manuscripts. Ideally it will inspire other historians to become involved in such research, thereby hastening the day when a better book on Olivi can be written.

Since this work is based largely upon manuscript sources, I have had to face the problem of how citations should be footnoted. After experimenting with several unwieldy arrangements, I finally decided to give folio numbers for one manuscript of each work and cite that manuscript in the bibliography at the end of the book. Thus only one manuscript is listed for each title, even though in most cases the manuscript listed in the bibliography was compared with at least one other.

It goes without saying that this work depends upon the efforts of more people than I can mention here. I am indebted to Warren Lewis for allowing me to check my citations from Olivi's commentary on Revelation against his own critical edition of that work, a valuable piece of scholarship which should be in print by the time this study appears. I am also grateful to David Flood for his encouragement and his massive effort to keep me informed on the state of Olivi scholarship in Europe. The advice and encouragement proffered by Beryl Smalley, Decima Douie, E. R. Daniel, and others were also appreciated.

Although I myself am the major contributor in the financial realm, several organizations have offered considerable help. Preliminary investigations were done in the summer of 1968 at the Southeastern Institute of Medieval and Renaissance Studies, Duke University. In 1969 a grant from the American Philosophical Society allowed me to examine the manuscript sources in Italy and purchase a number of microfilms. In 1970–1971 a grant from the Duke–University of North Carolina Cooperative Program in the Humanities enabled me to spend a year using the library at Duke University. Finally, research funds from Virginia Polytechnic Institute and State University were used for another trip to Italy in 1972 and more microfilms in 1973.

Various libraries and librarians have been of incalculable service. In this country I am particularly thankful for prompt service by the interlibrary loan office at Virginia Polytechnic Institute and State University and for the cooperation extended by librarians at Duke University and Holy Name College during my brief, hectic research trips to these schools during the last few years. Among Italian libraries I am particularly indebted to those who aided me during extended stays at the Biblioteca Laurenziana and Biblioteca Nazionale in Florence, the university library in Padua, and the communal library in Assisi.

Finally, there is the home front. During the last few months I have learned the difference between researching a work like this one and actually completing it. Part of that difference lies in sheer stamina and a concentration approaching monomania. Such excesses can be achieved only in the proper environment, and I shall be eternally grateful to my wife and children for providing that environment.

D. B.

ABBREVIATIONS

Olivi's Works

Amplior declaratio	*Amplior declaratio quinti articuli, qui est de divina essentia* (the appendix on the divine essence sent to the Paris masters along with the 1285 *apologia*)
Apoc.	*Lectura super apocalypsim*
De perf.	*Quaestiones de perfectione evangelica*
Eccl.	*Lectura super Ecclesiasten*
Gen.	*Lectura super Genesim*
Isaiah	*Lectura super Isaiam*
Jn.	*Lectura super Ioannem*
Job	*Lectura super Iob*
Lk.	*Lectura super Lucam*
Letter	*Epistola ad R.*
Minor Prophets	*Lectura super prophetas minores*
Mk.	*Lectura super Marcum*
Mtt.	*Lectura super Matthaeum*
Quodl.	*Quodlibeta*
Responsio I	*Responsio quam fecit P. Ioannis ad litteram magistrorum praesentatam sibi in Avinione* (Olivi's reply to the *Littera septem sigillarum*)
Responsio II	*Responsio P. Ioannis ad aliqua dicta per quosdam magistros Parisienses de suis quaestionibus excerpta* (Olivi's 1285 *apologia*)
Rule Commentary	*Expositio super regulam fratrum minorum* (as edited by Flood in *Olivi's Rule Commentary*)
II Sent.	*Quaestiones in secundum librum sententiarum* (as edited by Jansen, with volume and page numbers in parentheses)

Other Works

Archiv	Heinrich Denifle and Franz Ehrle, *Archiv für Litteratur-und Kirchengeschichte des Mittelalters*
Historia	Angelo Clareno, *Historia septem tribulationum ordinis minorum*

THE PERSECUTION OF PETER OLIVI

David Burr

CONTENTS

	PAGE
I. Time and place	5
II. In defense of poverty	11
III. The shaping of history	17
IV. Scholarly imperatives	24
V. Controversy and censure, 1274–1285	35
VI. Controverted issues: theology	44
VII. Controverted issues: philosophy	52
VIII. Controverted issues: poverty	61
IX. Rehabilitation and later life	67
X. Olivi and the council of Vienne	73
XI. The condemnation of the Revelation commentary	80
XII. Some final observations	90
Bibliography of works cited	93
Index	97

I. TIME AND PLACE

Petrus Iohannis Olivi is little more than a name to most students of medieval history. He is one of those significant second-rate figures who are mentioned but not explored in the major works dealing with his time. To those who have searched more deeply, however, he is an important man indeed. Modern Olivi scholars, having pursued their quarry through the thickets of unpublished manuscript and inaccessible incunabulum, often develop an almost fanatical devotion to the man.

There is nothing particularly novel about this phenomenon. Any number of Olivi's contemporaries would have sympathized completely. In fact, many of them were fanatics when it came to assessing Olivi and his place in history. Conversely, his person and writings seem to have been attacked with something less than scholarly objectivity by those who opposed him.

What little we know about Olivi rests upon the joint effort of his followers and opponents. Many manuscripts of his works are extant because sympathetic readers preserved them at some personal risk, while others have survived because responsible authorities, reacting to charges against Olivi, collected his writings in order to judge them. Our limited biographical information is culled largely from the polemics of defender and attacker alike. Thus it is fitting that the earliest and latest biographical notes should be provided by the fourteenth-century Dominican inquisitor Bernard Gui, who quotes Olivi's followers in the process of attacking them.

It should be noted, however, that the Beguines read, cause to be read, and willingly and frequently hear in their conventicles a certain small work entitled *The Passing of the Holy Father*, in which one finds the following: In the name of our lord Jesus Christ who is blessed in this world, in the year of his incarnation 1297 on Thursday, the day before the ides of March, at the sixth hour in the city of Narbonne the most holy father and most illustrious doctor brother Peter John Olivi left the world in the fiftieth year of his life and thirty-eighth year as a brother minor. He was born at the castle of Serignan, a mile from the sea in the diocese of Béziers, and his most holy body rests in the middle of the choir in the church of the brothers minor at Narbonne. . . . Just before his death, after receiving holy unction, the venerable father said in the presence of the brothers minor of Narbonne that he had received all his knowledge from God through infusion, and that at Paris, in the church at the third hour, he had suddenly been illumined by the lord Jesus Christ.[1]

Since the new year then began at Easter in Olivi's home territory, he died in March, 1298, by our reckoning. Thus he must have been born in 1247 or 1248 and entered the Franciscan order in 1259 or 1260 at the age of twelve, one year younger than the earliest age at which youths were normally admitted.[2] A later reminiscence on Olivi's part establishes that his novitiate was performed at Béziers.[3]

---

[1] Bernardus Guidonis, 1886: p. 287: "Notandum est autem incidenter in hoc loco quod Bequini et Bequine in conventiculis suis legunt aut faciunt legi et audiunt libenter et frequenter quemdam parvulinum libellulum quem intitulant: Transitum sancti Patris; in quo ita scriptum legitur et habetur: In nomine Domini nostri Jhesu Christi que est benedictus in secula. Anno incarnationis ejusdem M°.CC°.XCVII°., pridie ydus martii, die veneris, hora sexta, civitate Narbona, migravit a seculo pater sanctissimus ac preclarissimus doctor frater Petrus Johannis Olivi, anno etatis sue quinquagesimo, anno vero ingressus sui ad religionem Fratrum Minorum XXXVIII°, qui fuit oriundus de castello Serinhani quod per miliare distat a mari in dyocesi Bitterrensi, cujus sacratissimum corpus in Fratrum Minorum Narbone ecclesia in medio chori venerabiliter requiescit. Cujus viri sanctissimi mirandum sue conversionis progressum perfectissimum, necnon et sue conversationis finem gloriossissimum melius fore judico sacro silentio venerandum quam mordacium canum latratibus exponere conculcandum. Unum autem pretermittendum non puto quod dictus pater venerabilis, circa finem sui transitus, post sacram inunctionem receptam, astante sibi conventu Fratrum Minorum Narbone, dixit totam scientiam suam per infusionem recepisse a Deo, et Parisium in ecclesia hora tertia subito se fuisse illuminatum a Domino Jhesu Christo." The document quoted by Gui is also found elsewhere, most notably in MSS. Florence, Bibliotheca Laurenziana, S. Crucis plut. 31 sin. cod. 3, f. 175rb, and Pistoia, Fort. D298, ff. 253v–255v, both of which differ from the excerpt provided by Gui. See the discussion and edition of the Florence manuscript in Heysse, 1918: pp. 263–269, as well as my own comments later in this work.

[2] See Olivi's comments on the proper age of admission in *Mtt.*, f. 118va–vb and *Mk.*, f. 32v.

[3] *Lk.*, f. 20r.

Although Olivi is sometimes referred to as "Petrus Iohannes" in contemporary writings, "Petrus Iohannis" is more common and probably correct. Thus his name was not "Peter John" but "Peter, son of John." The name "Olivi" has been characterized as a latinization of "Olieu."[4]

However one may react to the announcement of Olivi's Parisian illumination, it is clear that he did study there in the 1260's. How early he arrived or how late he stayed remains a mystery, but he himself furnishes evidence that he attended the general chapter meeting of 1266 and heard Bonaventure's *Collations on the Seven Gifts of the Holy Spirit* in 1268.[5] These years in one of the intellectual capitals of Christendom must have had a profound effect upon the young friar, but it is difficult to gauge that effect by his own testimony. His attitude toward Paris will be the subject of some attention in chapter three. For the moment we must be content with the more prosaic question of how far Olivi's education actually progressed.

It is clear that he did not become a master. Olivi himself acknowledges that fact.[6] Bartholomew of Pisa describes him as a *bachalarius formatus* at Paris,[7] but Bartholomew was writing in 1385 and may have assumed as much from the existence of Olivi's commentary on Peter Lombard's *Sentences*. There is no evidence from Olivi's time to suggest that he taught at Paris as a bachelor. In fact, Valens Heynck argues that the evidence points in the opposite direction, since no one attained the baccalauriate before the age of thirty. Olivi was already back in southern France by that time. Moreover, it is significant that the criticism of his views leading up to the censure of 1283 was apparently directed against distinct *quaestiones*, not a *Sentence* commentary. There is, in fact, no evidence of a *Sentence* commentary by Olivi prior to the one he produced in Florence in 1287/88.[8] Heynck concludes that Olivi's teaching career began in the 1270's at Montpellier, where he was a *lector* in the order *studium*. This period of probation would have led to the teaching of the *Sentences* at Paris and eventually to the *magisterium* if Olivi's orthodoxy had not been questioned.

Heynck's argument is hardly conclusive. Extant documents tell us surprisingly little about academic requirements in Olivi's time.[9] It is not even all that clear what "attaining the baccalaureate" would have meant for a Franciscan in the 1260's and 1270's or how it would have related to lecturing on the *Sentences*. The most we can say is that our earliest evidence of Olivi's teaching career places him in southern France in the later 1270's. Heynck specifically mentions Montpellier, but does not document this choice. Certainly Olivi was there at least some of the time before his censure in 1283, but there is no reason to assume that he could not have been elsewhere as well. In fact, other evidence places him at Narbonne.[10]

Olivi's years as a student and teacher formed part of a period in which men inside and outside his order were seeking answers to several important questions. The lot of a Franciscan scholar was not an easy one, and it could often be a dangerous one. Any responsible Franciscan intellectual had to come to terms with at least three important issues.

First, there was the problem of Franciscan poverty. This problem had existed since the earliest days of the order in the sense that the question of more or less strict observance had been inescapable, but its terms changed as the years passed. Saint Francis wanted to emulate the life of Christ and his apostles and saw absolute poverty as a central element in that life. He founded an order which would presumably follow his example and which claimed to do precisely that. Nevertheless, most modern scholars choose to view thirteenth-century Franciscan history as the story of how an original Franciscan ideal was altered by such factors as the needs of the new Franciscan apostolate, increased size and complexity, or simple human frailty. Opinion on this matter is not exactly unanimous. Despite (or perhaps because of) the volume of research done on the thirteenth century, one can see no real consensus emerging. Painstaking research on the relationship between Francis's own aims and those of the early Franciscan order has revealed a set of source problems remarkably similar to the ones faced by New Testament scholars.[11]

The history of the order in the later thirteenth century is perhaps somewhat less beclouded by controversy at the moment, but even here there are serious differences. Some degree of confusion has resulted from the widespread tendency to oversimplify the poverty question by reading it in terms of a dispute between two clearly

---

[4] See Thomas, 1913: pp. 68–69.
[5] For references to his Parisian interlude in Olivi's own works see *Letter*, f. 51 (63) v; *De perf.*, q. 16, f. 71rb; *Quoniam contra paupertatem*, f. 56r; *Apoc.*, f. 69ra.
[6] *Letter*, f. 51(63)v.
[7] See Ehrle, 1887, "Petrus Johannis Olivi," p. 412.
[8] Heynck, 1956: p. 371–398.
[9] See Felder, 1904.

[10] The *Series condemnationum factarum de erroribus quos frater Petrus Iohannis docuit*, a fourteenth-century document published in Amorós, 1931: pp. 495–512, says (p. 502) that the minister general, Jerome of Ascoli, "called a meeting of the brothers" in Montpellier and that some of Olivi's errors were condemned at the meeting. These condemnations, it says, are contained "in the acts of the brothers of the province of Provence." This passage suggests that Olivi was in southern France during at least part of the period 1274–1277, when Jerome was minister general, but it does not conclusively place him in Montpellier. He is definitely located there by his *Letter*, which was composed in Montpellier and, as will be seen shortly, was written in the early 1280's, probably before 1283. Carter Partee, 1960: p. 217, notes a comment in Olivi's II *Sent.*, q. 36 (I, 633): "esto quod angelus velit me videre qui sum Narbonne." These words appear in the question as it is found in MS. Vat. Borgh. 322, f. 19va, a manuscript which antedates the censure of 1283. Thus Olivi must also have spent some time in Narbonne before that date.
[11] For a survey of research to date see Lambert, 1961: ch. 1.

distinguishable parties in the order perduring throughout the thirteenth century. This temptation is understandable but unfortunate. Various groups and individuals were indeed given a high degree of coherence in retrospect by Angelo Clareno and others from the early fourteenth century on, but once one ceases to view the thirteenth century through the eyes of the fourteenth-century polemicists one finds little evidence for the constant existence of a well-defined "spiritual" movement with a common set of assumptions and goals. Much less can one map the history of a "conventual" movement.

Nevertheless, the opportunity for disagreement was always present. One can see portents of things to come as early as the 1240's, when the March of Ancona became the scene of serious conflict.[12] The same area exploded again in the 1270's[13] while Olivi was in southern France. The situation in Olivi's own area is less clear. From what we know regarding Hugh of Digne it is certain that the more rigorous interpreters of the Franciscan rule were represented in Olivi's territory by the middle of the thirteenth century, but there is no evidence that the Italian conflict in the 1270's had a French counterpart. Least of all is there any evidence of a "spiritual party" which Olivi could join and later head. Here too, however, the poverty question was undoubtedly a live issue, and what we shall soon recognize as evidence of trouble in the early 1280's makes it at least likely that the brethren in southern France were beginning to take sides during the preceding decade.

It is not entirely clear why the early years of Olivi's teaching career should have marked the point at which the poverty dispute began to acquire new dimensions. Some historians tend to feel that Bonaventure's accession as minister general in 1257 marked a major turning point inasmuch as the more rigorous course previously charted by John of Parma was abandoned in favor of a more moderate approach which seemed to ensure stability, prestige, and privilege for the order but eventually contributed to the alienation of those who wished to pursue the more primitive Franciscan life style.[14] Others emphasize (probably correctly) the continuity between Bonaventure and John of Parma, arguing that the succession had less impact than the later spirituals assumed.[15] Malcolm Lambert suggests that Bonaventure could not have exerted any significant effect upon the course of events, since his freedom to act was severely limited by the fact that "the main pattern of observance had already been set for him by the existing Franciscan constitutions and the papal legislation of the previous thirty years."[16] This legacy, Lambert says, "contained a basic contradiction—between the needs of the apostolate and the ideal of poverty." The unresolved contradiction would eventually frustrate Bonaventure's efforts and lead to the difficulties of Olivi's time.

However fruitful it may be to search for critical moments before or during Bonaventure's generalate, one must recognize the extent to which Olivi's own period was unique in itself and exerted its own influence upon the course of Franciscan history. In some respects the 1270's can be seen as the end of an era. These years saw the clear-cut victory of the mendicant orders over those who would question their Biblical, theological, or philosophical underpinnings. When Bonaventure died at the Council of Lyons in 1274, he and his order had gone a long way toward achieving that victory. They had powerful allies. At Lyons, attacks against the mendicants failed because Pope Gregory X defended the friars. In 1279 Gregory's successor Nicholas III gave official sanction to the Franciscan self-understanding in the bull *Exiit qui seminat*. In 1282 Martin IV again backed the Franciscans in the bull *Ad fructus uberes*. By the early 1280's the opposition had not disappeared, but its fangs had been pulled. Thus relieved of attacks from the secular clergy, the mendicant orders were free to turn upon one another and upon themselves. Dominicans and Franciscans, once united against their assailants among the secular clergy, could now find time to examine one another's shortcomings, as in fact they had already been doing in England since the late 1260's or early 1270's. Moreover, in the following decades Franciscans could explore the ways in which they differed from other Franciscans. The enemy without could be replaced by the enemy within.

The battles of preceding decades had given Franciscans in the late 1270's and early 1280's not only the leisure to attack one another but the weapons with which to do so more effectively. In the course of the secular-mendicant controversy Bonaventure and others had elaborated a doctrine of Franciscan poverty which made explicit what had been only hazily stated before. Thus the contestants of Olivi's day were given a relatively sophisticated intellectual context in which to discuss the issues that divided them.

The late 1270's mark an important change in another respect. It was the Franciscans' tragedy that at the moment when they were surmounting external challenges and might have turned to internal consolidation their period of strong leadership came to an end. Bonaventure had been minister general for seventeen years. He was succeeded by Jerome of Ascoli, a man who, although competent enough, was kept busy doing other things for a succession of popes. Thus during a critical five-year period the order was left to drift. Bonagratia

---

[12] See Angelo Clareno, 1886: pp. 256 ff.

[13] *Ibid.*, pp. 301–305.

[14] For a recent example of this view see Moorman, 1968. Bonaventure's contribution is, of course, described with varying degrees of enthusiasm by such historians. Some see him as the savior of his order, others as its perverter.

[15] See, for example, Lambert, 1961: ch. 2.

[16] *Ibid.*, p. 124.

of St. John in Persiceto, who became minister general when Jerome resigned in 1279, tried to exercise firm and positive leadership but died in the attempt. His demise in 1283 was followed by a two-year vacancy, then a succession of two short generalates by Arlotto of Prato (1285–1286) and Matthew of Aquasparta (1287–1289). One wonders how much difference it would have made if Bonaventure had been followed by an equally imposing figure whose generalate lasted an equally long time.

Olivi's years as student and teacher also encompassed some of the most spectacular moments in another great debate, the argument over Aristotelian philosophy. By Olivi's time Aristotle had been the object of intense study for over a century, and at no time had the reactions been consistently favorable. Nevertheless, all the ingredients of a first-rate confrontation were not present until the later thirteenth century.[17] The translation, dissemination, and assimilation of Aristotle's works was a gradual affair. His *logica vetus* had been known since the days of Boethius and his *logica nova* was readily available by the end of the twelfth century. By the early years of the thirteenth century most of his other works were in circulation and a number of commentaries on his writings could be consulted.

By that time churchmen at Paris had signaled their alarm by banning the teaching of Aristotle's natural philosophy. It is not clear when (or even whether) this ban was formally lifted, but we know that Roger Bacon lectured on Aristotle's physics at Paris around 1250 and that the rest of his philosophy was being taught shortly thereafter. By that time Aristotle's commentators, particularly the Islamic philosophers Avicenna and Averroes, were also widely used.

If all the new elements were thus introduced by the middle of the thirteenth century, it was during the second half of the century that real differences regarding their assimiliation began to appear. Many historians of medieval philosophy have found it useful to describe these differences in terms of the interaction of three major points of view. First, there was the essentially Aristotelian orientation displayed by Thomas Aquinas and others, who tended to approach Aristotle with a measure of confidence that his thought, properly interpreted, would be found generally consistent with the Christian faith. Second, there was the essentially Augustinian approach which reached its highest development in the writings of Bonaventure. This position tended to regard Aristotle with suspicion, although its adherents made use of Aristotelian philosophy. Finally, there was the Averroist point of view espoused by Siger of Brabant and others, according to which Aristotle as interpreted (in a strikingly non-Christian way) by Averroes was to be regarded as the voice of natural reason.

During the last thirty years this typology has been subjected to repeated attacks by Fernand van Steenberghen, who denies the validity of the "Augustinian" and "Averroist" categories and raises significant questions about the motives and intellectual sophistication of the various parties. The battle has continued down to the present without resolution, leaving observers a bit confused as to which differences are substantive and which merely terminological.

At any rate, it is clear that in Olivi's time scholars at the University of Paris were coming to grips with a series of questions which involved Aristotle yet pointed beyond him. As to Aristotle himself, the main question was whether his philosophy was consistent with the Christian faith, and this issue involved the subsidiary question of what Aristotle actually said. Did he or did he not espouse such ungodly notions as the eternity of the world? The real dimensions of the problem are revealed, however, only when Aristotle is seen not as an individual but in his role as natural man engaged in the quest for truth without benefit of Christian revelation. At this level the question was not one of Aristotle's personal failings but rather of the limitations of even dangers of human reason in matters of ultimate concern. The debate over Aristotle was, in short, a springboard to more basic issues such as the relationship between faith and reason or nature and grace. In the course of the later thirteenth and early fourteenth centuries continued meditation on these matters would radically alter the shape of medieval theology.

In the meantime, religious leaders were not above trying to end debate by coercive legislation. The most famous of these attempts were the two condemnations of 1270 and 1277 by Stephen Tempier, bishop of Paris,[18] and the parallel action in 1277 by Robert Kilwardby, archbishop of Canterbury.[19] The battle was joined on several levels and the University of Paris itself attempted to establish norms which would limit the dangers of philosophical speculation.[20] The religious orders also reacted to the crisis, and the nature of their response is of central importance for the matter at hand.

By the time Olivi arrived in Paris, both mendicant orders had established the right to exercise supervision over their members' intellectual activities. The general chapter held by the Franciscans at Narbonne in 1260 prohibited circulation outside the order of any new work which had not been examined and given official approval. The same chapter probably also forbade the assertion of views commonly rejected by Franciscan masters.[21] The Dominican order had already prohibited publication of works without official permission.[22]

---

[17] For a brief survey of this matter see Steenberghen, 1970 or Leff, 1968: ch. 5.

[18] *Chartularium universitatis parisiensis* (hereafter *Chart.*), 1889: 1: pp. 486–487 and 543–558.

[19] *Ibid.* 1: pp. 558 f. The battle in England was continued by Archbishop John Pecham. See *ibid.* 1: pp. 624–627 and 634 f.

[20] *Ibid.* 1: pp. 499 f., 586 f., and 538 f.

[21] See Bihl, 1941: p. 73.

[22] See *Acta capitulorum generalium ordinis praedicatorum*

The condemnations of 1277 left the two orders in notably different positions. Since one of the Dominicans' most illustrious scholars, Thomas Aquinas, held some of the views condemned at that time, it is understandable that the order should have embarked upon a campaign to protect his name. In reality, the Dominicans went well beyond a simple defense of Aquinas's orthodoxy. Despite the diversity of philosophical and theological outlooks within the order—a diversity made glaringly apparent by the fact that Kilwardby was a Dominican—the general chapter of 1278 began the movement toward establishment of Thomism as the only acceptable stance within the order when it dispatched two friars to England to investigate those criticizing Thomas's writings.[23] The next chapter was somewhat more explicit, calling for the punishment of those who spoke irreverently of Thomas or his writings.[24] In 1286 still another general chapter commanded that all brothers study and support Thomas's views insofar as they were able. Those doing the opposite were to be punished and suspended from their offices and privileges.[25] General chapters in 1309, 1313, and 1315 commanded that his views be taught and prohibited teachers from contradicting him or even citing contrary views without explicitly refuting them.[26] By the latter date individual members of the order had already learned the price of disobedience, as is seen in the well-known case of Durandus of St. Porciano (censured in 1314)[27] and the less famous but hardly less striking case of Ubertus Guidi, a bachelor in Florence who, having publicly contradicted Thomas on several issues, was called upon to retract his statements, removed from his academic functions for two years, and shipped off to the convent at Pistoia, where he dined on bread and water for ten days.[28]

It must be noted that the Dominicans were not the only order to follow this course. The Augustinians found themselves in an analogous position insofar as their most promising scholar, Aegidius Romanus, was censured at Paris shortly after the condemnation of 1277.[29] The parallel was completed in 1287 when a general chapter of the order commanded that masters and scholars assent to and defend "the opinions, positions and views written and yet to be written" of Aegidius Romanus, a reminder that their chosen authority still had a long academic career ahead of him at the time.[30]

The Franciscan order found itself in a rather different situation after 1277. Its leading theologians were not seriously threatened by the events of that year. In fact, Franciscan scholars had been among the most zealous opponents of an uncritical Aristotelianism, and their opposition probably constituted an important part of the background from which the official action of 1277 emerged.[31] The Paris condemnation soon made its appearance in the official decisions of the Franciscan order. In 1279 the general chapter at Assisi explicitly alluded to it in prohibiting opinions rejected "by the bishop and the Paris masters."[32] The next general chapter, held at Strasbourg in 1282, limited the reading of Thomas Aquinas to the more educated brethren, who were to read it with the help of William de Mare's corrections.[33] It also commanded that ministers report to the general minister any brother who pertinaciously defended unsound opinions.[34] The following year, the order officially discovered such opinions in the writings of Peter John Olivi.

It is unlikely that Olivi was the first Franciscan to be so treated, since Roger Bacon was probably imprisoned for doctrinal reasons somewhere between 1277 and 1279. It is unfortunate that we know so little about this event, since it might well cast some light upon Olivi's case. Given the present evidence, however, we must confess almost total ignorance.[35]

If Olivi's generation was involved in the debate over Aristotle, it was also involved in the dispute over another figure—this time a Christian—whose orthodoxy seemed questionable to many. Joachim of Fiore was hardly the first man to discover the joys of apocalyptic speculation. For centuries Christian authors had been exploring the prophetic possibilities of such Biblical sources as Daniel and Revelation, not to mention non-Biblical sources like the sibylline oracles and prophecies of Merlin.[36] By the thirteenth century there was a healthy tradition of such scholarship and thus there was nothing inherently ridiculous about the notion that a careful examination of Daniel 7 or Revelation 6 might enable the Christian to construct a theology of history which would explain the past, illuminate the present and even predict the future.

(hereafter *Acta*) **1**: pp. 69 and 78 in: *Monumenta ordinis fratrum praedicatorum historica*, 1898: 3.

[23] *Ibid.* **1**: p. 199; *Chart.* **1**: pp. 566 f. Their powers were more than simply investigative, since they could remove men from office and send them out of the province.

[24] *Acta* **1**: p. 204.

[25] *Acta* **1**: p. 235; *Chart.* **2**: p. 6.

[26] *Acta* **2**: pp. 38 and 64; *Chart.* **2**: pp. 166 f. and 173.

[27] See Koch, 1927: pp. 412 f.

[28] *Chart.* **2**: p. 174.

[29] See Hocedez, 1932: pp. 34–58.

[30] *Chart.* **2**: p. 12. A similar obligation was imposed in 1290. See *Chart.* **2**: pp. 40–42.

[31] See Hadrianus a Krizovljan, 1957: pp. 121–165 and *idem*, 1961: pp. 133–175.

[32] Bihl, 1929: p. 80.

[33] Fussenegger, 1933: p. 139.

[34] *Ibid.*, p. 137. Fussenegger claims (p. 130) that this command refers "without doubt" to Olivi. It is of course possible but, considering the temper of the times, by no means definite.

[35] See the differing interpretations offered by Crowley, 1950, and Easton, 1952.

[36] See Southern, 1972, for an informative overview of this matter.

Nevertheless, it was Joachim more than any other writer who set the tone for avante-garde apocalyptic speculation in the thirteenth century. While his trinitarian views had been condemned at the fourth Lateran council in 1215, his theology of history had emerged unscathed and soon gained currency throughout the west. There is some debate among scholars as to precisely what is unique in Joachim's historical outlook, but little question as to its impact. Up to the 1240's interest centered upon his *concordia* between the New and Old Testaments and his prophecies regarding the Antichrist. After that date attention came to be focused on his tripartite division of all history into the ages of father, son, and holy spirit.[37]

According to Joachim, history was trembling on the brink of the third age. The immediate prospect was a frightening one. The elect would suffer extreme persecution at the hands of the ungodly. In the long run, however, this persecution would have a positive effect, purifying the spiritual men who, armed with a new understanding of the faith, would become leaders of the church in the new age.

As early as the 1240's Joachim's thought had begun to exercise a peculiar fascination for some Franciscans, who thought they detected in it a valuable tool for interpreting the historical significance of their own order.[38] Such interest seemed warranted by the fact that Joachim had assigned an important role to two future orders of spiritual men, a prophecy easily applied to the mendicants; yet Joachim's appeal to Franciscan sensibilities was based on affinities more fundamental and pervasive than any particular prediction or speculation. Joachim expected something very important to happen in the near future. Franciscans thought something very important had happened in the life and work of their founder. In the twilight of history, as a deteriorating world staggered toward the Antichrist and judgment, God had sent a new order to renew the life of Christ and his apostles.

There were, of course, significant differences between the emerging Franciscan theology of history and the one offered by Joachim. The early Franciscan view placed greater emphasis on renewal, return to the apostolic pattern, while Joachim's outlook was more evolutionary, stressing a progressive development in history.[39] Nevertheless, the affinities were strong enough to make Joachim an important source for some Franciscans who sought to deepen their own self-understanding.

There was no single, characteristic Franciscan use of Joachim. Modern historians are understandably tempted to concentrate their attention on the more radical and therefore more interesting Joachimism developed by Gerard of Borgo San Donino, whose condemnation in 1255 caused his order a great deal of embarrassment and contributed to the fall of a minister general, John of Parma. Gerard, proceeding from Joachim's tripartite division of history, anticipated the imminent dawning of an age of the holy spirit in which the Franciscans would supplant existing clerical orders and Joachim's writings would replace the New Testament.[40] In such a view the progressive aspects of Joachim's thought, developed in a way Joachim would have found disturbing, led to a repudiation of existing ecclesiastical structures and even the Christian faith itself as previous generations had known it.

Nevertheless, Joachim's influence was also felt in the most respectable circles. Bonaventure, while rejecting Joachim's trinitarian errors and the excesses of the radical Franciscan Joachimites, was himself willing to utilize Joachimite perspectives in contemplating the historical significance of his order, making particularly effective use of Joachim's division of history into seven ages of Old Testament and seven of the New Testament.[41] Thus for a large number of scholars in Olivi's time the question was not whether to employ Joachim's theories but how to employ them and which to employ.

It would be nice to know more than we do about Joachimite currents in southern France prior to Olivi's day. It is clear that such existed. Salimbene reports that Hugh of Digne was an ardent Joachimite.[42] Nevertheless, we are not entirely sure what kind he was and the connection between Hugh and Olivi, if such existed, remains hidden from modern historians.

In any case, Olivi's early years as a teacher were certainly a period in which important debates were being carried on within his order. A number of issues furnished occasion for controversy and recrimination. Moreover, there was a strong temptation to foreshorten debate through the use of official coercion. How successfully Olivi maneuvered in such perilous waters will become evident in chapter four, when we examine the events leading up to the censure of 1283. First, however, something should be said to delineate Olivi's own attitude toward his order and his task as a Christian scholar.

---

[37] See Reeves, 1969, part 1, ch. 4–6.

[38] For the beginnings of Joachimite influence on Franciscan thought see Daniel, 1968: pp. 671–676; *idem*, 1975: pp. 76–80; Reeves, 1969: p. 184.

[39] This point is emphasized by Daniel, 1975: p. 27.

[40] On Gerard see Denifle, 1885: pp. 49–142; Reeves, 1969: pp. 59–70 and 187–190.

[41] See Ratzinger, 1959; McGinn, 1971: pp. 42–45; Reeves, 1969: pp. 179–181. It should be noted that throughout this work the word "Joachimite" will be used to describe views considered characteristic of Joachim, like the tripartite division of history into ages of the father, son and holy spirit and the parallel sets of seven Old Testament and New Testament periods. This is a somewhat narrower sense than the one given to the word "Joachite" by Reeves, 1969, but broader than those assigned to "Joachite" and "Joachimite" by Daniel, 1975: p. 76 and McGinn, 1971: p. 35.

[42] Salimbene, 1966: p. 339.

II. IN DEFENSE OF POVERTY

Wherever Olivi may have been teaching in the late 1270's and early 1280's, the period was an extremely fruitful one for him. A surprising number of his extant writings seem to date from this period. Their relation to his teaching career is hardly obvious, however.

Certainly he lectured on various books of the Bible. His commentaries on Matthew and Isaiah belong to this period, and he probably dealt with other books as well. In addition he may have lectured on the *Sentences*, although there is no evidence that he did so. A number of the *quaestiones* which are now considered to represent his *Summa* or *Questions on the Sentences* (as distinguished from the extant *Sentence* commentary dating from a later period) were written during this period,[1] but it does not inevitably follow that these questions arose from classroom lectures on the *Sentences*. In fact, a later remark by Olivi seems to indicate that they were written, not for dissemination in the classroom, but for his own private edification and, as it were, for private circulation within a limited circle.[2] Olivi's way of citing these early questions, his comments on his own activities, and the available manuscript evidence all seem to indicate that they were originally conceived as discrete examinations of particular issues connected with the *Sentences*.

At this time Olivi was also turning out a series of works on the Franciscan life in general and Franciscan poverty in particular. In 1279 his aid was solicited in connection with the writing of *Exiit qui seminat*, the papal bull which gave enthusiastic support to the Franciscans in their struggle against secular opponents. It seems that Olivi, who was in Rome at the time, was asked by his provincial minister to contribute something for the edification of the ministers and masters gathered at Soriano to advise the pope.[3] It has been suggested that during this same Italian excursion Olivi visited Assisi and wrote his treatise on the Portiuncula indulgence.[4] If so, perhaps here too his advice was useful to a pope, for the indulgence was confirmed shortly thereafter by Martin IV.

During the same period Olivi produced his treatise beginning with the words *quoniam contra paupertatem evangelicam*,[5] an important polemic which reflects the increasing strife within the order over whether the rule binds Franciscans to a limited use of the resources at their disposal. By the time he wrote it he had already written a good number of what are now known as his *Questions on Evangelical Perfection*, perhaps the most important source for his understanding of the Franciscan life.[6] There is at least some haziness involved in the very notion of the *Questions on Evangelical Perfection*. The title is usually used in reference to seventeen questions found in manuscript Vat. lat. 4986 and elsewhere—all seventeen in 4986, various questions elsewhere—and described as a unit by modern scholars. The number and order of these questions vary in different manuscripts and there is no agreement among scholars as to which arrangement represents Olivi's final redaction; yet it is widely held that the first ten or eleven questions were composed as a unit in their present order before 1279 and that sixteen of the seventeen questions were written early in Olivi's career, probably by 1282.[7] The first part of this view is at least open to question, but the manuscript evidence indicates that, whatever the circumstances of their composition, Olivi had placed the first ten questions in their present order by a very early date.

A final category of Olivian writings from this period remains to be mentioned: The polemical works undertaken in connection with a bitter dispute between Olivi and a group of detractors in southern France. These works and their relation to the writings already mentioned in this chapter can be ignored for the moment, since they will be discussed at length in chapter five.

No one can examine Olivi's early career without being impressed by the number and quality of the works produced by him before 1283. By that year he had accomplished most of the writings given particular attention by modern scholars. The achievement is particularly impressive when we recall that by 1282 he was still under thirty-five years of age.

Olivi's view of his order and its mission emerges clearly from these writings. It is found, not merely in the works explicitly devoted to that topic, but in the Bible commentaries as well. In fact, for reasons that will become apparent in the next chapter, some aspects of his view are more sharply delineated in the Bible commentaries than anywhere else. Nevertheless, the main source for his view of poverty and its role in Franciscan life is certainly the *Questions on Evangelical Perfection*, particularly questions eight and nine. The *Questions on Evangelical Perfection* as a whole actually transcend the question of poverty, placing it and other issues within the context of a more encompassing vision of the Christian life at its most intense. The eighth and ninth questions deal explicitly with poverty, but see it as part of a single *Gestalt* in which various aspects of the Christian life mutually reinforce one another. At the same time, in these two questions poverty is placed in its Biblical context by relating it to Christ and the apostles and in the context of Olivi's own historical

---

[1] For discussion of the dating see Heynck, 1956: pp. 371–398 and *idem*, 1964: pp. 335–364.

[2] *Responsio* II, p. 132.

[3] This information is furnished by Olivi himself in *Rule Commentary*, p. 159. The work contributed by Olivi is extant. It is the treatise *Quod regula fratrum minorum excludit omnem proprietatem*, edition cited in bibliography.

[4] *De veritate indulgentiae de Portiuncula*, pp. 139–145.

[5] It is found in MS. Vat. lat. 4986, ff. 49r–57v.

[6] For bibliographical data on these questions see the bibliography at the end of this book.

[7] For example, see Emmen and Simoncioli, 1963: p. 385.

situation by relating it to St. Francis, his order, and their place in Christian history. Finally, in the course of these questions Olivi considers practically every imaginable argument for the superiority of wealth and provides some sort of response from the Christian perspective.

It is important to emphasize that for Olivi poverty is not simply one more ideal readily separable from other aspects of the Christian life, but rather a major link in the complex chain of elements which combine to produce evangelical perfection. For example, poverty is closely related to humility. Among carnal men nothing is more contemptible than poverty, and the poor man is counted as nothing in the eyes of the world. Thus he who voluntarily chooses poverty performs an act of highest humility because in doing so he wills his own abnegation and, as it were, his own annihilation.[8] He has robbed himself of the greatest occasion for wordly reputation and pride.

It is noteworthy that Olivi argues not simply for poverty but for absolute poverty effected by means of a vow. Perfect humility is achieved by complete lack of ownership as opposed not only to private ownership but to common ownership as well, for the corporate wealth of a monastery can also be an occasion for pride. Again, it is best achieved by a vow of poverty, for such a vow removes not only present wealth but the hope of future wealth, and elimination of this hope schools the passions by decreasing desire. Olivi notes that, while flying is in itself more desirable than riding a horse, possibility makes men yearn to ride rather than to fly.[9]

Olivi's attitude toward vows constitutes an important element in his treatment of poverty and merits at least passing reference. In the fifth of the *Questions on Evangelical Perfection* he asks whether it is better to perform an act with or without a vow and decides for the former.[10] In his consideration of the question he takes full account of the strongest arguments for the opposite view. For one, a vow places man in danger of sin through exposing him to the possibility of breaking that vow. Again, vows seem to rob their accompanying actions of precisely that voluntary element which determines the measure of their merit. Again, by prohibiting that which was formerly licit vows increase concupiscence in good Pauline fashion, introducing the law where it was previously unknown. Again, Christ neither vowed nor told his disciples to do so.

Olivi's positive argument is a masterly attempt to neutralize such objections. The value of a vow is seen in what is surrendered through it: Not only our works but our freedom, which is of the highest value. The merit of a vow in Olivi's eyes depends upon the fact that freedom is simultaneously given and retained in it.

On the one hand it involves an infinity of merit because, in the moment of vowing, man surrenders his freedom not only for that moment but for every future moment. On the other hand, the subject does retain his freedom in the sense that he remains capable of free choice. Thus in voluntarily adhering to the vow in future moments he perenially ratifies it. The merit involved in a vow is, then, a multiple of infinity, with the subject constantly giving free consent to the act by which he surrenders his freedom for all time.[11]

In considering the question of whether vows decrease the merit of good works by making them easier to perform, Olivi distinguishes between two kinds of difficulty, the subjective type arising from impediments in the doer and the objective type based on the nature of the work to be done. The latter increases merit, the former does not. Thus it is more meritorious for a poor man to give a certain sum to charity than for a rich man to give the same amount, but it is no more meritorious for a miser to give that sum than for a generous man to do so. The value of a vow is seen in the fact that the extra difficulty added by it is of the objective sort, thereby increasing merit while it actually lessens subjective difficulty.[12]

As to the matter of whether Christ vowed or demanded vows, Olivi argues that wherever Christ commended the acts of evangelical perfection he presupposed that they would be assumed through a vow, "for no one perfectly surrenders all things if he retains the power to acquire them again, nor does he perfectly make himself a eunuch if he is still able to marry." [13]

Olivi acknowledges that what is better in the abstract may not always be preferable in a particular case. While fine in itself, a vow may not always be expedient. If there is serious risk of transgression or if the vow involves something which might possibly be evil at some future time, it is more expedient not to vow.[14]

Poverty is also closely related to chastity. The married man must have sufficient wealth to provide for his wife and children. He must provide a decent inheritance for the latter, "for they should not be forced into poverty by the father." [15] Thus marriage calls for a degree of wealth, and poverty precludes marriage. "By natural order," Olivi says, "the election of poverty includes in itself the election of chastity."

The connection does not apply only in the case of marriage. Poverty and chastity are also related insofar as wealth provides greater opportunity for unchastity outside wedlock. Just as a man who finds himself alone with women is in more danger than one who avoids such situations, so a man who has some chance of succeeding with women is more easily tempted than one

---

[8] *De perf.*, q. 8, ff. 5rb–vb.

[9] *Ibid.*, f. 5vb.

[10] *De perf.*, q. 5: "An sit melius aliquid facere ex voto quam sine voto."

[11] *Ibid.*, f. 97 f.

[12] *Ibid.*, f. 106.

[13] *Ibid.*, f. 107.

[14] *Ibid.*, f. 101.

[15] *De perf.*, q. 8, f. 7rb–va.

who can expect only rejection. In this area as in others, money talks. Thus the rich man is tempted to exploit his advantage to his own detriment.

Poverty is also closely related to the love which unites men in fellowship, just as wealth is a powerful destroyer of that love. "Nothing," Olivi says, "corrupts the truth and fidelity of friendship like the love of wealth." [16] As examples he points to the prince's joy when the throne is vacated through the death of the king; the son's pleasure when his father dies and leaves an inheritance; and—closer to home for Olivi—the priest's elation over the death of one who will be buried under his auspices and thus enrich the church.

Wealth brings with it fraud and deceit. The rich man is surrounded by a swarm of sycophants indistinguishable from his friends. Only through financial disaster can the two groups be sorted out. The rich man's predicament in this respect stems from his status not only as a source of gain but also as an object of fear. The poor fawn upon him because they know that he can destroy as well as build. The deceit practiced by others leads almost inevitably to self-deceit. The wealthy, constantly exposed to flattery, are more likely than the poor to overlook their own flaws, since no one dares to expose them.

Wealth also destroys love by ushering in discord and contention. Where there is property, people will fight over it. Olivi duly notes that here, as elsewhere, common possession is no solution. He points to the spectacle of religious houses battling with one another over property or within themselves over rights and powers.

Poverty is also closely related to liberality. The professor of voluntary poverty gives most happily because he has no love for possessions. He gives most promptly because he wants to surrender his property even when there is no one to whom he can give it. He gives most abundantly because he surrenders for all time all of his own possessions and all that he or others ever wanted or could want. By persevering in his vow he constantly surrenders all past, present, and future possessions.[17]

Poverty is also closely related to fortitude, for it implies "not only the surrender of possessions but a great contempt for all carnal life, and nothing so renders a man timid, inconstant and fearful in undertaking arduous and difficult enterprises as does fear of losing his possessions or his life." Again, the vow of poverty encourages fortitude through fear of public derision, "lest it be said that this man began to build and could not complete his work." [18]

Poverty is closely related to faith. Voluntary surrender of one's worldly possessions implies the highest faith in Christ's teachings and in divine providence. Poverty turns the mind from sensible to eternal things, and faith is itself "the firm application of the mind to invisible and eternal things." [19]

The reverse is also true. Luxury and heresy both spring from the same root, excessive preoccupation with the things of this world. Olivi argues that almost all the intellectual errors which may arise among philosophers and theologians are rooted in an overvaluation of sensible things. Thus the errors so hotly debated in his own time, those stemming from Aristotelian philosophy, arose because Aristotle, overvaluing the things of this world, put his faith in sense experience and considered impossible anything which seemed inconsistent with the data gained through empirical observation.[20]

Aristotle is hardly the only guilty party in this respect. Olivi argues that "the overvaluation of private wealth is the singular foundation of . . . the sect of Antichrist and of all the Judiac and Saracen errors." It strikes at the heart of Christianity, the doctrine of Christ, for if wealth is superior to poverty Christ is not the messiah promised by the Old Testament. Here Olivi links poverty not only with Christianity but with the sort of Bible exegesis he considers to be characteristically Christian. The Jews, who interpret the Old Testament carnally, look for a messiah who will give them wealth and dominion. The Christians, worshiping a messiah who rejected wealth and power, interpret the Old Testament spiritually, referring the critical passages to spiritual rather than temporal riches. The spiritual interpretation assumes the superiority of poverty over wealth, just as the carnal interpretation assumes the superiority of wealth over poverty. Thus the exaltation of poverty is not only a characteristically Christian idea but is, in fact, a cornerstone of the faith.

Finally, poverty is related to contemplation. In turning the mind from sensible things it prepares man for that wisdom which is hidden from human eyes. In turning him from the pursuit of wealth it gives him more time and desire for study. In showing him the vanity of temporal and sensible things it teaches him to look for the spiritual or contemplative sense in Biblical passages which discuss such matters and thus offers a key to the interpretation of scripture.

The preceding comments hardly do justice to the complex web of interrelationships by which Olivi binds poverty to other aspects of the Christian life. Those wishing to explore the matter further need only look at the eighth of his *Questions on Evangelical Perfection* to appreciate how many other elements he puts into play. This sort of treatment represents only one aspect of his brief for poverty, however. Like other Franciscan apologists of his day Olivi tries to give his order Biblical

---

[16] *Ibid.*, f. 7vb.

[17] *Ibid.*, f. 9ra–va. Note the connection with Olivi's argument in q. 5.

[18] *Ibid.*, ff. 11vb–12ra.

[19] *Ibid.*, f. 12vb.

[20] For this and the following see *ibid.*, ff. 12vb–16rb.

sanction by showing that Christ and his disciples practiced evangelical poverty.[21]

The discussion of poverty in New Testament times includes both offensive and defensive tactics. On the one hand, Olivi marshals all available passages from the Bible and the fathers to show that Christ and his disciples were absolutely without possessions. Christ's benediction upon evangelical poverty is seen in his decision to be born of parents so poor that they could afford nothing better than a stable at the time of his birth, so poor that they had to offer doves rather than a lamb. Olivi contends that Christ himself begged in his youth. At the end of his life he spent the night in Bethany because he was too poor to find lodging in Jerusalem. He died without clothes or disciples, bereft of all things. Had he possessed anything one would expect him to have given it to his mother at the end; yet nothing was forthcoming. Olivi argues at length that the same poverty displayed by Christ in his own life was strongly emphasized in his teaching and practiced by his disciples.

The defensive element in Olivi's discussion arises from the fact that certain Biblical texts could be cited against the Franciscan reading of apostolic poverty. For example, there was the embarrassing fact that Christ and his disciples carried a purse. Olivi says, among other things, that they had it for purposes of pastoral care and used it for themselves only in case of necessity, as in Samaria where hostility toward them made it necessary to buy food rather than live from alms. In parrying such objections Olivi is always intriguing, often ingenious, and sometimes convincing.

The proper interpretation of such passages was obviously important to Olivi and his fellow Franciscans, since they claimed to practice the same poverty embraced by Christ and the disciples. The New Testament situation held even greater significance for Olivi, since he saw it as one major element in a complex pattern of historical development which, properly understood, would enable him to interpret past and present events and even anticipate the future to some extent. His attitude toward his order and its practice of poverty can be appreciated only when it is viewed in relation to his theology of history. Nevertheless, the latter subject is such a complex one that it deserves its own chapter and must be bypassed for the moment.

So far we have seen how Olivi argued in favor of absolute poverty against the proponents of private or common possessions. This sort of argument was dear to Franciscans of his time. In the second half of the thirteenth century it had a fair amount of existential significance, since the Franciscans really did have to defend themselves against attacks from outside the order. By the late 1270's and early 1280's, however, another great battle was beginning. This one was largely a fraternal affair and was centered around the question of *usus pauper*. Olivi had a great deal to say about this problem too, and the discerning reader will see in his writings an index of how the poverty dispute had changed in the single generation that separated Bonaventure from Olivi. By Olivi's time Franciscan scholars were still engaged in the secular-mendicant controversy, but their efforts on this score represented little more than mopping-up operations. The really live issue was now *usus pauper*.

Olivi's thoughts on this matter are most clearly stated in two works written sometime in the late 1270's and early 1280's. One of them, the ninth of his *Questions on Evangelical Perfection*, can be dated before March, 1279, since it antedates *Exiit qui seminat*.[22] Here Olivi asks whether *usus pauper* is included in the council or vow of poverty in such a way as to be a substantial part of it [23] and answers, of course, that it is. In the process of responding to the question he explicitly deals with such specific issues as money, clothing, procurators, debts, and the obligation of Franciscan prelates to observe *usus pauper*.

The other work, the treatise *Quoniam contra paupertatem evangelicam*, is later than *Exiit qui seminat* (which it cites profusely) but was probably written before the censure of 1283.[24] Although the later of the two writings, this one offers a better introduction to the dispute as Olivi saw it and will be examined in some detail.

Olivi begins with a historical survey of the Old Enemy's attacks on evangelical poverty in the recent past. First there was the attack on mendicancy by leading members of the secular clergy. Next there was the denial on the part of certain pseudoreligious imbued with the magisterial office (here Olivi seems to be thinking of certain Dominicans, perhaps including Thomas Aquinas) [25] that the poverty contained in the Franciscan rule was perfect or was the same poverty practiced by Christ and the apostles. Finally, most recent and most abominable, there is the allegation by certain Franciscans that poor or moderate use (*usus pauper seu usus moderatus*) is not included in the profession and vow of the rule, nor is it a substantial part of the rule, but that it is merely accidental to it. These pseudoreligious also claim that Christ did not impose *usus pauper* on his apostles.

Olivi responds in several ways. First, he launches a massive attempt to smother his opponents with authorities, citing Franciscan leaders like Bonaventure, John Peckham, and Bonagratia of St. John in Persiceto; gen-

---

[21] See *De perf.*, q. 8, ff. 23rb–vb, 40vb–45va, 49rb; q. 9, ff. 64rb, 65ra, 68ra–rb, 70ra–71va.

[22] *De perf.*, q. 16, f. 96b explicitly says so.

[23] *De perf.*, q. 9, f. 50vb: "Queritur an usus pauper includatur in consilio seu voto paupertatis evangelice ita quod sit de eius substantia et integritate."

[24] Olivi cites it in *Responsio* II, p. 386. Thus it was certainly written before 1285, probably before 1283. The problem of its dating will arise again in the next chapter.

[25] Olivi explicity criticizes Thomas in a passage in *Mtt.* edited by Alverny, 1974: pp. 207–218.

eral chapters of the order like those at Narbonne and Assisi; various thirteenth-century popes (particularly Nicholas III and *Exiit qui seminat*); various non-Franciscan authors including Jerome, Bernard, and Hugh of St. Victor; and the Bible. None of these authorities had to deal explicitly with the question of *usus pauper* as Olivi faced it. Thus the main intent of his citations is to demonstrate that the words of pope, master, and chapter imply acceptance of *usus pauper* as a substantial element in the vow, while the Bible and its interpreters credit Christ and the apostles with the sort of poverty which implies a vow of *usus pauper*.

Having thus arrayed his authorities, Olivi attempts to show how his opponents' position would compromise the order.[26] Denial of *usus pauper* would neatly destroy all the arguments offered by Olivi and others for the virtues of poverty. Moreover, it would suggest that the Franciscan order is not perfect and that one could aspire to a higher sort of *religio*, in fact that one should expect such at the end of time. In short, his opponents' view would compromise the eschatological interpretation accorded the Franciscan order by Olivi and others. (Here again we must apologetically leave the matter hanging until the next chapter.)

Olivi argues that his opponents' position would not simply imply the future existence of a superior order. It would also suggest that superior orders have existed in the past. If Franciscan poverty allows riches, it is not only inferior to the old anchorites but even to those orders which allow possessions in common but without opulence.

Olivi next turns to the task of refuting his opponents' arguments. This section is an important one because, along with the objections refuted in the ninth of the *Questions on Evangelical Perfection*, it offers some insight into what Olivi's adversaries actually thought about the subject. Olivi presents and refutes eleven different objections, but the basic issues can be summarized more simply.

In the first place, Olivi's opponents point to practices in the order at it stands. The brothers actually do eat, drink, and make merry, yet the pope has approved their state. Bonaventure himself and others who wrote about poverty lived laxly.

A second approach concentrates upon the way in which the rule binds one to obedience. It is argued that, according to Nicholas III and others, Franciscans are bound only to that which they explicitly vow, and *usus pauper* is not explicitly demanded in the rule. It is also suggested that Franciscans are bound only to what they intend to vow, at least when their intention is in line with the reasonable sense of the words used in the vow.

Third, Olivi's opponents argue that the inclusion of *usus pauper* in the vow would involve extreme peril to the vower's soul. Since the level of obligation cannot be determined precisely, the vower would never know exactly what was demanded of him and thus would be in constant danger of sinning. Moreover, the sin would be mortal, since Franciscan masters agree that all deviation from a vow is such. Thus whoever once exceeded the limit by eating good bread, chicken, or white wine would sin mortally. Again, the obligation of *usus pauper* would rob the order of the flexibility required for the care of diverse brothers with different abilities in varied situations.

Olivi observes that his opponents, having offered the aforementioned arguments, add that "the use of possessions, while not directly contrary to the vow or precept of the rule, is nevertheless against the mind of it." They also say that *usus pauper* is "very perfect, very useful, and so necessary for avoiding faults that the profession of poverty has little or no utility without it." [27]

Olivi's response to the first type of argument is largely predictable. He rejects the idea that papal approval extends to Franciscan luxury. As to Bonaventure's purported life style, he notes that

it was hitherto customary to cite solemn men as examples of perfection; yet today, alas, they are cited as examples of laxity. . . . I say, therefore, what I know of the aforesaid father. He was of the best and most pious inner disposition and, as is clear from what has been said above, always preached that which is of the highest purity. Nevertheless, his body was frail and perhaps smacked of something human, which he himself humbly confessed, as I have often heard him do. For he was not greater than the apostle, who said, "We all offend in many things." [28]

Olivi goes on to say that Bonaventure certainly was not among those defending laxity in his time and that he himself had heard Bonaventure bewailing it at the Paris general chapter meeting.

In response to the second line of attack Olivi notes that Franciscans do not explicitly vow to abdicate common possessions and eschew the use of money; yet such things are commonly accepted as a substantial part of the rule. As to the brothers' intentions, *usus pauper* certainly is commonly intended by those vowing to observe the rule, and if the gentlemen in question did not intend such they are not true friars minor. Even if one does not intend this explicitly, it is enough to do so implicitly by intending that which the founder of the order intended.[29]

Olivi's reply to the third objection is probably the most significant part of his treatise, since it reveals a

---

[26] *Quoniam*, ff. 54v–55a.

[27] *Ibid.*, f. 55r.

[28] *Ibid.*, f. 56r: "Dicendum quod hactenus solebant omnes advertere viros sollempnes in exemplum perfectionis, sed heu domine deus hodie ab istis indicuntur in exemplum laxationis. . . . Dico igitur, quod de predicto patre sentio. Fuit enim interius optimi et piissimi affectus et in doctrine verbo semper predicans ea, que sunt perfecte puritatis, sicut ex supradictis ab eo satis liquere potest. Fragilis tamen fuit secundum corpus et forte in hoc aliquid humanum sapiens, quod et ipse humiliter sicut ego ipse ab eo sepius audivi, confitebatur; nec maior fuit Apostolo dicente: 'in multis offendimus omnes.'"

[29] *Ibid.*, f. 56v.

strikingly different attitude toward vows and the obligations entailed through them than the one apparently held by his opponents. In the first place, he denies that all transgressions of a vow are mortal. Some modern masters do hold such an opinion, he says, but it is not the opinion of the *sancti*. Olivi quotes William de Mare's *Correctorium* to the effect that those transgressing the rule do not necessarily sin mortally any more than the Jews do in violating any single part of the law. Such transgressions may be mortal or venial, depending upon the situation.[30]

Again, Olivi denies that *usus pauper* is violated by a single chicken dinner any more than Christ violated it by eating with publicans. One does not forsake *usus pauper* simply by enjoying something one could do without. In fact, Olivi notes that the idea of "being able to do without something" is more complicated than one might suppose. There are those things without which a man can live and those things without which he can fulfill all things befitting his station and office. The two are by no means the same. *Usus pauper* is "that use which, all things considered, befits the evangelical poor and mendicant," but even the evangelical poor must operate in a variety of places, times, and conditions. Some things are certainly prohibited. Personal possessions and the use of money are excluded. Many other things are simply restricted and the extent of this restriction depends upon the situation. Thus use must adjust to circumstance.

Moreover, *usus pauper* itself is not an absolute. It exists according to diverse grades and can be observed worthily even with an admixture of venial sin. In this life one can barely observe it in any other way. Indeed, transgression becomes mortal only when one uses what he could do without so frequently or to such a degree that his use of it is unreconcilable with *usus pauper*.

If these considerations seem to leave the required degree of observation dangerously undetermined, the problem is not unique to *usus pauper*. To what extent, for example, must one avoid consorting and talking with women, or resist the lure of carnal thoughts? To what degree can one transgress the simple word of a prelate without mortal sin? Such things cannot be determined fully, yet every Franciscan must deal with them. Even if one is not a Franciscan, the problem remains. At what point does pride or wrath become a mortal sin? There are no convenient yardsticks for this sort of measurement.[31]

The same basic attitude is apparent in the ninth of Olivi's *Questions on Evangelical Perfection*. Here too he argues that *usus pauper* falls under the vow indeterminately, so that a small deviation involves venial sin and mortal sin occurs only when the deviation is so great that, given the circumstances, the use involved should be judged rich use (*dives usus*) rather than poor use, just as a violation of the precept of temperance is not mortal unless it is so great that through it the man should be judged intemperate rather than temperate. The perfection of evangelical vows lies precisely in their indeterminacy. They involve no danger that a small violation will entail mortal sin, yet they bind one to the apex of perfection. In doing so, they enliven and lead to perfection according to the proportion of virtue and grace given to each man, causing different friars to practice *usus pauper* more or less strictly as their abilities and inclinations allow.[32]

In this work Olivi is careful to ward off the suspicion that *usus pauper* may entail physical danger. He defines it as "manifestly existing or imminent need of such a sort that the proper state of one's body or person cannot be maintained without its satisfaction,"[33] but he acknowledges that "present necessity" cannot be taken too strictly or too broadly. It is taken too strictly when nothing is deemed necessary for the present moment except what is needed at that moment, and too broadly when all that is necessary for an entire life is taken as present necessity.

Thus *usus pauper* does not rule out intelligent planning. Here again there can be no single rule covering all things. Vegetables and oil are needed in small and inexpensive amounts, cannot commonly be found in the form of a gift, and thus can be conserved for a part of the year without compromising *usus pauper*, unless they are stored in large amounts. A barn full of wheat or a cellar full of wine is another matter, since these things are in common use and can be given by most people. Houses and clothes last longer than food and stockpiling in these areas is quit unnecessary. Books, which have only spiritual utility, can be kept as long as excess is avoided. Here excess is harder to determine, except perhaps in the case of unnecessary duplication or of ornate books which appeal to vanity rather than spirituality.[34]

The difference between Olivi and his opponents is obvious in some respects, unclear in others. The unclarity lies mostly in the area of his opponents' intentions. Their position as he presents it involves a recognition that *usus pauper*, while not included in the vow, is nonetheless perfect, useful, and necessary for proper observance of Franciscan poverty; yet his discussion of the matter is interlaced with hints of duplicity on their part.[35] Thus he draws a line between their official protestations and their actual aims, leaving us to decide whether we should accept his story or theirs.

The central point of debate is clear enough. Olivi's opponents argue that any obligations incurred through a vow must be precisely determinable or the vower

---

[30] *Ibid.*, f. 55v.
[31] *Ibid.*, f. 55r.

[32] *De perf.*, q. 9, ff. 62vb–63ra.
[33] *Ibid.*, f. 63rb.
[34] *Ibid.*, f. 67ra–vb.
[35] *Quoniam*, f. 55r: "Ne autem videntur . . . rem horrendam dicere dicunt . . . ; . . . cum passio (*sic*) multe duplicitatis dicunt . . . ; . . . quasi in dolo subdicunt. . . ."

would be in constant danger of sinning. They think of a vow as a straightforward, well-defined affair which the subject can observe and indeed must observe if he is to avoid mortal sin.

Olivi feels that his opponents' precisely determinable obligations constitute a recipe for mediocrity. He himself is willing to sacrifice well-defined limits in return for a rule which aims at perfection and is observed in varying degrees by weaker and stronger brethren. According to his view the difference between allegiance to the rule and apostasy from it cannot be defined in terms of minute distinctions. When Olivi speaks of *usus pauper* he contrasts it with opulent living. Words like *habundantia rerum*, *divitias*, and *opulentia rerum* are constantly used to characterize the condition opposed to it. He is not interested in isolating that precise moment when the opposites meet.

It would be reasonable to conclude that Olivi is no fanatic on the subject of *usus pauper*. He insists that the rule demands it, but in such a way as to inspire us rather than damn us. The Franciscan binds himself to the highest sort of poverty knowing that he may achieve a good deal less. If kept within reasonable limits, his insufficiency will be a venial sin in no way erasing his allegiance to the rule. It is possible to envisage various levels of *usus pauper*.

During the rare moments when Olivi applies his ideas to concrete situations, one does not get the impression that *usus pauper* should be equated with extreme self-denial. He seems to anticipate a life of pious study in a well-ordered monastery which will feed him without pampering him.[36] It is all very well to talk about the lilies of the field, but when it come to provisioning a measure of good sense will be appreciated.

III. THE SHAPING OF HISTORY

In the course of the previous chapter we noted in passing that Olivi's attitude toward his order and its mission must be understood in relation to his theology of history. We must now turn to that subject. Here the principal sources for our investigation are not his writings on poverty but his Bible commentaries, and they present a peculiar problem. That problem stems from the fact that the key work, Olivi's commentary on Revelation, was written around 1297, shortly before his death.[1]

Thus the question naturally arises as to whether it is legitimate to project the views of the Revelation commentary back upon the Olivi of the 1280's. The answer is that, with certain reservations, it is perfectly proper to do so. The Revelation commentary represents Olivi's most thoroughgoing attempt to delineate the religious significance of past, present and future history. Perhaps it is also, as Raoul Manselli suggests, "the work to which, more than any other, he consigned all of his grief, hopes and ideals."[2] Nevertheless, in most respects it marks no serious break with the past. Olivi did not turn from other interests to apocalyptic speculation in his declining years. The evidence seems to indicate that, far from losing interest in other types of scholarship as he grew older, he was still polishing his *Questions on the Sentences* during the final years of his life.[3] Moreover, he did not discover apocalyptic in 1297. Both the interest and the basic themes are found throughout Olivi's writings from the earliest to the latest. He simply did not develop them as fully in other works. Thus the Revelation commentary is generally consistent with other writings, but goes beyond them in the richness of detail with which Olivi sketches the course of history.

It is an oversimplification to say that Olivi imposes a pattern upon history. In reality he employs several more or less complementary patterns. At times he utilizes the traditional division of world history in terms of the world-week, with the sixth age beginning with Christ and running to the final judgment.[4] His more common tendency, however, is to use the sevenfold pattern in a different way stemming from Joachim of Fiore *via* Bonaventure and others. Here the seven ages of the Old Testament are followed by seven ages of the church. The two sets of sevens are thought of as paralleling one another to some extent, with Old Testament events foreshadowing events of the new dispensation.[5] There are also similar parallels between each of these sevenfold patterns and the sevenfold pattern of world history.

Threefold patterns are also popular. Divisions derived from the images of childhood, adulthood, and old age or morning, noon, and night are imposed upon individual periods or upon the sevenfold pattern as a whole.[6] History as a whole is described in terms of three periods characterized by the laws of nature, scripture, and grace.[7] It is also divided into the ages of the father, son, and holy spirit.[8] Finally, Olivi speaks of Christ's three advents in the flesh, spirit, and judgment.[9]

---

[36] David Flood, in his introduction to *Rule Commentary*, p. 88, says, "Olivi . . . makes unreflective movements . . . which suggest where best he would feel at home: in a modest monastery with a good library and a regular kitchen, in a quiet room kept in order by a working friar devoted to the master, where he could give himself to study in the interests of God and Christ's chosen Order."

[1] *Apoc.*, f. 84ra, where Olivi remarks that there are only three years left in the thirteenth century.

[2] Manselli, 1955: p. 178.
[3] See Heynck, 1964: pp. 335–364.
[4] *Apoc.*, f. 13rb.
[5] For example see *Apoc.*, f. 2ra–va.
[6] For example see *De perf*, q. 8, f. 47ra–rb.
[7] *Lk.*, ff. 8r, 31v; *Mtt.*, ff. 107vb, 153ra.
[8] *Mtt.*, f. 109va; *Lk.*, f. 8r; *Gen.*, f. 108vb; *De perf.*, q. 8, f. 33rb–va; *Apoc.*, f. 55rb.
[9] *Apoc.*, f. 7vb; *Mtt.*, f. 107rb–va; *Job*, f. 13a; *Minor Prophets*, ff. 21b, 22vb–23ra, 24rb, 26va, 28vb, 35vb; *Gen.*, f. 85va.

The various divisions fit together rather neatly. The seven ages of Old Testament history correspond to the first five ages of the world-week, the age of the father, and the laws of nature and scripture. The seven ages of the church correspond to the sixth age of the world-week, the ages of the son and holy spirit, and the law of grace. Within these seven ages of the church, the first five correspond to the age of the son and end with Christ's second coming in the spirit. Then follows the age of the holy spirit, which corresponds with the sixth and seventh ages of the church and culminates in Christ's third coming in judgment.

Note that all of these divisions are scriptural as far as Olivi is concerned. Together they form a conceptual framework which will allow the scholar to make sense of the Bible. Approached in this manner, exegesis becomes an exciting game in which individual passages are related not merely to one period but to several simultaneously. The parallelism of various sevenfold and threefold patterns allows simultaneous application of passages to correlated periods within different patterns (e.g. the third age of various sevenfold patterns) or even to different periods within the same pattern (e.g. the first and sixth of the seven periods of church history). Thus human history is like a carefully wrought musical composition. It is based on a series of themes which appear throughout in rich counterpoint and with almost inexhaustible variations.

While it is both convenient and appropriate to speak in terms of clearly defined periods or ages, it is also slightly misleading. Olivi grants that the distinctive characteristics of each period, although particularly pronounced at that time, are found in other periods as well. Moreover, the divisions between periods are not clearly marked. The end of the preceding period coexists with the beginning of the succeeding one.

Thus it should hardly be surprising that Olivi's periodization is a bit bewildering at times. Nevertheless, the basic pattern is clear enough, particularly in relation to church history. The first period was that of the primitive church. In this period the church was opposed by the first of the hostile forces it would encounter, Judaism. Pressure from the Judaizers finally obliged the apostles to leave Palestine and preach to the pagan world, an event which ultimately entailed the transfer of primacy from Jerusalem to Rome.[10]

The second period of the church found it opposed by the persecution of the pagans. During this period a new Christian hero arose to meet the challenge, the martyr.[11] This period was brought to an end by Constantine and the rise of Christian empire, but the dawn of the third period witnessed a new enemy, the heretics, who were countered by the *doctores*. Although Olivi mentions a number of major heretics by name, he is especially interested in Origen and Arius, particularly the latter.[12]

Even while the heretics were being vanquished by the *doctores*, another battle was raging. In the fourth period of the church the hypocrites were opposed by the anchorites. Here the complexity of Olivi's periodization is obvious. He notes that the two periods are distinguished more by activity than by chronology, since Anthony and Athanasius were contemporaries, while the writings of Jerome and Augustine show the existence of anchorites in their time.[13]

The third and fourth periods soon gave way to the fifth, which was destined to be much longer and more damaging to the church. This period, the beginning of which Olivi identifies with the rise of Frankish empire,[14] was one of *condescensio*. In it the church came to terms with the world in a manner that assured comprehension at the cost of rigor. The church grew wealthy and in the process began to decay until "around the end of the fifth period practically the whole church is infected from head to toe, confused, and turned into a new Babylon as it were."[15] The shift in tense is significant. Olivi feels that he stands at the end of the fifth period and beginning of the sixth.

The *condescensio* of the church was not an unmitigated evil. Olivi regards the acquisition of temporal possessions during this period as natural and rational *for that time*. Nevertheless, the effect was laxity among ecclesiastics, monks, and laity, leading in turn to the Manichean and Waldensian revolts against the Catholic Church.[16] In Olivi's own time an even more deadly thing was happening.

These first five periods of the Church, proceeding from Christ's first coming in the flesh, comprise the age of the son. They follow the pattern of infancy/maturity/senility or morning/noon/night, with the third and fourth periods representing the apex and the fifth witnessing a gradual decline.[17] By the end of the fifth period the stage is set, not only for a new period of the Church, but for a new age of the holy spirit as well.

We come again to the fact that the periods overlap. Olivi lives in the final days of the fifth period, but the sixth has long since dawned. Olivi sees about him the signs, not only of a progressive deterioration, but of regeneration as well. In his own time two great forces are colliding in an encounter which is of central importance for mankind.

---

[10] *Apoc.*, f. 26ra. Here Olivi sees the possibility of a move from Rome in the sixth age. For fuller treatment of this and other matters see Manselli, 1955. Despite the distortion occasioned by Manselli's desire to safeguard Olivi's orthodoxy by distinguishing him as clearly as possible from Joachim of Fiore, his work remains the best treatment of Olivi's apocalyptic thought.
[11] *Ibid.*, f. 27va.
[12] *Ibid.*, ff. 48vb–49ra, 63ra–va.
[13] *Ibid.*, ff. 9rb–10va. See also ff. 49vb–50ra.
[14] *Ibid.*, ff. 46vb, 51vb, 93ra.
[15] *Ibid.*, f. 7rb.
[16] *Ibid.*, ff. 6va–7rb, 64va, 68rb–va.
[17] *De perf.*, q. 8, f. 47va–vb; *Apoc.*, f. 7va.

Olivi's period marks the beginning of the third great age of world history, that of the holy spirit. In this age "the holy spirit will reveal itself as a fiery furnace of divine love and a wine-cellar of spiritual intoxication." Whereas the first age was characterized by bodily works typical of laymen and the second by the sort of scholarship practiced by clerics, in the third age "there will abound that chaste and sweet contemplation typical of monks or religious."[18]

The new age is being ushered in by an impressive advance along two fronts. On the one hand, it involves a new illumination of the intellect, particularly in regard to the meaning of scripture. This phenomenon, along with the related turn to contemplation which characterizes the age, is closely connected with Olivi's attitude toward learning and thus will be reserved for the following chapter.

The other advance bears close examination at this point: Olivi feels that the dawning third age (or sixth period) is characterized by a resurgence of the evangelical and apostolic life. After centuries of accommodation to the ways of this world, centuries in which the church quietly choked on its own possessions, evangelical perfection (involving, of course, apostolic poverty) is again being pursued rigorously by at least a handful of Christians. The age of condescension is giving way to a new quest for the Christian life in all its fullness.

In accordance with his refusal to draw sharp lines between periods, Olivi recognizes not one but several beginnings for the sixth period. First, it had "a certain prophetic beginning" in the revelation of the abbot Joachim and those like him. Second, it was established and began to grow with the renewal or the evangelical rule by St. Francis. Third, it is spread about and flourishes in the preaching of spiritual men. Fourth, the beginning of its clear distinction from the fifth period will come with the destruction of Babylon.[19]

Thus the first dawn of the new era is connected with two individuals, Joachim and Francis. Olivi's attitude toward the first has been the subject of continued debate, and in the course of this debate a number of recent scholars have been unduly influenced by Manselli's tendency to play down any great dependence and argue that "Olivi considers Joachim an authority like all the others."[20] In reality, Olivi looks upon Joachim as something other than one more authority. His use of the word *revelatio* in connection with Joachim is not to be taken lightly. In a significant passage Olivi says that Joachim's position at the very beginning of the third age explains both his great gifts and his mistakes. It should hardly be surprising, Olivi observes, if "the great light given him in the dawn, as it were, of the third age was mixed with shadows in the knowledge of future events, particularly since the night shadows of the fifth period engulfed his time."[21] In two other places he accepts Joachim's own assertion that the *concordia* of the New and Old Testaments was revealed to him at a particular moment in time, then goes on to explain Joachim's errors by observing that the veracity of the revealed principles does not insure the truth of conclusions inferred from these principles by probable conjecture.[22]

Thus Joachim, although hardly an infallible authority, is an important harbinger of the new age. Nevertheless, he is dwarfed in significance by St. Francis, the principal *renovator* of evangelical perfection. Francis is in a class by himself. There were, to be sure, various divine messengers like Anthony, Benedict, and Bernard who, like Old Testament judges and prophets, came to draw some Christians back to the apostolic life.[23] Again, Olivi's supple interpretative framework leads him to recognize Francis's career as one of several beginnings of the new age. Again, Olivi occasionally bows toward Joachim's expectation of *two* future orders.[24] Nevertheless, in the final analysis Olivi accords Francis a position so unique as to make him the most important figure to appear after the time of Christ.

Francis is given apocalyptic significance by identifying him with the angel bearing the seal of the living God in Revelation 7:1, the angel with a face like the sun in Revelation 10:1, and Enoch or Elijah.[25] He is occasionally seen as a new John the Baptist.[26] Most important, he is identified with Christ himself, an identification sometimes carried to extraordinary lengths. Olivi argues that there was almost nothing of excellence in Christ which was not embodied in Francis as well. He resembled Christ as a wax figure does the seal which impresses it. At one point Olivi asserts that no one after the apostles has manifested Christ's life as fully as Francis did.[27] At another he characterizes Francis as the greatest observer of the evangelical life since Christ and his mother.[28]

The comparison is detailed by Olivi in passages which cite abundant parallels between the two figures and their historical situations. One of the more obvious and more emphasized of these is the stigmata, a reminder that Francis has renewed not only Christ's life but his cross and suffering as well.[29] Olivi even suggests that the

---

[18] *Apoc.*, f. 31vb. Marjorie Reeves, 1969: p. 197 notes that this passage contains extensive borrowings from Joachim of Fiore. See also *De perf.*, q. 8, f. 33rb–va.
[19] *Apoc.*, f. 52va–vb.
[20] Manselli, 1955: p. 186.
[21] *Apoc.*, f. 84ra.
[22] *Apoc.*, f. 67ra; *Isaiah*, f. 15vb.
[23] *Jn.*, f. 38rb–va.
[24] *Apoc.*, ff. 68va, 76ra, 96rb. See also *Gen.*, ff. 96va, 107rb.
[25] *Apoc.*, ff. 52rb–va, 55rb, 72vb, 76ra.
[26] *De perf.*, q. 8, f. 29ra–rb.
[27] *Ibid.*, f. 29ra.
[28] *Apoc.*, f. 55rb.
[29] *Apoc.*, ff. 13rb, 52va; *Minor Prophets*, f. 32rb; *Mtt.*, f. 122va. For other comparisons of Francis and Christ see *Apoc.*, ff. 53va–54rb, 73ra–rb.

parallel may extend to a resurrection on Francis's part. He cites—without assertion but with some enthusiasm—the word of "a spiritual man" who had learned from brother Leo (one of Francis's earliest followers) and from revelation accorded to himself that when Francis's disciples are beset by temptation in the future tribulation he will rise and strengthen them, just as Christ did his own disciples.[30]

The parallelism is implicit in Olivi's historical perspective. Just as Christ came to usher in the sixth period of world history, Francis came to introduce the sixth period of church history. Again, just as Christ established the age of the son, Francis heralded the age of the holy spirit. The latter comparison may seem to have an ominous ring, since it appears to move Olivi dangerously close to Gerard of Borgo S. Donino's vision of a third age which abrogates the second, with an eternal gospel of the holy spirit superceding the New Testament. His view differs from Gerard's in important respects, however. Olivi is always careful to subordinate Francis to Christ. Even in reporting the legend of Francis's impending resurrection he emphasizes that it will differ in degree of dignity from those of Christ and his mother. The basic point to be appreciated is that Francis is important as the *renovator* of the life style established by Christ, not as the initiator of a new, superior life style.

Here it is important to remember the way in which Olivi's threefold and sixfold patterns complement one another. The age of the holy spirit is composed of the sixth and seventh periods of Christ's church. The ages of the son and holy spirit are introduced by Christ's advents in the flesh and spirit respectively. Thus Christ is the lord of all history and the pattern for all holy men after his incarnation.

If Christ is related to all periods of history, he is particularly identified with the sixth and seventh periods. This is to be expected, since they are the *finis* of the first five. Thus it is proper that the life of Christ should singularly flourish in these periods and the love and contemplation of Christ should be particularly enjoyed in them. Olivi counters the objection that such a view would make the state of Christ and the apostles inferior to that of the sixth period by observing that, although Christ is in one sense part of the first period, in another part of the last, and in any case universal lord of all time, he belongs more to the sixth and seventh periods "according to the fullness of his presence in the Christiform life." The latter part of the statement applies also to his disciples and apostles, who were *universalia vasa* of Christ. While it was necessary for Christ, the disciples and the apostles to establish the pattern of perfection in the first period of the church, that pattern will be realized in a singular manner by the church of the sixth and seventh periods.[31] This identification of Christ with the sixth and seventh periods is so important for Olivi that he sometimes views the relationship between John the Baptist and Christ as prefiguring that between the ages of the son and holy spirit.[32] Thus Christ is at times identified more with the age of the holy spirit than with that of the son.

The new age is hardly uncontested. Far from surrendering the field, the enemies of evangelical perfection are mustering their forces for a final great assault which will almost carry the day. To some extent their opposition is typical of the conduct demonstrated by leaders of the old order whenever anything really new develops. In such cases there are always those who point presumptuously to their own antiquity, just as the scribes and pharisees did when confronted with Christ and his church.[33] Such people fail to appreciate the dynamic nature of God's action in history.

There is more involved than simple misunderstanding, however. Olivi sees the strife of his own day as one more round in a continuing battle between the powers of light and darkness. Carnal men have opposed God's work throughout history, and in Olivi's own time the fruition of evangelical perfection has called forth a similar supreme effort on the part of the carnal church, that element of the visible church which is Christian in name but not in fact. The battle is being waged on two major fronts. On the one hand, the revival of evangelical poverty is attacked by those who attack the mendicant orders, say that Christ and his disciples had common possessions, or deny the necessity of *usus pauper*. Franciscan poverty is being challenged from inside and outside the order. The external threats are seen most spectacularly in the assaults of the secular masters at Paris. Extending the Christ-Francis parallel, Olivi notes that in the infancy of the order, while the kings of the world were adoring Christ's poverty in it, the new

---

[30] *Apoc.*, f. 55a. Identification of Francis with Christ was a common practice among Franciscans in Olivi's time. See Stanislao da Campagnola, 1971. Moreover, even the most impeccably orthodox writers might include the resurrection among those aspects in which Francis was assimilated to Christ. Bonaventure does so in the third of his *Sermones de S. patre nostro Francisco*, in: *Opera* 9: pp. 382–385, and more obliquely in the *Legenda maior*, cap. 15, in: *Opera* 8: p. 347. Nevertheless, Bonaventure gives the term "resurrection" a highly metaphorical sense when applying it to Francis and does not refer it to any future occurrence. On the other hand, the *Arbor vitae* and *Speculum vitae* look forward to a possible resurrection *in corpore glorioso*, to strengthen the brethren in time of persecution. See Ubertino da Casale, 1961: pp. 442 ff.; and Little, Mandonnet and Sabatier, 1903: 1: pp. 378 f. Both documents report the testimony of Ubertino, who in turn cites Conrad of Offida, who cites Brother Leo, who received a revelation from St. Francis. Thus Olivi's "spiritual man" may be Conrad of Offida, with whom (as we shall see) he was acquainted. Olivi himself is hardly precise on this matter. Note his prophecy concerning Francis's future spiritual descent in *Apoc.*, f. 73rb, which should perhaps be read in conjunction with his remarks on Francis's resurrection.

[31] *De perf.*, q. 8, ff. 29va–30va. Compare *Apoc.*, f. 46va–vb.
[32] *Lk.*, ff. 8r, 24v.
[33] *Gen.*, f. 104va; *Jn.*, f. 21rb; *Mtt.*, ff. 105vb, 112rb, 132ra.

Herod was seeking to kill it.³⁴ By his own day, however, the order has been in existence long enough to develop its own carnal element and no longer has to look outside itself to find enemies of apostolic poverty. The controversy over *usus pauper* provides ample evidence of this fact.

At the same moment, the carnal church is attacking on another front. The generation that witnessed the secular-mendicant controversy at Paris also saw the appearance in the same university of certain "philosophical or rather pagan errors"³⁵ which have since developed into a major threat to Christian orthodoxy. He refers, of course, to Aristotelian philosophy as interpreted by Islamic philosophers and as accepted by many scholars in his own day. This matter is an important one which will be given extensive treatment in the next chapter. For the moment it need only be said that in this respect as well Olivi feels that the carnal church has infiltrated his own order and is subverting it from within.

The two challenges are closely related in Olivi's mind. Those who espouse philosophical error employ it to attack evangelical poverty.³⁶ Here we have the reverse side of the connection between poverty and doctrinal orthodoxy noted in the preceding chapter. Those who attack orthodoxy will also attack poverty. Olivi notes that all heresies eventually turn publicly or secretly to carnal things, no matter how they may feign chastity and austerity. He who does not taste true spiritual delights in God will inevitably seek carnal pleasures.³⁷

Thus, as has been pointed out elsewhere,³⁸ Olivi reduces the various challenges of his day to a basic encounter between carnal and spiritual man. The spiritual man is a Christian, accepts the spiritual interpretation of scripture, worships Christ as the messiah, and recognizes the superiority of evangelical poverty and chastity over carnal delights. The carnal man appears in various guises. He is the Jew, who follows a carnal interpretation of the Bible and seeks a messiah who will bring him earthly power and wealth; the Moslem, who awaits a heaven of carnal pleasures; Aristotle, who based his philosophy upon sense experience and was thus blind to spiritual truth; and the Cathar, whose carnal interpretation of the Bible leads to the sort of hypocritical sanctity practiced by their *perfecti*.³⁹ Like all great attempts to reduce experience to a few basic categories, Olivi's scheme has its difficulties, and his inclusion of the Cathari alongside the Moslems and Jews in a carnal hall of fame is one point at which it seems to produce particularly odd results.

If the spiritual-carnal confrontation has been a perennial feature of church life, it has been manifested in a series of specific situations. The historical parallels between Olivi's own period and the travails of other times are not lost upon him. In a sense his own age faces the same challenges encountered in every period, but in a more intense form. In his period the culmination of evangelical perfection will be achieved, making that period the *finis* of all preceding periods. Thus it is fitting that his age should also be the *finis* of all preceding periods in the negative sense, with the greatest virtue being countered by the greatest temptation.⁴⁰

There are, however, certain obvious parallels with particular periods in the past. We have seen how thoroughly Olivi exploits the model of the early church, casting Francis and his order in the role of Christ and his disciples while allowing the opponents of evangelical perfection to play the part of the scribes and pharisees. We have seen that these comparisons are no casual literary conceit, but are deeply rooted in his theology of history. Other parallels are also important. Olivi is aware that the dangers and glories of the third and fourth periods are, in more intense form, characteristic of his own day. In the third period the great doctors combatted heresy, while in the fourth the anchorites opposed carnal luxury. In his own time those faithful to evangelical perfection must evade the pitfalls of Aristotelian hetorodoxy and carnal luxury, which, as we have seen, are not clearly distinguishable but spring from the same basic mindset and mutually reinforce one another. (Thus it is hardly surprising that the third and fourth periods were not clearly distinguishable.)

Olivi feels that the danger of these challenges in his own day is intensified by the fact that the forces of darkness are proceeding to monopolize positions of leadership in church and state. In the days to come, great monasteries and churches will be subverted by a carnally oriented ecclesiastical authority which will operate at the highest levels, including the papacy. Whereas papal favor toward evangelical poverty once prevented opponents from attacking it, the Franciscans will be naked to their enemies.⁴¹ Olivi raises the possibility that future tribulations will be presided over by no less than two pseudopopes, one connected with the temptation of the mystical Antichrist and the other with that of the great Antichrist.⁴²

This deterioration will be aided by secular authority. Olivi reports without explicit approval the opinion that a descendent of Frederick II will rule the empire and France, draw several other kings to him, and install as pseudopope an apostate *religiosus* who will use his power to support the descendents of Frederick and attack

---

³⁴ *Apoc.*, f. 54ra–rb. It is not clear whether Olivi has one person in mind (e.g. William of St. Amour) or is using the name "Herod" to designate the whole group.

³⁵ *Apoc.*, f. 83vb.

³⁶ *Ibid.*, f. 66rb.

³⁷ *Ibid.*, f. 29vb.

³⁸ Burr, 1971, "Apocalyptic Element," p. 26.

³⁹ See *Apoc.*, ff. 13rb, 68ra–rb; *De perf.*, q. 8, ff. 12vb–16rb; and chapter four of this work.

⁴⁰ *De perf.*, q. 8, f. 30va.

⁴¹ *Apoc.*, f. 70ra.

⁴² See *ibid.*, ff. 91ra–rb, 93ra–rb, 101ra–rb.

evangelical perfection. This pope will be "pseudo" because he errs heretically regarding evangelical poverty and perfection and perhaps also because he will not be canonically but schismatically elected.[43]

Caught in this situation, the true Christians will be sorely tried by the most exquisite temptations. They will, of course, be coerced. Those who defend the gospel will be anathematized, excommunicated, and punished by the secular authorities.[44] In this respect they will parallel the martyrs in the second period of church history; yet the martyrs of the early church never had to undergo the subtle temptations to be experienced in coming days by Christians, who will find themselves opposing apparently legitimate ecclesiastical authority, the moral authority of those who were once considered leading proponents of evangelical perfection, and the arguments of eminent scholars. They will be confronted not only with physical torture but with ostensibly sound philosophical arguments, twisted interpretations of scripture, false piety, and bogus ecclesiastical authority. In such straits even the elect will barely be saved from error.[45] Here the parallel with Christ takes on a new dimension already implied in Francis's stigmata. The true sons of St. Francis, those who follow Christ's life, will be assimilated to his cross and relive Christ's suffering.[46]

The forces of darkness will be led by the mystical and great Antichrists. Here Olivi describes the future in terms of apocalyptic imagery which, like much of the imagery he employs, remains relatively undefined despite the amount of time he spends discussing it, partly because he is often content to cite various theories on the subject without explicitly accepting or rejecting them. In the Revelation commentary he makes it clear that the mystical Antichrist will precede the open one and that the destruction of Babylon (the carnal church) will follow the reign of the former and inaugurate that of the latter. The destruction of Babylon will mean the end of the corrupt church which has developed in the fifth period. It will be accomplished through a real military attack by non-Christians which will devastate Rome. Thus the unchristian carnal church will be eliminated by non-Christian enemies in a blow actually aimed at Christianity itself. The elect will still be in extreme distress, since they will then have to endure the persecution of the great Antichrist, but once he is destroyed by Christ they will be free to enter fully into the peaceful, joyful, contemplative religion of the third age.

The complete dawning of the third age is indeed something to anticipate. In the meantime, however, the temporary ascendency of the carnal church will lead to a movement of great importance in the divine plan of salvation. Under pressure from the carnal church in the Latin west, spiritual men will go to the Greeks, Moslems, and Jews. There they will find converts, albeit at the cost of many martyrs.[47] Olivi sees these events as a reversal of the process which took place at the beginning of the church. In the Revelation commentary he says that in the time of the apostles the *processus* was principally *quasi dexter* to the pagans, and only secondarily *quasi sinister* to the Jews, since the apostles felt that the Jews were not such a likely target for evangelization. In the coming days, however, the message will not be heard so readily in the carnal church of the Latins as among the Greeks, Saracens, and Jews.[48] In his commentary on John, Olivi offers an even more elaborate analysis. There he identifies the three languages in which Christ's title was written on the cross with Judea, Samaria, and Galilee and with Jews, Greeks, and Latins. Just as Christ went from Judea to Galilee by way of Samaria, the Christian faith went from the Jews to the Latins by way of the Greeks. It will finally return from the Latins to the Jews, who will be converted, and it is hardly surprising that it will do so by way of the Greeks, showing them their errors. The Greeks will be illumined by spiritual men who will come to them from the Latin world at a time when the malicious jealousy of many Latins compels them to go.[49]

Thus the ultimate conversion of the Jews, a Biblical motif which assumes tremendous importance in Olivi's eschatological scenario, is connected with a more general mission to the infidels spurred in part by persecution at home. This mission is not simply the result of persecution, however. The Franciscans are called to such activity by the example of both the apostles and Francis himself. In commenting upon that passage of the rule which deals with friars "inspired by God to go among the Saracens or other unbelievers," Olivi remarks that this was said

not only as a concession, but also as a council or incitement or even prophecy; for just as the apostles were first sent among the Jewish faithful . . . and then to the infidel Gentile nations, so after preaching to the Latin faithful the order is, I believe, to be sent to the infidel nations so that, just as the world was converted around the beginning and middle of the church by the person of Christ suffering in assumed flesh, so the fullness of the Gentiles will enter into the church and all Israel be saved through the life and rule of Christ suffering in his members.[50]

---

[43] *Ibid.*, f. 93ra. At 91rb, speaking of the great Antichrist (who may or may not be a pseudopope), Olivi predicts that he will be *apostata a statu . . . altissime religionis*, which seems to indicate that he will be a Franciscan. It is less clear that in calling the earlier pseudopope a *falsus religiosus* Olivi wishes to make him, too, a Franciscan.

[44] *Ibid.*, ff. 92vb–93ra.

[45] *Ibid.*, ff. 9va, 92vb.

[46] *Ibid.*, f. 55va; *Mtt.*, ff. 107rb-va, 140vb.

[47] *Apoc.*, ff. 73ra, 98rb; *Jn.*, f. 22ra; *Quodl.* II, q. 7.

[48] *Apoc.*, f. 73va.

[49] *Jn.*, f. 32vb. Does this passage reflect the journies undertaken by Angelo Clareno and other rigorists from the March of Ancona during the generalate of Raymond Gaufredi?

[50] *Rule Commentary*, p. 193: "Aestimo autem hoc non esse hic positum solum concessive, sed etiam consultive seu incitative aut etiam prophetice, quia sicut apostoli primo missi sunt inter

Thus the role of the Franciscans at the dawn of the sixth period of church history is indeed a glorious one. They are the shock-troops of the new age. An equally important role awaits them once Babylon has fallen, the great Antichrist is slain, and the third age of world history has fully dawned. Needless to say, they are the pattern for the spiritual religion of that time. They will rule by more than example, however, for in that age internal and external authority will be so beautifully correlated that ecclesiastical power will be given to them.[51]

The preceding paragraphs ought to raise some interesting questions about Olivi's attitude toward the church. After all, he continually announces that the spiritual men will be persecuted by the carnal church, which he also likes to describe as Babylon and the great whore. Granting that terms like "carnal church," "Babylon" and "great whore" are used by Olivi in such a way as to frustrate any simple identification with the hierarchical church of his day, it would be hard to read the Revelation commentary without recognizing that Olivi considers the hierarchy in his time to be extremely corrupt and getting more so by the day. Nor is it the sort of corruption Christians can and must live with, the frailty to which all flesh is heir. It is, in Olivi's eyes, part of a mounting crescendo of wickedness which purposes to block the fulfillment of evangelical perfection. The forces of darkness are seizing control of the institutional church and will even control the papal chair in Rome. Good Christians must face persecution by their own purported shepherds.

This evil situation will be ended, not through reform, but through the destruction of Rome by non-Christian armies. The carnal church will then be uprooted and the years of hypocritical religion ended, leaving the spiritual church to develop on its own. Although Olivi recognizes a continuity between the churches of the second and third ages—the church of Christ is, after all, one in all periods—he often speaks in terms which underline the discontinuity between the two. He talks of the *end* of the church at the close of the second age and the beginning of a *new* church at that time.[52] He occasionally likens these events to the transition from synagogue to church at the beginning of the second age,[53] a comparison which can only emphasize the radical novelty of the religious situation in the third age. The discontinuity may even be dramatized by a relocation of the principal seat of the church, with Rome losing this honor to Jerusalem or some other city, although Olivi is not committed to this idea.[54]

Such statements on Olivi's part confront the historian with a real dilemma, not only because they are hard to interpret in themselves but because they must be judged in the light of other passages which suggest a veneration for ecclesiastical authority in his own time. For example, we have his question on papal infallibility, which Brian Tierney considers to be the earliest serious attempt to formulate that doctrine.[55] Again, there is his question written in 1295 defending the legitimacy of Celestine V's abdication, the argument of which will be considered in chapter nine of this work. Again, there is his letter of the same year attacking the spirituals who withheld obedience from Boniface VIII, which will be discussed in the same chapter. Finally, there are a whole series of occasional remarks reflecting a respect for ecclesiastical authority in general and papal authority in particular, not the least striking of which is the closing passage of the Revelation commentary, in which Olivi submits that work to the Roman church for correction.[56] This respect for authority is in harmony with a profound commitment to the idea of hierarchy manifested throughout Olivi's writings.

Thus we are left with what seems to be a peculiar bifurcation of Olivi's thought regarding the church. On the one hand, he was an avowed supporter of papal authority. On the other, he saw widespread corruption in the church and anticipated a day when that corruption would reach the papacy itself, with the church being presided over by a pseudopope. On the one hand he bowed to ecclesiastical authority. On the other, he felt that the ecclesiastical hierarchy was being subverted by the carnal church and would eventually be largely controlled by it. How does one go about reconciling these positions?

In the first place, Olivi's time scale is important. It is one thing to say that the degradation of the church will reach its culmination in three centuries and quite another to say that it will happen next week. In the former case the matter remains highly theoretical, while in the latter it calls for serious attention and perhaps some weighty decisions. Olivi's attempts to attach dates to his apocalyptic timetable are usually quite tenta-

---

Iudaeroum fideles ex quibus erant nati, et tandem post mortem Christi et Iudaeorum aliquantam ad Christum attractionem missi sunt ad gentium infidelium nationes; sic, prout aestimo, post praedictionem latinorum fidelium mittendus est ordo ad in fidelium nationes, ut sicut per Christi personam patientem in carne assumpta circa principium et medium ecclesiae conversus est orbis, sic per Christi vitam et regulam in suis membris passuram plenitudo gentium intret et omnis Israel salvus fiat." Olivi goes on to cite the example of Francis, giving the chronology of his mission to the Moslems a mystical significance also found in *Apoc.*, f. 73ra. Daniel, 1975 stresses the importance of missionary activity for the Franciscans.

[51] *Apoc.*, f. 75ra: "Huic ordini prefato datur potestas et discretio regendi ecclesiam illius temporis; *ibid.*, f. 96vb: . . . principaliter designat hic evangelicum ordinem sanctorum Christo et eius vite similium et regiam seu pontificalem coronam seu auctoritatem circa finem seculi habiturorum cum potestate et officio collegendi finalem messem electorum."

[52] See *Mtt.*, f. 124ra; *Apoc.*, f. 7vb.

[53] For example *Apoc.*, f. 33vb.

[54] *Ibid.*, f. 106va.

[55] "An romano pontifici in fide et moribus sit ab omnibus catholicis tamquam regule inerrabili obediendum," now considered the thirteenth of the *Questions on Evangelical Perfection*. See Tierney, 1972: ch. 3.

[56] *Apoc.*, f. 123rb–va. There is also a similar assertion in his purported deathbed confession, as we will see in chapter nine.

tive. He considers himself better off in this respect than those living in previous centuries, since the new light available from the beginning of the sixth period provides greater understanding of prophecy concerning future events. He is even better off than Joachim of Fiore, whose estimable gifts were compromised by his position at the very beginning of the sixth period. Nevertheless, a generous degree of uncertainty remains in Olivi's time, and he is accordingly rather tentative in his efforts to determine precisely when events will occur.

This is not to say that he has no idea of the time scale. He knows that he is living in a time of mounting opposition to evangelical perfection, and he does have certain Bible passages which offer definite numbers apparently related to coming events.[57] By juggling these numbers he can come up with at least a rough idea of when to expect the two Antichrists and the fall of Babylon. On the basis of his calculations it will be neither next week nor three centuries hence, but it will be much closer to the former than to the latter. On the whole his calculations seem to suggest that these events will occur during the first half of the fourteenth century.

Thus for Olivi the earliest of these events, such as the pseudopope preceding the destruction of Babylon, might be expected in the relatively near future. Brian Tierney is probably correct in suggesting that Olivi's attitude toward papal authority in such documents as the questions on papal infallibility and Celestine's resignation, far from being at variance with this notion of imminent apocalyptic tribulation, fits rather well with it. The Franciscan rule, that key element in the burgeoning third age, had been approved by a series of thirteenth-century popes. In Olivi's own time Nicholas III had placed a papal blessing upon Franciscan poverty in *Exiit qui seminat*. Nevertheless, Olivi's apocalyptic studies led him to suspect that this cozy relationship would end at some future date when a pseudopope working for the carnal church attacked evangelical perfection. Anticipating this crisis, Olivi tried to protect his order by arguing that the decisions of preceding popes on faith and morals were inerrant and therefore unchangeable. Thus future popes were limited by *Exiit qui seminat*.

The coming pseudopope, of course, would hardly recognize this limitation. Here the real value of Olivi's notion of papal inerrancy comes to light. It not only supports the authority of true popes but offers a criterion for sniffing out false ones. Unfortunately Olivi's question on papal inerrancy is incomplete, but by the time it breaks off the general direction of Olivi's thought seems to be established and that direction is confirmed by his remarks in other questions like the one concerning Celestine's resignation.[58] The burden of Olivi's message is that a true pope is inerrant on matters of faith and morals, and therefore a man who errs on such matters is not true pope. It follows that any future occupant of the chair of St. Peter who attacks evangelical poverty as defended by *Exiit qui seminat* will automatically declare himself to be a false pope. Thus we see the significance of Olivi's announcement in the Revelation commentary that the future pseudopope "will be 'pseudo' because he will err in a heretical manner against the truth of evangelical poverty and perfection."[59]

Olivi, then, had only the highest veneration for authority as it ought to be, used to be, and would be again. Even in its somewhat debased present state, ecclesiastical authority was seen as legitimate and therefore worthy of respect. At the very highest levels it had shown itself to be on the side of the angels in the poverty dispute. In the early 1280's Olivi could cite papal authority with apparent confidence that Peter's successors stood at his side in the battle against enemies inside and outside the order. Even at that time, however, he recognized that growing corruption in the church would eventually culminate in an attack on poverty by a false pope. At that time the elect would find themselves in the uncomfortable position of acting against the wishes of one who, as far as external appearances went, seemed to be the supreme pontiff. Fortunately, however, that time was still in the future.

Clearly Olivi retained this basic perspective throughout most of his life. Did he retain it throughout all of his life? There is some difference of opinion on this matter, as we shall see in dealing with his final years.

IV. SCHOLARLY IMPERATIVES

Olivi was not only a Franciscan but an intellectual as well. By the late 1270's he was a *lector* with a growing reputation in scholarly circles. For this reason he had to come to terms not only with the Franciscan mission in history but with his own mission as a Franciscan scholar. He attacked the problem in a series of works which provide both an evaluation of scholarship in the abstract and an analysis of its role in Christian history.

Those wishing to understand Olivi's attitude toward scholarly activity could do worse than to start with the first four of his *Questions on Evangelical Perfection*, in which he attempts to place study within the broader context of the Christian life. In the first of these he asserts the superiority of the contemplative over the active life.[1] Through contemplation we attain our ultimate end, knowledge and love of God, directly. Through the active life—works performed to promote the physical and spiritual well-being of creatures—we are merely disposed to attaining it. Again, external

---

[57] See *Apoc.*, ff. 12ra–rb; 27rb; 54ra–rb; 82rb–85rb; 89rb–va; 92vb–93rb; 113ra–114ra.

[58] See chapter nine. *Quodl.* I, q. 18 is also important.

[59] *Apoc.*, f. 93rb.

[1] "An contemplatio sit melior ex suo genere quam omnis alia actio," edition cited in the bibliography. The following comments represent a slightly abridged version of what I said earlier in Burr, 1971, "Petrus Ioannis Olivi."

works derive their meritorious nature from their relation to the contemplative life, since the latter is the source of that love which makes our external acts meritorious.

Having established the importance of the contemplative life, Olivi turns in the second question to the relative role of intellect and will within it.[2] The question is an important one for him, since he feels that Christian orthodoxy demands a psychology in which the intellect is related to the will as instrument to agent. Olivi concludes that in contemplation the will predominates inasmuch as it turns the intellect to its object and inasmuch as the crowning glory of the contemplative life is a union of love which goes beyond any *visio dei* in a strictly intellectual sense.

In the third and fourth questions Olivi examines the place of study in the Christian life.[3] He argues that study is good only when it is pursued in order to consider divine things, understand those things by which we are ordered immediately to God, or learn those things which aid us in such an understanding. In every case one must consider not only its effect upon the intellect but its effect upon the will. Its value is to be determined by its contribution to *caritas*. The role he assigns it is, on the whole, an estimable one. Study is less valuable than internal acts of the will like compassion and obedience, which are meritorious in themselves; yet legitimate study is superior to all external acts except preaching and the exercise of ecclesiastical authority.

What sort of study is legitimate? A general answer is provided by Olivi's announcement that study is good only when it is pursued in order to consider divine things, understand those things by which we are ordered immediately to God, or learn those things which aid us in such an understanding. Particular determinations are more difficult, depending upon specific situations. It is clear that the Bible is absolutely central. Beyond it, there are those disciplines like grammar and logic which aid us in understanding the Bible, and it is in these areas that one can encounter ambiguity. In general one could say that two criteria must be employed. First, there is the objective criterion of necessity or at least usefulness for the study of scripture. Second, there is the subjective criterion of attitude. Pagan philosophy can be valuable for the man who employs it carefully and fatal for the man who lets it come between him and Christian dogma or piety. Even the most innocuous studies can be harmful if they are pursued at the expense of more essential activities such as prayer. In every case one must consider not only the effect of study upon the intellect but its effect on the will. Its value is to be determined by its contribution to *caritas*.

This characterization is still a bit overgeneralized. Olivi had to face, not grammar and logic in general, but grammar and logic as they were pursued in western Europe during the final quarter of the thirteenth century. His stance as an intellectual depended, not only upon his views concerning study in the abstract, but also upon his attitude toward what was happening around him. What was happening around him was, of course, an intellectual revolution. Aristotle had come to Paris and was raising some important questions there. These questions inevitably involved dispute over "pagan philosophy" as an entity and over specific Aristotelian views. In such matters Olivi, like the rest of his generation, had to take a stand.

In the course of his writings Olivi responds to the problem in a number of ways. At times his reaction is a protest of indifference. Philosophical questions are secondary affairs, unworthy in themselves of a Christian's serious attention.[4] It is easy enough to see how such an attitude accords with Olivi's view of study and its place in the Christian life. *Purely* philosophical problems are so much intellectual froth, unrelated to Christian truth and therefore without importance. It is also easy to see how the attitude is connected with his veneration of poverty. The true lover of evangelical perfection avoids excessive involvement with the things of this world, whether these are conceived as possessions valued by the carnal rich or the sense experience upon which pagan philosophers based their thought. We are again reminded of the connection between luxury and pagan philosophy.

Nevertheless, anyone familiar with Olivi's works will feel it necessary to exercise some caution at this point. The impressive amount of space devoted to philosophical concerns in his *Questions on the Sentences* seems a rather odd way of expressing indifference. Like other scholars of his time, Olivi did spend a great deal of time pondering philosophical questions, and it is understandable that he should have. Such questions found their way into thirteenth-century *Sentence* commentaries because theologians thought they were relevant to Christian doctrine and therefore fair game. Olivi thought so too.

It is, of course, ill advised to expect too much consistency in these matters. Olivi seems to have been a born intellectual whose scholarly endeavors often revealed an enthusiasm not entirely explicable in terms of his own theories on the nature of Christian scholarship. At times he pursues philosophical questions with a gusto that seems to reflect the sheer joy of intellectual exploration rather than any serious concern for their theological application. Nevertheless, many of the philosophical detours taken by him were warranted by his own theological preoccupations. Such issues were philosophical without being purely so, and their implications for

---

[2] "An contemplatio principalius sit in intellectu quam in voluntate," edition cited in the bibliography.

[3] "An studere sit opus de genere suo perfectum," and "An aliquod opus vitae activae praeter regimen animarum et predicationem sit melius ex suo genere quam studium," editions cited in the bibliography.

[4] See his *Responsio* I, p. 130 and *Responsio* II, p. 134.

Christian orthodoxy might be weighty indeed. In such cases Olivi could feel quite at ease in the philosophical lists. In fact, he could feel a definite responsibility to be there. Here we come to the fact that Olivi's decision to take a stand on numerous questions was spurred in part by his strong conviction that philosophy as accepted by many of his contemporaries constituted a menace to Christian life.

Olivi's most sustained critique of pagan philosophy is his treatise *How to Read the Books of the Philosophers*.[5] The work is, in a sense, a meditation on Paul's assertion that "God has made foolish the wisdom of this world." Olivi notes that these words reflect four major aspects of "worldly philosophy": The falsity of its errors, the truth of its reasoning, the emptiness of its teaching and the limited nature of its examination. The treatise then proceeds to examine these four aspects in order.

As to the falsity of its errors, Olivi argues that the teaching of the philosophers is false "in the principles on which it depends, the arguments by which it reasons, and the conclusions at which it arrives." Its principles are false because they are taken from sense experience. Building upon such a foundation, the philosophers could not attain truth, since "the principles of truth are most spiritual and most abstract, and the unspiritual man cannot grasp them because discernment or experience of them is spiritual rather than sensual." In dealing with the other two points Olivi simply marshals a variety of Biblical quotations to show that faulty arguments and conclusions follow from faulty premises.

Regarding the truth of its reasoning, Olivi notes that "worldly philosophy . . . contains wisdom in its matter or subject, in its form or mode, and in its proximate end." It has wisdom in its subject because its subject is being rather than nonbeing and because it divides sciences and substances according to types of being on the one hand and our mode of apprehension on the other. Since, he says,

> they saw that one sort of being did not come from ourselves, another sort came from our reason, and still another sort came from our will and action, they divided the sciences into real, rational, and practical, the real comprising the quadrivium, the rational the trivium, and the practical metaphysics and ethics or politics. And since, in dealing with things, our intellect ascends through three degrees, apprehending some things with the help of sensible qualities, others with the help of imaginable quantities, and others through the idea of intelligible essences—or, to put it another way, it apprehends some things with motion and quantity, others without motion yet with quantity, still others without either motion or quantity—they divided the real or speculative sciences into the categories of natural, mathematical, metaphysical or divine. Since reason by its very nature searches for the true, proper, and persuasive, they divided the rational sciences into grammar, which searches for the proper wording; logic, which seeks and sits in judgment upon true syllogisms; and rhetoric and poetry, which strive to produce persuasive syllogisms through the use of the various rhetorical and poetic techniques. Since our will seems to concern itself with three things—namely the soul, the life of the body, and external matter—the philosophers divided the practical sciences into the categories of ethical or political, medical or curative, and metaphysical.[6]

When Olivi attributes wisdom "in its form and mode" to worldly philosophy he means that "it investigates matters in an orderly way, moving from the general to the specific, from the obvious to the obscure," proceeding "by means of proof or ratiocination." When he allows it wisdom "in its proximate end," he means that each of the sciences is directed toward a goal which is really worth attaining. In the speculative sciences that goal is "the contemplation of real truth," while in the rational sciences it is "the formation of proper and fitting statements or, to speak in higher and subtler fashion, the proper ordering of the acts performed by our reason." In the practical sciences it is "the advantage of human regimen insofar as it pertains to this life." Nevertheless, its truth in these respects "is mixed with a great deal of pernicious falsity," since worldly philosophy, lacking true knowledge of God, "is improperly related to man's final end both in the speculative sciences, where the final end is perfect contemplation of God, and in the practical sciences, where the final end is perfect care and provision for human salvation."

In dealing with the third major point, the emptiness of worldly philosophy, Olivi wishes to impugn both the way in which philosophers proceeded and the end they envisaged for man. As to the former, Olivi argues that "they taught with temerity and presumption, without due reverence for the supreme master" and without observing "the simplicity befitting speech about divine matters." As to the latter, he maintains that man's end as the philosophers envisaged it is an empty one, "for if

---

[5] "De perlegendis philosophorum libris," edition cited in the bibliography.

[6] *Ibid.*, p. 40: "Unde quia viderunt quoddam esse ens non a nobis, quoddam vero essen ens nostrae rationis, quoddam vero esse ens nostrae voluntatis et actionis, idcirco diviserunt scientias in realem, rationalem seu sermocinalem et in practicam, reales attribuentes quadrivio, sermocinales trivio, practicas vero metaphysicis et ethicis seu politicis. Et quoniam circa res noster intellectus triplici gradu ascendit: quaedam enim apprehendit per adjutorium sensibilium qualitatum, quaedam vero per adjutorium imaginabilium quantitatum, quaedam vero per speciem intelligibilium quidditatum, seu quaedam apprehendit cum motu et quantitate, quaedam sine motu et cum quantitate, quaedam vero sine utroque, ideo scientias reales seu speculativas diviserunt in naturalem, mathematicam, metaphysicam seu divinam. Quoniam etiam ens rationis fuit circa intentionem veri, congrui et persuasivi, ideo diviserunt scientias rationales seu sermocinales in grammaticam, quae insistit circa inventionem congrui sermonis, in logicam, quae insistit circa inventionem et dijudicationem syllogismi verisimilis, et in rhetoricam simul et poeticam, quae insistunt circa inventionem syllogismi persuasivi et attractivi per locos rhetoricos et per tropos figurales et poeticos. Quia autem ens nostrae voluntatis et actionis videtur versari principaliter circa tria, videlicet circa animam, circa corpus vitale seu circa corporis vitam et circa exteriorem materiam, ideo practicam diviserunt in ethicam seu poeticam et in medicinam seu curativam et in metaphysicam."

there is no end beyond the one posited by worldly philosophy all things occur to wise and foolish alike and 'the wise man dies just as the fool does.'"

Finally, Olivi deals with "the particularity or limitation of its examination," claiming that the philosophers discovered "little concerning corporeal nature, less concerning rational or human nature, and least of all concerning intellectual or separate nature." As to the first, they were limited to what could be gleaned through the senses by repeated observation of external accidents. Thus they could say nothing precise about specific differences and forms or about those properties of bodies unobservable by our senses, and they could say little or nothing in cases where distance or other impediments rendered observation imprecise.

Their ignorance regarding human nature was even more abysmal. "How little they wrote about the origin . . . or powers of the soul!" Moreover, they knew nothing of "the cause of our natural corruption, or any number of other things relating to mankind, such as the division of languages, the original settlement of various lands, and matters of that sort." Their poorest showing was in the area of separate intellectual substances, which they regarded as gods. Their knowledge of the first cause was so limited that they were silent, not only concerning difficult matters like the trinity, but about such basic issues as God's justice, mercy, rewards, providence and creative power.

Olivi concludes with a summary of the philosophers' contribution to moral and political thought.

What they discovered regarding morality and the political rule of men is clear enough, for they taught us a false beatitude and consequently false virtues. I pass in silence over such things as the redemption and restoration of mankind, the grace of God our savior, angelic protection, the battle against demons, and the victory over temptations, concerning which the philosophers neither knew nor wrote anything that was true. Nor is this surprising, when all so disgracefully strayed from the worship of the true God that they were all equally enslaved by idolatry.[7]

The total picture is not encouraging. The philosophers were competent in grammar, logic, and rhetoric, and their knowledge of the physical sciences was adequate insofar as it could rest upon empirical observation. Beyond this point their achievement was a highly dubious one, a mixture of some truth and much error placed in the service of an improper end in the speculative and practical sciences. The result, Olivi observes, is about what one would expect from non-Christian man.

Nor should it be surprising if worldly philosophy is such, since its authors were such. For they have some share in the light of natural intelligence and thus were able to write some things that were true; yet they had it darkened by original and actual sin, causing them to mix truth with falsity. They had it in modest quantity and closely tied to matter, thus forcing them to proceed through attention to particulars. They had it without the light of faith and divine grace or friendship, and thus they were enslaved by empty falsehoods.[8]

Note that the blame falls upon pagan philosophy, not Aristotle alone. Olivi does not attempt to compare Aristotle unfavorably with Plato. In fact, the work closes with a quotation from Augustine which condemns both in the same breath. If either is favored it is Aristotle, since he is at least quoted from time to time, usually as a witness to the limitations of pagan philosophy. One emerges with the feeling that Aristotle deserves credit for having recognized, at least in part, the modesty of his own achievement.

Serious as Olivi's indictment may be, it is not intended to deter Christians from the study of pagan philosophy. Olivi is interested in determining *how* to study it, not *whether* to do so.

Since this philosophy is foolish, it must be read cautiously. Because some spark of truth is found in it, it must be read discreetly. Because it is useless in itself, it is to be used as a means rather than as an end. Because it is mean and, as it were, childish or slavish, it is to be read in a dominant rather than servile spirit, for we must be its judges and not its followers.[9]

The basic stance is, again, that of St. Augustine's *On Christian Doctrine*, which Olivi cites with approval. Pagan philosophy is destructive when pursued as an end in itself, valuable when used as a means. It must be restricted to an ancillary role.

Olivi's own handling of pagan philosophy in general and Aristotle in particular is largely explicable in terms of his determination to observe the Augustinian dictum himself and his pervasive fear that contemporaries are not doing so. He is not consistently hostile toward pagan philosophy. Anyone bothering to inspect all of the references to it in his works would probably discover that the majority are rather straightforward appeals to Aristotle's authority. He would certainly discover that

---

[7] *Ibid.*, p. 44: "Quid de moribus et de toto regimine hominum politico invenerunt, patet, quia falsam beatitudinem ac per consequens falsas virtutes nobis tradiderunt, ut taceam de redemptione et reparatione humani generis et de gratia Dei Salvatoris et de custodia angelica et de pugna contra daemones et eorum tentatione vincenda, de quibus nihil omnino veri sciverunt aut scripserunt? Nec mirum, quando omnes in cultu veri Dei sic turpiter erraverunt, ut cuncti pariter idolatriae deservirent."

[8] *Ibid.*, p. 37: "Nec mirum si mundana philosophia talis est, quia auctores ejus tales fuerunt. Habuerunt enim aliquid de lumine naturalis intelligentiae, et ideo potuerunt aliquid veritatis scribere. Habuerunt tamen illud cum obtenebratione originalis culpae et actualis maculae, ex quo multum falsitatis habuerunt veritati immiscere; habuerunt etiam in modica quantitate et multa materialitate, et ideo particulariter habuit eorum perscrutatio in veritate intrare; habuerunt etiam illud sine lumine fidei et divinae gratiae seu amicitiae, et ideo habuerunt vanitati deservire."

[9] *Ibid.*, pp. 37 f.: "Quoniam igitur haec philosophia est stulta, ideo perlegenda est caute. Quia vero est aliqua scintilla veritatis fulcita, ideo perlegenda est discrete. Quia vero est vana, ideo perlegenda est transitorie seu cursorie utendo ea ut via, non ut fine seu ut termino. Quia autem est modica et quasi puerilis seu paedagogica, ideo legenda est dominative, non serviliter; debemus enim ejus esse judices potius quam sequaces."

the majority of them make no explicit reference to the fact that the sources cited are pagan.[10] Moreover, anyone comparing Olivi's philosophical views with Aristotle's will recognize that he is anything but doctrinaire in his acceptance or rejection of Aristotelianism. Orazio Bettini has shown that while Olivi felt called upon to reject a number of theses associated with Aristotelianism in his own time, in other cases he rejected views held by Bonaventure in favor of a more Aristotelian position.[11]

Despite these facts, historians continue to perpetuate the image of Olivi as anti-Aristotelian. That reputation is not entirely unearned, either. At times he displays a striking personal animosity toward Aristotle, even when the Stagirite is apparently on his side. In one work he closes a long series of references to Aristotle's works with the comment that "there are many other ways in which this point could be defended by reference to Aristotle and his commentator, but I omit them for the sake of brevity and through dread of his authority."[12] On another occasion he remarks, "It seems that Aristotle was not of that opinion, although his authority displeases me greatly."[13]

The bitterness is, of course, hardly abated when he finds that Aristotle is in disagreement with him.

Aristotle does not seem to have been of this opinion, although it does not matter to me what he thought, since his authority, like that of any infidel and idolator, is nothing to me, especially in those things directly or indirectly related to the Christian faith.[14]

Sometimes he is not above a straightforward reply *ad hominem*.

If, however, it should be said that Averroes accepts the opposite view . . . and that he seems to draw it from the words of Aristotle, it should be noted that he similarly posits one intellect in all of us and was a Saracen, while Aristotle was a pagan and idolator.[15]

Olivi's rancor is partially explained by his suspicion that Aristotle's authority, far from displeasing his contemporaries, pleased a number of them too much. He protests against those who follow Aristotle as if he were "the god of this world,"[16] accepting him "as the infallible measure of all truth."[17] For the Christian, only the Bible and the Catholic faith should be granted such authority.[18] Olivi expresses his amazement that modern men, blessed with the advantage of Christian hindsight, should follow Aristotle into errors which he, as a pre-Christian philosopher, was unable to avoid. "These things," he says, "do not surprise me in a pagan born and bred in idolatry, but it is too astonishing that Christians who are theologians and even in religious orders should so esteem and practically adore his views on matters pertaining to theology or metaphysics."[19]

Thus Olivi rejects the *cult* of Aristotelianism with its unquestioning acceptance of Aristotle's opinions as the voice of truth. He opposes it because he sees it as a form of idolatry. He also opposes it, however, because he is convinced that in some areas Aristotelian philosophy is in direct opposition to the Christian faith. Thus Aristotle's uncritical worshipers are following him straight into heresy.

There is, for example, the issue of whether natural reason suggests that the world has existed from eternity. This question had attracted a great deal of attention in Olivi's time and was one of the important points in dispute at the University of Paris in the 1260's and 1270's. Like Bonaventure (and unlike Thomas Aquinas), Olivi sides with those who try to argue philosophically for the impossibility of an eternally existing world. In the process he makes it quite clear that he is arguing against Aristotle and that Aristotle's opinion on the subject is part of a larger complex of ideas compromising several Christian doctrines. He notes that

the error of the eternity of the world as posited by the philosophers of the world is based upon an impious foundation. As can be seen in Aristotle and his followers, it is especially founded upon three wicked notions. The first is that God does whatever he does necessarily, so that he could do it in no other way. . . . The second is that for everything which acts on some occasions but not on others (or acts in a certain way on some occasions but not on others) there must be some cause why it does so. . . . Because Aristotle saw that inferior causes varied in acting and not acting, it seemed to him that all inferior causes could be reduced to some cause which could uniformly cause contraries in other things, and it seemed to him that this was the eternal motion of the heavens. . . . The third is the idea that things emanate from the first cause in such a way that eternal and incorruptible things depend upon it more immediately than temporal and corruptible things; and among eternal things intellectual substances are more immediately related to it than corporeal substances; and among intellectual substances those which are supreme and more similar to it are more immediately related to it, these being so like the first cause that they considered and called them gods and hence they say that no inferior thing can be done by the first cause except through the intermediate superior substances.[20]

---

[10] Those wishing to engage in a limited experiment along these lines need only check the tables provided by the editor in the third volume of Olivi's II *Sent*.

[11] Bettini, 1958: pp. 176–197.

[12] II *Sent.*, q. 31 (I, 551).

[13] *Ibid.*, q. 31 (I, 548).

[14] *Ibid.*, q. 16 (I, 337).

[15] *Ibid.*, q. 57 (II, 341): "Si autem dicatur quod Averroes ponit primam, Super VIII Physicorum et alibi, et quod videtur eam trahere ex verbis Aristotelis: sciendum quod similiter ponit unum intellectum in omnibus nobis et fuit Saracenus, Aristoteles autem paganus et idolatra." Olivi does go on to add, in passing, that the view in question is presupposed rather than proved by Aristotle.

[16] *Ibid.*, q. 58 (III, 482). See also q. 54 (II, 269).

[17] *Ibid.*, q. 27 (I, 479). See also *Letter*, f. 52(64)r.

[18] II *Sent.*, q. 16 (I, 343).

[19] II *Sent.*, q. 6 (I, 131).

[20] *Ibid.*, q. 5 (I, 96 f.): "Nec mirum, quia error de aeternitate mundi, prout a philosophis mundi est positus, habet fundamentum impium; prout enim patet ex dictis Aristotelis, et sequacium eius, praecipuum fundamentum sumpserunt ex tribus nefariis. Primum est quod Deus quicquid agit necessario agit, ita quod nullo modo posset aliter agere nec amplius aut minus,

These principles lead to the denial, not only of creation as Christians affirm it, but also of divine and human freedom as accepted by the faith.

For if God does all things necessarily and cannot act otherwise, all fear and reverence, friendship and gratitude, hope and imprecation are useless and he has no real lordship over the course of things. And if freedom to choose between opposites is taken from him, even more is it taken from all those creatures beneath him.[21]

Nor do the impious conclusions stop at this point. Given such basic premises, "practically all the articles of the Christian faith are denied in a single breath."

For [this position] denies original sin, since it posits no first man, and thus it also denies the work of redemption. It posits either unity of the intellect, transmigration of souls through diverse bodies, or infinite souls, many of which remain eternally separate from the body. Moreover, since it assumes an eternal duration for the world and for human procreation, it clearly allows man no felicity except in this life.[22]

Let us take another example, the question of how one should go about distinguishing between *tempus* and *aevum*. The problem is essentially that of how the idea of time is related to beings like angels and heavenly bodies which, although created, are nontheless incorruptible. The scholastic theologians solved the problem to some extent by allowing them a special category, aeviternity (*aevum*), which was to be distinguished from both time (which was applicable to corruptible beings) and eternity (which was applicable to God alone).

The solution was only partial, however, since one still had to explain how these categories differed. Bonaventure decides that *tempus* differs from *aevum* inasmuch as the former implies a succession of before and after with variation while the latter involves a succession of before and after without variation.[23] Thomas Aquinas, finding it hard to imagine succession without variation, argues that there is no succession of before and after in *aevum*, although it differs from eternity inasmuch as before and after can be joined to it.[24]

Olivi stands solidly behind Bonaventure, largely because he is interested in establishing a clear-cut distinction between God and his creatures. He realizes that the Bonaventuran position is flawed by its failure to distinguish adequately between *tempus* and *aevum*, but he announces that he will accept it anyway because the opposite view "involves greater, more dangerous and (I believe) more evident problems."[25] He observes that "the view which involves smaller and less evident problems should not be avoided by accepting one with greater and more obvious difficulties, as some people have done in this matter."

Olivi has his own suspicions as to why some people have chosen the more dangerous view.

I believe that they were deceived by the pagan philosophers, who were forced to posit simple duration in the intelligences because they thought that they issued necessarily and eternally from God.... Moreover, as is apparent to anyone carefully studying their views and particularly those of Aristotle's followers, they felt that the operations of these intelligences were intrinsic, invariable, eternal, and even consubstantial with them. Nor is this surprising, since they thought them to be gods of a sort, although inferior to the highest God. Having accepted these affirmations—affirmations which negate the entire catholic faith in the most direct fashion—they were driven to hold that the duration of these intelligences was both simple and actually infinite. These [modern Christian philosophers], accepting those views of the pagan philosophers which did not seem to conflict with the faith, do not seem to have seen the contradiction involved in accepting one part of a view while rejecting another part which openly contradicts the faith.[26]

---

loquendo de immediata actione ipsius. Secundum est quod omnium quae aliquando agunt, aliquando non agunt aut quae aliquando sic agunt, aliquando vero non sic oportet reddere causam quare aliquando sic, aliquando vero non sic. . . . Quia igitur Aristoteles vidit inferiores causes in agendo et non agendo varie se habere: ideo visus est omnia inferiora reducere ad aliquam causam quae cum uniformitate posset esse in aliis causa contrariorum; visumque est ei quod haec erat motus caeli aeternus. . . . Tertium est, quia ut visum est eis, res per ordinem habent necessario emanare a prima causa, ita quod res aeternae et incorruptibiles immediatius sunt et dependent ab ea quam res temporales et corruptibiles; et inter aeterna intellectuales substantiae immediatius sunt ab ea quam substantiae corporales; et in intellectualibus illae quae sunt supremae et magis ei similes immediatius sunt ab ea illique in tantum similes quod eas deos putaverunt et vocaverunt; et hinc est quod ut dicunt, nullum inferiorum potuit esse a prima causa nisi per intermedias substantias superiores; videnturque sibi per hoc mirabilem ordinem ac concordiam et concatenationem ponere in toto universo."

[21] *Ibid.*, q. 5 (I, 97): "Si enim Deus omnia quae facit necessario facit nec aliter agere aut non agere potest: omnis timor et reverentia, amicitia et gratia, spes ac deprecatio seu imploratio frustra habetur ad eum nihilque veri dominii habet in rebus; et ex quo ab eo libertas in opposita tollitur, multo magis ab omnibus quae sunt sub ipso; ex quo iterum vorago infernalis impietatis consurgit, sicut in materia de libertate voluntatis humanae est abunde monstratum."

[22] *Ibid.*, q. 5 (I, 98): "Sicut autem habet impium fundamentum, sic habet et processum, quia omnes aut fere omnes articulos fidei catholicae uno flatu abnegat et de medio tollit; tollit enim peccatum originale, quia nullum primum hominem ponit et per consequens tollit totum opus redemptionis; ponit etiam aut unitatem intellectus aut revolutionem earundem animarum per diversa corpora aut infinitas animas et plures earum in aeternum manere separatas a corpore; et cum cursum istius saeculi et humanae generationis ponat in aeternum manere; patet quod nullam felicitatem statuit homini nisi in vita ista." This concatenation of ideas is reminiscent of Bonaventure. See *Collationes in hexaemeron, collatio* 3 and *collatio* 7 in *Opera* 5, where Bonaventure cites such errors as the eternity of the world, unity of the intellect, lack of any notion of reward and punishment after death, limitation of God's knowledge to himself, denial of divine prescience and providence, and fatalism. See also collatio 8 of the *Collationes de donis spiritus sancti* in: *Opera* 5, where he cites the errors of fatalism, the eternity of the world and the unity of the intellect.

[23] II *Sent.*, d. 2, pars 1, art. 1, q. 3 in: *Opera* 2.
[24] *Summa theologiae*, I, q. 10, art. 5.
[25] II *Sent.*, q. 9 (I, 177).
[26] "Via autem philosophorum paganorum, quantum credo, decepit istos; illi enim coacti fuerunt ponere in intelligentiis durationem simplicem, quia posuerunt eas exire a Deo necessario et aeternaliter et eas impossibile destrui et habere quandam

A final example, the question of whether each angel is a separate species, shows Olivi pursuing the same basic concern. Here again he opposes the Thomistic view, which he identifies with the pagan philosophers.

> To the first question it must be said that although some people, following the pagan and Saracen philosophers on this matter, have said and continue to say that each angel is a species in himself, . . . nevertheless I, following the sounder and more catholic teachers in this matter, believe that this position is not only contrary to reason and truth but dangerous for the faith.[27]

The Thomistic position is again attacked because it compromises the distinction between God and his creatures.

> How dangerous this error is can be gathered from what has been said. It posits in a creature eternity (according to before and after), immeasurable locality or presence, and immeasurable simplicity. It posits that there is no particular accident in these creatures, that there is no receptivity in them, that whatever is in them is substantial to them, and that as far as nature, grace, and glory are concerned they infinitely transcend the soul of Christ and all other souls. . . . And if one carefully studies the views of the philosophers regarding the plurality of gods, he will see that error contains all these others wtihin itself.[28]

In both the second and third examples the Thomistic view is challenged partly because Olivi spies in it the half-submerged ruins of Greek polytheism. He knows that Aristotelian philosophy was born in an alien religious environment and thinks Aristotle absorbed more of that environment than was healthy for him or his Christian followers. Thus it is clear to him that, while some aspects of Aristotelian thought are useful to the Christian, others are extremely dangerous and must be resolutely rejected.

Why, then, are so many purportedly wise Christians enthralled by the Aristotelian menace? Olivi thinks he has an answer. In the course of his question on the eternity of the world, after exposing the full implications of the opposing position, he remarks that wise men consider this error to be "one of the principal articles introductory to the infernal sect of the Antichrist."[29] He goes on to cite in rather garbled fashion Bonaventure's interpretation of the number 666 in Revelation 13:18 as a reference to certain errors of Aristotelian philosophy.[30] The passage is hardly the only one in which Aristotle is given eschatological implications. Comments of this sort are scattered throughout Olivi's writings and are most prevalent, as one might guess, in his Revelation commentary. Remember that the apocalyptic scenario for Olivi's time calls for a two-pronged attack upon the faith. While evangelical poverty is being challenged by luxury, Christian doctrine is being threatened by intellectual errors so subtle and enticing that in the days to come even the elect will be sorely tempted. Olivi rejects the notion that these errors could be caused by Catharism, since the sect contains so many "stupid and patently absurd errors" that the wise can in no way be seduced by it.[31] Besides, from the time of St. Francis and St. Dominic the Cathari have been so successfully combatted by evangelical men that they are now "about buried."[32]

Olivi himself is inclined to support the candidacy of Aristotelianism in the form espoused by his uncritical contemporaries. The threat from this quarter is so insidious that he describes it as the temptation of the mystical Antichrist, which in turn predisposes those tempted by it to ensnarement in the sect of the great Antichrist.[33]

It was noted earlier that the problems of Olivi's day are seen by him as analogous with those encountered in the third and fourth periods of church history, and that his favorite heretics of the third period are Origen and Arius. In the Revelation commentary his interest in

---

rationem universalitatis in sua essentia seu totum ambitum suae speciei, qui comprehendit, quantum est de sui ratione, totam aeternitatem tam a parte ante quam a parte post; universale enim secundum rationem suae universalitatis excedit omne tempus et omnem locum. Posuerunt etiam in eis operationes intrinsecas invariabiles et aeternas, immo etiam eis consubstantiales, sicut apparet inspicienti subtiliter dicta eorum et maxime sequacium Aristotelis; nec mirum, quia posuerunt eas tanquam deos, licet inferiores Deo summo. Istis autem positis quae directissime evacuant totam catholicam fidem necessarium fuit tenere durationem earum esse simul simplicem et actu infinitam; isti autem in parte dicta eorum accipientes, pro quanto videlicet visa sunt eis non repugnare fidei, visi sunt non attendisse quod contradictio implicabatur in accipiendo partem dicti cum abiectione partis alterius quae fidei aperte contrariabatur."

[27] Ibid., q. 33 (I, 596–597): "Ad quaestionem primam dicendum quod licet quidam sequentes in hac parte paganos philosophos et Saracenos dixerint et dicant quod quilibet angelus comprehendit totam suam speciem secundum totum suum ambitum, . . . sequendo tamen doctores in hac parte saniores et magis catholicos credo quod haec positio non solum est rationi et veritati contraria, sed etiam in fide valde periculosa."

[28] Ibid., q. 33 (I, 604): "Ex omnibus autem praedictis satis colligi potest quam periculosus sit iste error, quia ex hoc ponitur in creatura immensa aeternitas secundum ante et post, immensa localitas seu praesentialitas, immensa simplicitas et quod nullum in eis est accidens particulare et quod in eis nulla passio vel receptio et quod quicquid est in eis est eorum substantia et quod quantum ad naturam, gratiam et gloriam transcendunt in infinitum animam Christi et omnem aliam animam. . . . Et si quis bene inspexerit omnia dicta philosophorum de pluralitate deorum, recte ille error omnia illa in se includit." Olivi goes on to note that the argument used by his opponents would, if applied to the human intellect, lead to the Averroist conclusion that there is a single intellect in all men.

[29] II Sent., q. 5 (I, 98).

[30] See Bonaventure, *Collationes de septem donis spiritus sancti*, in *Opera* 5: p. 497. Olivi again alludes to the Bonaventuran interpretation, this time accurately, in *De perf.*, q. 16, f. 99r. For an extensive discussion of this and the following matters see Burr, 1971, "Apocalyptic Element."

[31] Apoc., f. 67rb.

[32] Apoc., f. 68va.

[33] Ibid., f. 67ra–rb. See also ff. 50va, 56vb, 83vb and 101ra, in which Olivi relates Aristotelianism, poverty, the mystical Antichrist and the great Antichrist in similar yet slightly different ways.

the Arians is closely connected with his conviction that their heresy was founded on an improper use of philosophy. At the Synod of Nicaea, he says, "many philosophers rent the church with horns of pride, impugning the catholic faith with diabolical arguments."[34]

The real source of the Arian heresy was Origen. Arius was a great scholar, but he was "puffed up with the errors of Origen."[35] Origen in turn was misled by Plato. In his commentary on the gospel of John, Olivi remarks that the Platonists posited one principal word but did not consider it to be consubstantial with the highest God. Thus Origen and Arius concluded that the word of God is a creature of lesser stature than God himself.[36]

Olivi puts all the pieces together in a *quodlibet* dealing with Saul's visit to the sorceress in I Samuel 28. He interprets the passage as a reference, among other things, to the "many philosophizing Christians who . . . consult a sorceress, that is, the philosophy of Aristotle."

And since truth is mixed with falsehood and there is present some image of the wisdom of Christ—which, nevertheless, the sorceress did not know—Saul recognized Samuel (i.e. Christ) and, bowed down toward the earth (i.e. to earthly writings), adored Christ there. . . . The sorceress will finally give him a calf to eat, that is, the error of Antichrist which lies in it in seminal form, of which Christ speaks in the Psalms when he says, "I am poor and lamenting, but I shall praise the Lord with a song and it will please him more than a young calf growing horns and hoofs," that is, the beast with two horns similar to those of the lamb, which ascends from the earth. But they fail to note that the error of Origen and the Arians proceeded from that other sorceress, the mother of this one, the philosopher Plato, who was Aristotle's master. Thus the error of Antichrist is to the error of the Arians as the philosophy of Aristotle is to the philosophy of Plato.[37]

Olivi's identification of Aristotelianism with the error of Antichrist does not in any way compromise the centrality of the poverty issue, for, as we have seen, the two issues are connected in Olivi's mind. This connection is amply illustrated in a passage from one of Olivi's *Questions on Evangelical Poverty*, in which the equation Antichrist/Arians = Aristotle/Plato is interpreted in terms which include the poverty dispute.

Aristotle's view of riches and human happiness is, I believe, . . . the root of the error of Antichrist. . . . And just as from the erroneous doctrine of Plato the master proceeded the Arian heresy, so, according to some masters, from the erroneous doctrine of this one proceeded the heresy of the Antichrist, which is a disciple of the Arian heresy just as Aristotle is a disciple of Plato.[38]

What, then, should the Christian do in this situation? Certainly the solution cannot lie in a hasty retreat from the battlefield. Simple anti-intellectualism will not work.

This point is an important one, for Olivi's broadsides against pagan philosophy and his Christian zeal often lead historians to think of him as in some sense anti-intellectual. Even those who recognize his scholarly interests and abilities sometimes have subscribed to this image at least to the point of saying that young Olivi was a medieval academic dropout who voluntarily renounced the *magisterium* because he thought it inconsistent with the humility demanded by his status as a Franciscan. In fact this latter theory, propounded by Franz Ehrle in 1887,[39] is honored by some of the most illustrious Olivi scholars writing today. Efrem Bettoni not only accepts the explanation but attributes it to Olivi himself, while Raoul Manselli describes it as *l'hypothèse qui vaut*.[40]

Such a view is quite untenable. Olivi's writings reveal no serious doubts concerning the compatibility of either study or the *magisterium* with Franciscan vows, except in one passage which we shall examine below. On the whole it would be tempting to suggest that as far as learning is concerned Olivi is more directly a son of St. Bonaventure than of St. Francis. While he is careful to define and delimit the bounds within which study can be considered acceptable, within those bounds he considers it to be commendable and even necessary, not only for Christians in general but even for Franciscans in particular. The range of acceptable subjects is, to be sure, determined by one's situation. Olivi remarks that the study of law is valuable for prelates but not for friars, who have renounced temporal concerns and would be better off studying something less worldly.[41] Nevertheless, intellectual pursuits remain an important part

---

[34] *Ibid.*, f. 44ra.
[35] *Ibid.*, f. 63rb–va.
[36] *Jn.*, f. 3vb.
[37] *Quodl.* II, q. 5, f. 12v: "Secundum mysterium est de multis philosophantibus christianis qui apertis heresibus effugatis unam phitonissam idest Aristotelis philosophiam in terra dei consulunt, quasi necessitate advocandi sapientiam christi. Et quia ibi falsis vera commixta occurrit et ibi aliqua imago sapientie Christi, quem tamen phitonissa non novit sed Saul intelligit quod esset Samuel, idest Christus, et in terram, idest in scripturam terrenam incurvatus Christum ibi adorat, et quantum in se est plurimum inquietat. Phitonissa vero finaliter dabit ei comedere vitulum suum idest errorem antichristi, qui in ea seminaliter latet, de quo in psalmo Christus dicit, Ego sum pauper et dolens, tamen laudabo nomen dei cum cantico, et placebit domino super vitulum novellum cornua producentem et ungulas, ipse est bestia que ascendit de terra habens due cornua similia agni. Negligunt autem isti advertere quod error Originis et Arrianorum de altera phitonissa huius matre processit, scilicet de philosophia Platonis qui Magister Aristotelis fuit, sic se habet error antichristi ad errorem Arrianorum sicut philosophia Aristotelis ad philosophiam Platonis."

[38] *De perf.*, q. 8, f. 40rb: "Dicendum quod sententia aristotelis de divitiis et felicitate humana est ut credo fomentum et radix erroris antichristi sicut et alii errores eius, sicut suo loco in plenitudine habet tradi. Ipse enim magister fuit regis alexandri de cuius successione processit radix peccati antiochus qui dicitur silentium paupertatis et qui est imago antichristi. Et sicut ex doctrina erronea platonis magister eius processit heresis arriana sicut secundum sententiam quorundam magistrorum ex doctrina huius erronea procedit heresis antichristi, que est discipula heresis arriane sicut aristoteles platonis." 11

[39] Ehrle, 1887, "Petrus Johannis Olivi," p. 412.
[40] Bettoni, 1959: p. 12; Manselli, 1972: p. 70.
[41] *De perf.*, q. 3, p. 158.

of the Franciscan life, and Olivi goes so far as to label "heretical" the idea that among friars manual labor for one's own support is superior to study.[42]

Olivi's attitude toward books is probably significant in this regard. He is, of course, aware that they can be the object of undue affection,[43] and he is perfectly willing to cite the story of how Francis responded negatively to the brother who asked for a psalter;[44] yet he also finds it necessary to observe that, in applying the principle of *usus pauper*, excess is harder to recognize in the case of books than in other situations.[45]

Again, there is the sheer mass of his theological and philosophical writings. Olivi invested a great deal of time and effort in what are clearly recognizable as the normal scholarly exercises of his day. He accepted the basic forms of scholarship provided by his time and employed them without any obvious sign of discomfort. Nor can his activities along these lines be seen as a passing phase, a type of activity which ceased as he grew older and wiser. However tempting it may be to divide Olivi's career into segments and argue that he eventually turned his back on scholastic thought in favor of apocalyptic speculation, we have seen that such a view is unsupportable. Far from representing two different phases of his career, Olivi's apocalyptic speculation and his *Questions on the Sentences* represent two types of scholarship which seem to have occupied him throughout his life.

Just as there is no evidence of any serious rebellion on Olivi's part against the basic scholarly techniques of his day, there is no evidence that the *magisterium* in particular was offensive to him. Certainly his career suggests no animosity toward teaching in itself, since Olivi seems to have served without protest as a *lector* in several places. Perhaps he felt that a *lector* could remain humble while a master could not; yet it is hard to imagine why he should have thought so.

The only solid evidence ever cited for Olivi's refusal of the *magisterium* actually points in the opposite direction. In a letter written around 1281 or 1282 [46] Olivi claims that he has feared "Parisian ambitions" and rejoices in Christ's decision to frustrate the world in its decision to elevate him to the *magisterium*.[47]

Impressive as the words may sound, a careful examination of their context will reveal their insufficiency as evidence for any voluntary renunciation on Olivi's part. In the first place, his fear of "Parisian ambitions" is introduced by him to explain, not why he never became a master, but why he hesitated in the past to write defending himself against the charges being leveled against him. In the second place, his approbation of Christ's decision to prevent the world from endowing him with the *magisterium*, far from suggesting a voluntary renunciation, is part of a passage which strongly hints at a very involuntary one. God, he says, has moved the heart of his superior, causing him to hold Olivi's teachings suspect.[48] The entire statement seems to imply that God has foiled the world by causing Olivi's career to be impeded through censure. To be sure, Olivi heartily endorses God's action, recognizing as he does that the cross must precede the crown; yet his approval is necessarily *ex post facto*. His renunciation is voluntary only insofar as he willingly surrenders that which he has already lost. True, he seems to suggest that he predicted and approved of his failure to attain the *magisterium* long before it occurred, feeling that such a worldly honor would have to be considered a sign of divine reprobation rather than election. Nevertheless, the entire passage clearly assumes that, whether Olivi wanted the *magisterium* or not, his failure to attain it was primarily due to the intervention of others rather than to his own free decision.

It is not necessary to conclude that Olivi's references to "Parisian ambitions" and "the ambitions of a human *magisterium*" represent nothing more than sour grapes. They are probably that in part, but they are also consistent with other important aspects of his thought. In the first place, one is reminded of Olivi's thoughts on divine providence in his 1295 letter to the captive sons of Charles II,[49] where adversity is greeted with the consoling announcement that God chastizes those whom he loves and that suffering is nothing less than conformity with the pattern of Christ himself, or any number of his comments on the conformity with Christ's life and suffering to be experienced by the Franciscan order.

In the second place, Olivi's references to "Parisian ambitions" and "the ambitions of a human *magisterium*" probably reflect his attitude toward the situation at Paris more than toward the *magisterium* in general. It is hardly surprising that Olivi should have looked upon

---

[42] *Ibid.*, q. 4, p. 164.
[43] *Ibid.*, q. 8, f. 11ra.
[44] *Rule Commentary*, p. 189.
[45] *De perf.*, q. 9, f. 67rb.
[46] This letter is found in the Venice, 1509 edition of Olivi's *Quodliberta*, where it is listed as addressed to R. de Camliaco. It will be discussed at length in chapter five.
[47] *Letter*, f. 51(63)v: "Veritatem dico in Christo Jesu, non mentior, testimonium mihi perhibente consciencia in Spiritu Sancto quod quadam grandi erubescencia, quodam consciencie stimulo, Parisienses ambitiones perhorrescens, vobis et sociis vestris scribere non curavi, nisi aliquando et raro ex litteris mihi missis compulsus; et longe ante predixeram non ut vates propheticus sed instinctu interioris sensus inspiratus; quia et si mundus vellet me ad ambitiones humani magisterii sublevare, christus hoc nullatenus pateretur; addens quod et si hoc propter peccata mea permitteret quasi signum mihi esset reprobationis eterne, aut saltem abiectionis ab illa singulari electione de qua ille gloriatur psallens, Elegi abiectus esse in domo domini magis quam habitare in tabernaculis peccatorum."

[48] *Ibid.*: "Putasne innuisset deus in cor prelati mei ut me tanquam suspectum de veritate aut forte tanquam falsarium veritatis abiiceret diffamaret reprobaret ac condemnaret." In MS. Paris, Bibl. nat. nouv. acq. 774, f. 94r the first four words are *Putasne nisi misisset Deus*.
[49] *Epistola ad regis Sicilie filios*, edition cited in bibliography. See chapter nine of this work.

the Parisian academic scene with some distaste. He saw it as a place where the carnal church was offering particularly bitter resistance to the dawning third age. It was at Paris that the mendicant orders were beset by bitter opposition in the thirteenth century. Olivi seems to be thinking of this opposition when he observes that in the infancy of the Franciscan order, while the kings of the world were adoring Christ's poverty in that order, "the new Herod of the carnal doctors" was trying to kill it.[50] In another place he explicitly refers to the Parisian doctors' attack on the mendicants.[51]

Again, it was at Paris that the controversy over Aristotelian philosophy came to a head during Olivi's years as a student and teacher. The special connection in Olivi's mind between Paris and Aristotelian heterodoxy is specifically noted in his reference to the "many philosophizing clerics at Paris" who trust only in worldly philosophy, and in his observation that during the time of the mendicant controversy there appeared at Paris "many philosophical or rather pagan errors."[52]

Olivi's attitude toward Paris may well have been conditioned by still another factor which can be mentioned but not adequately described at this time, since a great deal of research must be done before the matter can be discussed intelligently. It is not impossible that Olivi's attitude toward the situation at Paris was affected by his southern French background. One must recall that the thirteenth century was marked, not only by the controversies regarding mendicancy and Aristotelian philosophy, but by the Albigensian crusade and the subsequent extension of Capetian authority in Languedoc. During the closing decades of that century, memories of relative political independence were still fresh and cultural differences between north and south still pronounced. Moreover, these cultural differences may have included significant differences in piety. Olivi was, of course, no friend of the Cathari, but a native of Olivi's region did not have to be a supporter of Catharism in order to be an enemy of the northern French crusaders. Here, however, the historian has little material to work with, since Olivi's attitude toward the Albigensian crusade never surfaces clearly in his works. He does mention the crusade in his Revelation commentary, where it is cited, along with the resulting sack of Olivi's own Béziers, as an example of the disruptive events which signaled the birth of the Franciscan order.[53] Olivi does not pursue the matter, however, and the passage leaves us without any notion of whether such events excited an emotional response on his part. One is tempted to assume that the fate of his native region can hardly have fired Olivi's enthusiasm for Paris, the major northern French political and cultural center, but Olivi offers us little in the way of evidence to support such an assumption.

At any rate, it is clear that Olivi saw the church threatened by error, attributed that error in part to carnal doctors, and thought Paris to be an especially good example of this phenomenon. The scholarly world of his day was, then, one of the major points at which the carnal church was attacking. Far from counseling retreat in this area, Olivi seems to have favored a determined resistance. The temptations introduced by the carnal doctors had to be opposed, not by a rejection of scholarship, but by the cultivation of a different type of scholarship, one more fully consonant with the Christian faith and virtues. The leaders in this battle would be the *doctores spirituales*. With the aid of a scholarship firmly anchored to the Bible and informed by Christian love and humility, these spiritual doctors would help to rescue the church from the errors plaguing it.[54] Despite his observation that since the time of St. Francis *idiotae* are more easily drawn to repentence than clerics or monks,[55] Olivi's essentially hierarchical world view conspires with his respect for learning and his experience of the *status quo* to convince him that some sort of *magisterium* is necessary. The real choice facing Christianity is one between two different types of *magisterium*. One type, that of the carnal doctors, judges the Bible in the light of worldly philosophy. The other type, that of the spiritual doctors, judges worldly philosophy in the light of the Bible. One despises evangelical poverty and humility. The other is so endowed with Christian humility and scorn for earthly rewards that the spiritual doctors will prohibit their disciples from honoring them. The disciples, of course, will therefore honor them all the more.[56] Thus Olivi envisages an ideal *magisterium* in which the claims of Christian humility are reconciled with those of the hierarchical principle. He firmly believes in both and feels that there is room for both in scholarship as in ecclesiastical government.

It is significant that the tense has begun to hover between present and future. Olivi's attitude toward the *magisterium* cannot be isolated from his conviction that the world is moving into another period. The coming years will witness great tribulation, for the carnal church will seek to mislead the faithful with intellectual temptations so complex and alluring that even the most learned of the elect will barely avoid succumbing; yet it will also witness an increase in the knowledge available to the elect and a change in the form of that knowledge. It would be an oversimplification to say that Olivi believes in a progressive illumination of God's people in history. The pattern he envisages is more complex, allowing for periods when knowledge and virtue wane as well as wax.[57] Nevertheless, the overall tendency is toward

---

[50] *Apoc.*, f. 54ra–rb.
[51] *Ibid.*, f. 83rb.
[52] *Ibid.*, ff. 67rb–va, 83vb.
[53] *Apoc.*, f. 53rb.

[54] *Ibid.*, ff. 74va, 118ra, 119ra, 121vb–122ra.
[55] *Ibid.*, f. 73va.
[56] *Ibid.*, ff. 121vb–122va. See also f. 118ra.
[57] See for example *De perf.*, q. 8, ff. 45va and 47ra–vb.

greater knowledge. Just as the Old Testament prophets could not grasp the mysteries of divine providence as fully as those living after the event of Christ, so those living in the first five periods of church history could not comprehend these mysteries as fully as those who will appear in the sixth and seventh periods.[58] Thus the doctors of the sixth and seventh periods will be able to disseminate and interpret Christian knowledge more satisfactorily than their predecessors, and it will be during this third general period of world history that Christianity will witness an event predicted by Paul and dear to Olivi's heart, the conversion of the Jews and infidels.

Note that the doctors' role includes both interpretation and dissemination. Far from spending their days sequestered in academic ivory towers, Olivi's spiritual doctors are preachers as well as scholars.[59] In the coming days they will place their learning at the service of Christian missionary activity. Here Olivi's understanding of the spiritual doctors is closely related both to his view of the relationship between contemplation and action and to his thoughts on the missionary task facing the Franciscan order.

The former matter need not detain us long. In the first of his *Questions on Evangelical Perfection*, having established the essential superiority of the contemplative over the active life, Olivi outlines the conditions under which one should temporarily abandon the former for the latter. The first (and for Olivi clearly the most interesting) of these is when the salvation of others can be furthered. He explicitly alludes to the preaching and defense of the faith.[60] Such activity robs the Christian of time which could be spent in contemplation, but it is not thereby entirely opposed to contemplation, since the concern for others implied in this service is motivated by contemplation itself, in which one comes to love God both in himself and in all his works. Thus contemplation leads to love for God and consequently for one's neighbor.[61] Again, he who takes interest in the salvation of others conforms himself with God, who governs and leads his creatures to perfection.[62]

This missionary imperative is particularly important for the Franciscan order. We have seen how Olivi makes the development of his order a major event in the unfolding history of the sixth and seventh periods. The founding of the order was a major sign of evangelical rejuvenation in the church. In the coming days, when the rejuvenation is opposed by the carnal church, the Franciscans—or at least a righteous remnant among them—will be prominent among those defending the gospel by their word and act.

The acts are obvious enough. By practicing absolute poverty the Franciscans incarnate evangelical perfection in a church and society long debased by worldliness and greed. Raoul Manselli contends that Olivi differs in this respect from many of the Italian spiritual Franciscans, who placed relatively greater emphasis upon the eremitic life and less on the idea of serving the faithful by example within the world. In Manselli's words, Olivi feels that "all his confreres should live among the faithful and for the faithful, . . . rigorously actualizing the gospel in order to attract souls to themselves."[63]

The ministry of the word to be performed by Franciscans in the sixth period is also important. We have seen how he interprets the Franciscan role in missionary activity as a continuation of the pattern set by Francis himself with his mission to the Moslems, and how he foresees a major *coup* among the Greeks, Moslems, and Jews in the days to come.[64] The important point to be made at present is that Francis's followers will be well prepared for this task, as Francis himself was, for they will possess knowledge surpassing that enjoyed by Christians in preceding periods. In commenting upon Revelation 10, Olivi remarks that the angel with a face like the sun will be clothed with a pure and celestial knowledge of scripture. Not only will he thoroughly understand the Bible, but he will be equipped with the ability to impart his knowledge to others. In the process Olivi makes it clear that he identifies the angel with Christ, Francis, and Francis's spiritual progeny.[65]

Thus in this passage, as elsewhere in his works,[66] Olivi insists that in the third general age there will be—in fact, there already is—a gradual increase in the knowledge enjoyed by God's elect. This increased knowledge is sometimes identified by Olivi with an improved ability to interpret the Bible, particularly its spiritual meaning.[67] Occasionally it is conceived at least partly as a fuller understanding of the course of history as prophesied in the Bible, especially Revelation.[68] Certainly it is closely tied with a new understanding of the Biblical teaching on poverty and contemplation.

Ultimately, however, it will include even more striking results. There will be a shift from the sort of scholarship which befitted clerics in the second general age to a "chaste and sweet contemplation more befitting monks." In this contemplation *affectus* and *intellectus* will be more closely allied than ever before. The elect, taught by the Holy Spirit and inflamed with divine love, will not only understand divine wisdom but will taste and feel it.[69]

The psychic change suggested here will be less radical than the reader might first imagine. Elsewhere, without

---

[58] *Ibid.*, ff. 8ra, 73rb, 119ra.
[59] *Ibid.*, ff. 68vb and 118va; *Mtt.*, f. 84vb.
[60] *De perf.*, q. 1, p. 422.
[61] *Ibid.*, p. 432.
[62] *Ibid.*, p. 422.

[63] Manselli, 1955: pp. 218 f.
[64] E.g. in *Apoc.*, ff. 72va–73va and *Rule Commentary*, p. 192 f.
[65] *Apoc.*, f. 73rb.
[66] For example *Lk.*, f. 13v and *Mtt.*, f. 155rb–va.
[67] *Apoc.*, ff. 60vb, 73rb.
[68] *Ibid.*, ff. 8ra, 43ra, 83rb.
[69] *Ibid.*, f. 31rb.

reference to any new age, Olivi distinguishes between *sapientia* as mere *cognitio* and *sapientia* which includes *gustum et affectionem seu amorem ordinatum ad ipsam sapientiam dei*.[70] In another place he speaks of study which involves not only intellectual but affectual adherence to the faith, "so that it is not only understood but tasted and devoured."[71] Olivi's works abound with references to *sapor* and *gustus* in relation to knowledge or contemplation. In the first of his *Questions on Evangelical Perfection* he notes that,

the union of our mind with God, called "contemplation" by the saints, is nothing other than the application of our intellect to God, the intellectual perception and apprehension of God, the intimate penetration of him through the fervor of our love, and the tasting of him, . . . a process begun in the intellect purified by faith and consummated in the act of love. . . . It always has joined with it a gustatory sense (*sensum degustantem*) which is called "taste" (*gustus*). Whether this sense is an act of the intellect or of the will or of some other power in us I do not intend to discuss at present.[72]

In the preceding passages Olivi is not simply talking about the third age but rather about true Christian contemplation in any age. Thus the contemplation of the third age will apparently develop from elements already present in the second. The element of continuity should not be overlooked.

Nevertheless, Olivi's line of thought is striking enough in any case. The general development he envisages for the third general period is in the direction of a state in which the spirit will teach the elect all truth directly without the need of books or of education as we know it. Olivi observes that this goal will be fulfilled *simpliciter* only in the church triumphant, but predicts that it will be fulfilled *secundum quid* in the church militant during the seventh period of church history.[73]

Such a happy state is, of course, very much in the future as far as Olivi is concerned. He considers himself to be living at a time when the sixth period is just dawning. Thus there is no reason to assume that his theology of history would lead him to espouse a *radically* different type of scholarship from that practiced by his predecessors. His extant works, and particularly his *Questions on the Sentences,* are evidence of the extent to which he accepted the academic forms prevalent in his own day.

This is not to say his scholarly methods were entirely unaffected by his apocalyptic predilections. One would guess that, if his eschatological presuppositions were to affect any aspect of his scholarly work, they would most strongly influence his Biblical exegesis. This is a delicate question and the answer to it would involve comparing Olivi's commentaries with those of other scholars in his time. Presumably future scholars will carry out this research, but no one has done it yet.

At any rate, it is clear that Olivi felt his position in history accorded him both special intellectual advantages and a special responsibility. He was a beneficiary of the new light available since the time of Joachim and Francis, and he had to use it in the service of the faith. The immediate task facing Christian scholars like himself was to identify and to combat the attacks launched against Christian doctrine and life by the carnal church and its doctors. Olivi had to wield the finest intellectual weapons at his disposal in the defense of theological orthodoxy and Franciscan poverty.

V. CONTROVERSY AND CENSURE, 1274–1285

In 1279, when Olivi made his contribution to the deliberations concerning *Exiit qui seminat*, he must have seemed a young man on the way up. Within the next four years his situation changed dramatically, and in 1283 he was severely censured by members of his own order. The story of this transformation is not entirely known, but certain elements are obvious and others can be deduced from the available evidence. The result is a picture of diverse factors combining to blight a promising career at its inception.

We must begin by acknowledging that all of Olivi's troubles did not begin in 1279. Even before that date he seems to have had one or more encounters with authority. Angelo Clareno furnishes some evidence in this regard when, in his *History of the Seven Tribulations of the Franciscan Order*,[1] he relates how Jerome of Ascoli, minister general from 1274 to 1277, asked to see some questions which Olivi had written on the Virgin Mary. These questions had been denounced, Angelo says, by envious brothers. Having received and examined them, Jerome ordered them burned. When the order had been carried out, Olivi departed with an unchanged face and a tranquil soul, rejoicing as if he had received a great honor, and celebrated mass. One of his friends, assuming that Olivi's spiritual state must have been profoundly affected by his experience, asked him how he could go straight from his humiliation to mass without resorting to confession on the way. He naturally assumed that Olivi would have thought a few things that urgently needed confessing before he partook of the eucharist. The friend was, of course, wrong.

---

[70] *Eccl.*, f. 5va.

[71] *Rule Commentary*, p. 188: "ita quod non solum intelligatur sed etiam saporetur et devoretur."

[72] *De perf.*, q. 1, p. 417: "Unio mentis nostrae ad Deum, quae a sanctis 'contemplatio' dicitur, nihil aliud est, nisi intellectus nostri applicatio ad Deum; et Dei intellectualis perceptio et apprehensio, ipsiusque per amoris fervorem intima penetratio; fortisque et firma ad nostra intima eius attractio iugisque degustatio; ab amore magis amicitiae quam concupiscentiae imperata; ab intellectu fide purificato inchoata et tandem in amoris actu perfecte quietative consummata. Qui semper habet adiunctum secum sensum degustantem, qui 'gustus' dicitur; sive hic sensus sit actus intellectus, sive voluntatis, sive alicuius alterius potentiae mentis nostrae; quod inquirere et discutere, non est praesentis intentionis."

[73] *Apoc.*, f. 120rb.

[1] Angelo Clareno, 1886: p. 288.

Olivi replied that he rejoiced over his treatment, regarding it is a spiritual benefit. He then added in somewhat more worldly fashion that the incinerated questions were no great loss anyway since he could easily reproduce them or write others on the same subject.

Angelo also reports that, when Jerome later became Pope Nicholas IV, Olivi's enemies tried to enlist his support against their innocent victim, but Nicholas replied with ample praise of Olivi's virtue and an announcement that his questions on the virigin were orthodox . Their burning was conceived as an exercise in humility.

It is hard to decide what should be done with this story, since Angelo is not exactly an impeccable source. The basic idea that Olivi's questions were inspected and burned seems to be based upon some real difficulty experienced by him, since it is hardly the stuff of which hagiography is made. Moreover, corroborating evidence is provided by a fourteenth-century list of Olivi's purported condemnations, according to which Jerome burned some of Olivi's writings at a gathering of brothers at Montpellier.[2] Other documents directed at the spirituals by the community in the early fourteenth century confirm that some of Olivi's writings were burned in Jerome's time.[3] Thus it is likely that Olivi actually was censured at some sort of meeting, perhaps a provincial chapter.

As to the rest of Angelo's story, the part about Olivi's response is at least consistent with what we know of his personality. Moreover, the final comment about producing more questions suggests a jauntiness not likely to have been invented by his followers. The least likely element is, of course, Jerome's later explanation of what the whole episode was about. Although not impossible, it is at least improbable that the minister general would summon a young scholar and destroy his works in front of his peers just to test his humility, particularly since at the time he does not seem to have let anyone else in on the inner meaning of the event. One is left with the suspicion that Jerome found something really objectionable about Olivi's questions and acted accordingly.

This suspicion is shared by various scholars, but for profoundly different reasons. Some, like Louis Jarraux, assume that Olivi sinned on the side of the angels by praising Mary too lavishly.[4] Others, following Victorin Doucet,[5] offer precisely the opposite theory. In the course of his explorations through the Olivi manuscripts at Padua, Doucet discovered an excerpt from a question in Olivi's *Sentence* commentary dealing with the Immaculate Conception. In this passage Olivi asserts that the Virgin needed purgation from all stain of original sin from the time she conceived Christ, but it was neither necessary nor fitting that she be so purged before his conception. He then cites a variant opinion according to which she was preserved from all original sin. The next fourteen lines of the text are erased, then the text continues with the words "honorific to the mother and son, nevertheless it is simply heretical, impious, and blasphemous." [6]

Doucet concludes that, although a pious reader tried to defend the Virgin's honor by selective erasure, the text still shows Olivi to have been a strong opponent of the doctrine of Immaculate Conception who attacked it in the strongest of terms. This conclusion is supported, he feels, by two other sources. First, an anonymous *Sentence* commentary now at Florence cites an unnamed Joachimite who says that the doctrine is heretical, impious, blasphemous, and insulting.[7] Second, Nicolaus Eymeric includes among those opposing the doctrine "Master Peter John, of the order of the brothers minor, who says in the third book of his *Sentence* commentary that . . . to say the blessed Mary was not conceived in original sin is insane, impious, blasphemous, and heretical." [8]

The Padua manuscript of Olivi's *Sentence* commentary is less satisfactory evidence than one might at first imagine, since it probably reflects Olivi's teaching during the years 1287/88, a full decade after the probable censure by Jerome.[9] Nevertheless, there is reason to hope that Olivi's opinion regarding the Immaculate Conception was not radically altered by censure, since, as we shall see in the next chapter, his views on marriage survived the censure of 1283 practically unscathed. Thus it is possible that the view promulgated in the 1280's was essentially the same one burned in the 1270's.

There is at least some evidence from the early 1280's that Olivi did not favor the doctrine of the Immaculate Conception. In his treatise on original sin, written sometime between 1280 and 1282,[10] he notes that a level of mental and bodily purity in which no trace of impurity remains can be effected by God alone, "as was done in the Virigin when she conceived the son of God." [11] Somewhat later he says that Mary's virtue was such that the *fomes* of sin was held bound and restrained from any vicious act before Christ's conception, yet could not be utterly eradicated.[12] In his Matthew commentary, which was written slightly before the treatise on original sin, Olivi says, "We hold without doubt that from the time she conceived Christ she was unable to sin." [13]

---

[2] Amorós, 1931: p. 502.

[3] Raymundus de Fronciacho, 1887: p. 13; Delorme, 1945: p. 86.

[4] Jarraux, 1933: p. 135.

[5] Doucet, 1933: pp. 560–563.

[6] MS. Padua, Univ. 1540, f. 262d.

[7] MS. Florence, Biblioteca Nazionale, D4.27.

[8] *Tractatus de conceptione B. Virginis*, MS. Vat. lat. 10497, f. 87b.

[9] See Heynck, 1956: p. 397.

[10] See Heynck, 1964: p. 344.

[11] II *Sent.*, q. 111 (III, 278).

[12] *Ibid.*, p. 284.

[13] *Mtt.*, f. 95 va.

Granting that Olivi rejected the Immaculate Conception, we are still left with the question of whether his view would have been thought to merit censure. Doucet's theory is sometimes challenged on the ground that the question was an open one in Olivi's time. Such is indeed the case. In fact, opposition to the doctrine within Olivi's order was sufficiently widespread for one modern scholar to argue that "not a single doctor of the Franciscan order who wrote in this period . . . held that our lady was immune from original sin."[14] Such an objection is not quite to the point, however, since Doucet locates Olivi's real offense not in his opinion but in the *hardiesses de langage* with which he defended it. These, Doucet feels, more than justified the measures taken against him. He is referring, of course, to the words "heretical, impious, and blasphemous."

Even if one gives Doucet's assertion the most benign interpretation and assumes that he means "justified" according to the standards of the time, there is the problem of whether such terminology actually would have been considered excessive enough to merit censure. Albert the Great uses the word "heretical" in connection with the doctrine[15] and, given the unsettled state of the question, it is entirely possible that the other words were used as well in Olivi's day. Nevertheless, we must avoid the error of crediting Olivi's age with a degree of consistency unachieved by any succeeding period including our own. When the Olivian views censured in 1283 are compared with those held by other theologians in the late thirteenth and early fourteenth centuries, it will be apparent that there is nothing incredible about the idea that Olivi was reprimanded for asserting about the Immaculate Conception what someone else had said with impunity. Such a situation is, in fact, precisely what we would expect from a time when the boundary between orthodoxy and heresy was vague and the faith was zealously guarded by those in authority.

There is good reason to believe that Olivi was questioned on other matters during Jerome's tenure as minister general. In a later work he parries a criticism of his view on marriage by protesting that he has already satisfied brother Jerome on that score and has said nothing about it since.[16] In another work, in the process of answering questions about his understanding of baptism and of the relation of existence to essence, Olivi explains in each case that he said something on the subject "before the time of Brother Jerome."[17] Thus he may have been challenged on several topics, although it is impossible to say whether he came to grief on the matter of the Virgin alone or on other issues as well.

However he may have been treated by Jerome, Olivi was to fare poorly indeed under his successor, Bonagratia of St. John in Persiceto. The story of his difficulties cannot be reconstructed completely, but a plausible theory can be spun around certain dates and documents. The key event took place in 1283, when Bonagratia ordered a commission of four masters and three bachelors of theology at Paris to examine Olivi's writings. Having complied, the commission censured some. Olivi was deprived of his writings and frustrated in his attempt to defend himself until 1285, when he finally addressed a letter to the commission.

These events, which we shall examine below, are very well documented. Starting with 1283 is, however, like arriving for the second act of a play. We cannot help wondering how Olivi worked himself into such a situation. How we answer that question—in fact, whether we try to answer it at all—will depend to some extent on what we do with a letter in which he answers attacks upon his writings and observes that he has been deprived of them. Both the recipient and the date of this letter are uncertain. The salutation of a sixteenth-century edition announces that it is addressed to "R. de Camliaco and his associates,"[18] but a manuscript copy says "Rdo. and dearest associates."[19] In the manuscript the letter is preceded by an announcement that it was sent to "Raymond Gaufredi and his associates before he became minister general." Gratien de Paris and others tend to accept this latter assertion as true,[20] but the matter is hardly closed. It would be nice to believe that the letter was written to Raymond Gaufredi, since that would tie a number of things together rather neatly, as we shall see later. Nevertheless, since Raymond was a famous man, it is entirely possible that the manuscript reads as it does because someone saw the abbreviated name "Rdo." and leaped to an unwarranted conclusion. Throughout this work we shall adopt the cowardly, awkward, and prudent expedient of referring to the document as "the letter to R."

The other great problem concerns the date. Franz Ehrle, knowing that Olivi was deprived of his writings after 1283 and assuming that the nineteen charges to which he responds in the letter represent a selection of those leveled by the Paris commission, concludes that the letter was written between 1283 and 1285.[21] Ehrle himself recognizes that his dating involves a serious problem. In the letter Olivi says that the general minister now possesses the self-defense he made before his provincial minister, yet there was no minister general between October, 1283, and the spring of 1285. Nevertheless, everything else seems to work out so well that Ehrle accepts the dating anyway.

Joseph Koch is more disturbed by the discrepancy and proceeds from it to a completely different dating.[22] He

---

[14] Carlo Balić, 1958: p. 196.
[15] *Commentarii in tertium librum sententiarum*, d. 3, a. 4, in: *Opera* 27.
[16] *Responsio* I, p. 127.
[17] *Letter*, ff. 51(63)v and 52(64)r.

[18] *Ibid.*, f. 51(63)v.
[19] MS. Paris, Bibliothèque Nationale, Nouv. acq. 774, f. 94r.
[20] Gratien de Paris, 1913: pp. 414–422.
[21] "Petrus Johannis Olivi," pp. 426 f.
[22] Koch, 1930: pp. 489–522.

argues that the minister is Bonagratia and the letter antedates the general chapter of 1282, at which a discussion of the Olivi affair led to the call for an investigation of his writings. Koch notes that Raymond of Fronsac refers to "two letters of brother Bonagratia" written against Olivi's errors.[23] The first, Koch surmises, contained the list of nineteen errors, while the second passed judgment upon these errors and called for the surrender of Olivi's writings. This judgment is, then, distinct from the one that came in 1283. Thus Raymond of Fronsac and Bonagratia of Bergamo later felt justified in claiming that Bonagratia of St. John in Persiceto had "conducted various processes" against Olivi's doctrine and followers.[24]

How, then, did Olivi come to be criticized before 1282? Koch points to another document, the so-called *Attack (Impugnatio)*.[25] This work begins rather enigmatically with a passage proclaiming that the first article threatening evangelical poverty has been proved erroneous and that the following articles will be dealt with briefly in the same order used in proposing them. Koch deduces from these words that Olivi has discussed the poverty question in a separate treatise and that the present work is a clarification of an earlier work which attacked the same series of articles.

Historians are practically unanimous in asserting that the *Attack* can be identified as the "explication of those things which I wrote against Brother Ar." mentioned in Olivi's letter to R.[26] They are much less than unanimous as to who Brother Ar. might have been. Sbaralea identifies him as Arlotto of Prato.[27] If so, Olivi's strictures came back to haunt him, since Arlotto became a member of the Paris commission and later was elected minister general. It is highly unlikely that he was the man, however. The trouble seems to have started in Olivi's own province, and it seems sensible to look in that direction for his chief opponent.

Ehrle fulfills at least that requirement when he nominates Arnold of Roquefeuil for the honor.[28] According to a fourteenth-century report, when Arnold was provincial minister he joined with thirty-five other brothers from the province of Provence in a document declaring that Olivi was the leader of a superstitious sect as well as a sower of dissension and error in Provence.[29] Thus he certainly qualifies as a major antagonist. Here again, if this choice is the right one Olivi was attacking someone who would be in a position to hurt him. Again, however, the identification is probably incorrect. Gratien de Paris notes that the Paris manuscript of Olivi's letter to R. refers to brother Ar. as *bone memorie*.[30] Thus Arnold of Roquefeuil, who was very much alive long after this letter could have been written, is not the man.

Gratien points to the fourteenth-century complaint by Raymond of Fronsac that "brother Peter Olivi carried on quarrels with brother Arnold Galhardi and many other good brothers who opposed his erroneous sayings."[31] Here we finally seem to have hit upon a strong candidate. The attribution is peculiarly unsatisfying, since it leaves us with little more than a name; yet it is probably the correct one.

Koch argues that the separate work on poverty alluded to in the opening passages of the *Attack* is none other than the treatise *Quoniam contra paupertatem evangelicam*. Thus in the realm of poverty the issue was *usus pauper*. Koch asserts that the quarrel between the two men began over this question, and the first extant writing connected with the quarrel is *Quoniam contra paupertatem evangelicam*, which was written between 1279 and 1282. Koch prefers to place it as early as possible in order to allow room for what followed. The treatise was meant for Bonagratia, the minister general. This opening round went to Olivi, since Bonagratia agreed with him on the issue of *usus pauper*.

Brother Ar., now at a decided disadvantage, saw that he would have to attack Olivi on some other issue. He turned to theology, an area in which Olivi was demonstrably vulnerable. The result was a list of nineteen questionable theses from Olivi's writings which Brother Ar. sent to Bonagratia. Olivi soon heard of this list and assembled his own. This one, also dispatched to Bonagratia, contained a list of suspect theses from Brother Ar.'s works.

It is impossible to say what Bonagratia did with Olivi's list, but he seems to have sent Brother Ar.'s on to the minister in Provence with a request that Olivi respond to it. This correspondence represented the first of the two letters by Bonagratia later mentioned by Raymond of Fronsac. Olivi defended himself to the provincial minister, who forwarded Olivi's response to the minister general. By this time Brother Ar. and his supporters were already describing the nineteen articles as heretical, so Olivi broke his silence and produced the *Attack*, which was also meant to convince Bonagratia. As he says in the leter to R.,[32] he hoped that both his and Ar.'s theses would be examined by the minister general.

It soon became obvious that Olivi's efforts were to no avail. Bonagratia sent the second letter mentioned

---

[23] Raymundus de Fronciacho, 1887: p. 13.
[24] Raymundus de Fronciacho and Bonagratia de Bergamo, 1887: p. 156.
[25] This work, a series of thirty-two articles directed against a single person, is found in *Quodl.*, ff. 42r-53r, where it is followed by five more articles aimed at less important figures associated with the scholar attacked in the earlier articles. These last five articles seem to be part of a longer work, the rest of which has long since disappeared.
[26] *Letter*, f. 52(64)r. The identification is based largely on the fact that Olivi cites the work as evidence of his view of quantity, which is amply discussed in the *Attack*.
[27] Sbaralea, 1908: p. 597.
[28] Ehrle, 1887: p. 478.
[29] Raymundus de Fronchiacho, 1887: p. 14.
[30] Gratien de Paris, 1913: p. 419.
[31] Raymundus de Fronciacho, 1887: p. 16.
[32] *Letter*, f. 52(64)v.

by Raymond of Fronsac. This one censured Olivi's theses and ordered that his writings be surrendered. Olivi had lost his battle with Brother Ar.

By this time news of Olivi's difficulties had long since been received by his friends. They wanted to help him, but needed information, so one of them wrote for himself and the others asking Olivi to comment on the charges against him. Olivi replied with the letter to R.

This letter provides evidence both for the disputed theses and for Olivi's official response to the censure. He begins by announcing that his friends, in their solicitude for him, are like Peter urging Christ to avoid the passion. Rather than mourning they should rejoice with him, since he takes his fate as a sign of divine favor and would be profoundly disturbed if things were going well. Much earlier he had predicted that, even if the world should wish to elevate him to the ambitions of a human *magisterium*, Christ would not abide it. At that time he added that if Christ should permit such a thing he would regard it as a sign of eternal reprobation. Now God has placed in the heart of his prelate a suspicion that Olivi is a falsifier of the truth, thus conforming him with the image of the suffering Christ. Fearing Parisian ambitions, he has hitherto been hesitant to write except rarely in answer to his friends' letters. Now, however, he has chosen to do so lest he encourage the idea that he is a falsifier of the truth, particularly of the Catholic faith. He will, he says, address himself to those articles concerning which he spoke before his minister.[33]

Olivi then proceeds to defend himself against nineteen charges, some of which will be discussed in the following chapter. Having done so, he closes his defense with a brief excursus on the nature and necessary limits of his obedience toward those who have censured him. He knows, he says, that the hierarchical order is fixed by divine law, so that inferiors are to be guided by superiors except in cases when the superiors abuse their authority or the inferiors are particularly inspired on some matter. If he is confronted with human opinions based on the human reasoning of superiors who are worthy of credence, he will listen humbly and with an open mind; yet he will not adhere to them as if to the Catholic faith itself. Anyone compelling him to do so would be asking him to commit idolatry.

Purely human opinions should never become the subject of empty disputation and sectarian allegiance. This stricture applies to Olivi as well as his censors. If it should be asked whether, in situations where he lists rival opinions without asserting any, he himself actually favors one more than another, his answer would be that he does so with the sort of belief appropriate to simple opinion, not with the belief appropriate to faith.

Olivi protests that he is ready to obey his superiors in all matters which violate neither the Christian faith nor the purity of his own conscience. The second condition is worth pondering, since Olivi obviously thinks of it as extending to more than established dogma. Even if violations of his conscience do not involve the faith itself, he says, he should lie for no man, particularly in doctrine.[34]

Olivi then turns to a matter about which his friends had not inquired, yet which, he says has been the source of accusations: "That I follow dreams and certain fantastic visions, and temerariously predict future events." Olivi replies that he follows no dreams or visions, nor does he believe they should be followed unless it is established that they are from God. As to the future, he has never asserted anything in the way of particular determinations regarding the time something will happen, the particular person involved, or things of that sort. Nevertheless, he is certain that through a Franciscan order purged of suffering and temptation the Christian religion will be renewed and the Jews and pagans converted.

Olivi closes by asking what he has done to his order that he should be attacked by his brothers and superiors. He himself has been guided by zeal for the faith and the rule. He concludes that his present sufferings were commanded by God to keep him humble.[35]

The letter was written at Montpellier and is dated four days before Easter. According to Koch's reckoning it must have been written early in 1282 at the latest, since the next important step in the process came with the general chapter of Strassburg at Pentacost, 1282. There Olivi's case was again considered and the order decided to turn the matter over to a commission of scholars. Thus in 1283 Bonagratia appointed the commission of seven.

Koch's reconstruction of the years 1279–1282 is a classic example of how a few isolated scraps of information can be combined to produce a coherent, believable narrative. It is creative scholarship at its best. Thus it seems almost churlish to point out that certain aspects of his theory rest upon rather slender evidence. Such is, however, the case.

For example, it is not all that obvious that the controversy began over *usus pauper* and then spread to other areas. Koch relies heavily upon the brief reference to poverty in the opening sentence of Olivi's *Attack*. He recognizes in this passage a reference to the treatise *Quoniam contra paupertatem evangelicam*, which is indeed about *usus pauper*; yet is it clear that the passage does refer to this particular treatise, or even to a separate treatise at all? Perhaps it does, but there is plenty of room for other hypotheses.

Koch's identification of *usus pauper* as the principal issue also rests to some extent on the role he assigns to Bonagratia. He takes Olivi's citation of Bonagratia in

---

[33] *Letter*, f. 51(63)v.
[34] *Ibid.*, f. 52(64)v.
[35] *Ibid.*, f. 53(65)r.

Quoniam contra paupertatem evangelicam as evidence that they agreed on *usus pauper*. Perhaps they did, but there is no strong reason to think so. Olivi cites a passage from "Brother Bonagratia our general, in the first letter which he sent to our order, beginning *a domino Jesu Christo normam rectitudinis*." [36] The passage demands greater conformity to the intention of Saint Francis, so that "in buildings, clothing and food, in which holy poverty should shine forth," the brothers should proceed "without sumptuosity, courtliness or superfluity." Bonagratia's demand shows that he thought the order bound to observe certain limits, but it does not show that he agreed with Olivi on the nature of those limits. Certainly there is no reason to conclude from it that the two men agreed on the question of whether *usus pauper* was required by the rule. Olivi himself simply suggests that his own view is logically implied by Bonagratia's statement. Moreover, Bonagratia's letter is extant [37] and anyone who reads it will recognize that Olivi quoted the most relevant passage in the entire work.

There is other evidence that Bonagratia agreed with Olivi on *usus pauper*. Ubertino of Casale, writing in 1311, explicitly says so.[38] He refers to a different letter which seems to have been written shortly after the general chapter of Strassburg in 1282. The same letter was apparently included by Raymond of Fronsac among the documents offered as evidence by the community.[39] It has been suggested [40] that Ubertino's assertion is indirectly corroborated by the fact that the community never challenged it; yet Ubertino's own comments suggest that the community *did* challenge it in a roundabout way by subscribing to Bonagratia's view as they themselves interpreted it. Even Ubertino seems to realize that Bonagratia's letter has its difficulties,[41] and he tells us little of its contents except that Franciscans are, by their profession, more bound to *usus pauper* than other orders. Thus we can come to no indisputable conclusion regarding the nature and limits of Bonagratia's agreement with Olivi.

There is, then, little solid evidence for Koch's view of the theological charges as a flanking attack in the battle over *usus pauper*. In fact, one could cite at least some evidence against such a thesis. If poverty was the central issue, one could ask why that issue is so strangely absent from Olivi's letter to R. It might be replied, of course, that the letter was written in response to his friend's request for clarification on specific issues, and it would be understandable if the questioner, sharing Olivi's views on poverty, required nothing on that score. Moreover, the issues discussed in the letter were those censured by Bonagratia and, as we have seen, Koch argues that those issues were introduced after Bonagratia proved uncooperative regarding the poverty question. Thus it is hardly surprising that poverty should be excluded from the nineteen articles.

Granting the force of this argument, it is still odd that Olivi's letter should have ignored the poverty question so completely. If the attack on his theology stemmed from a dispute over poverty, one might expect him to mention that fact in a letter defending himself on the former score written to friends who agreed with him on the latter one. When, in the closing passage, he asks what he has done to merit such abuse, one might expect him to come up with a rather definite answer.

Again, there is the indisputable fact that Olivi's theological views were already open to suspicion before the controversy with Brother Ar. and, as we shall see, continued to be attacked after his death by persons with no obvious stake in discrediting his stance on poverty. The case for poverty as the basic issue would be somewhat more persuasive if the theological and philosophical charges were obviously tenuous, but Olivi's contemporaries took them very seriously. Thus there is no reason why historians should, without evidence, automatically feel compelled to accord them a secondary role in the controversy with Brother Ar.

The preceding comments are hardly directed against Koch alone. The idea of poverty as the basic issue has a long and noble pedigree, stretching from present-day historians back through Ehrle [42] to Ubertino of Casale [43] and Angelo Clareno [44] in the fourteenth century. Far from reassuring the modern scholar, this fact should make him rather suspicious. Perhaps Ubertino and Angelo had more evidence on this matter than they submitted to posterity. We simply do not know. We do know, however, that by the early fourteenth century the question of Olivi's orthodoxy was being debated in a special context which made such a view quite understandable. As we shall see later, poverty *was* the central issue in the early fourteenth century. The leaders of the Franciscan order wanted to compromise the spirituals by discrediting their idol Olivi, and they tried to effect the latter by showing that his theological and philosophical heterodoxy was a long-established fact. Spirituals like Ubertino naturally retaliated by arguing that the theological and philosophical charges represented an attempt to obfuscate the real issue, poverty. For this reason it is somewhat risky to trust Ubertino and Angelo as authoritative guides to the reasons for Olivi's theological and philosophical difficulties in the late 1270's and early 1280's.

Whatever one might conclude regarding Koch's evaluation of the poverty issue, the fact remains that on the

---

[36] *Quoniam*, f. 51r.
[37] It is published in Wadding, 1931: **5**: pp. 83–85.
[38] Ubertino da Casale, 1886: p. 400. See also pp. 385 and 387 as well as *idem*, 1887, "Sanctitas vestra," p. 82.
[39] Raymundus de Fronciacho, 1887: pp. 13 f.
[40] See Malcolm Lambert, 1961: pp. 153 f.
[41] Ubertino da Casale, 1886: p. 387: ". . . tamen in illa lictera multa inconvenientia continentur. . . ."
[42] Ehrle, 1887: p. 416.
[43] Ubertino da Casale, 1886: p. 388.
[44] Angelo Clareno, 1886: p. 291.

whole his reconstruction of the period 1279–1282 is not only an impressive imaginative achievement but the most convincing interpretation of the documents offered to date. Perhaps new manuscript discoveries will eventually disprove it, but until that time it can be accorded a high degree of probability.

After 1282 we find ourselves on somewhat more solid ground. The *Chronicle of the Twenty-four Generals* informs us that,

in the year of our Lord 1283 this general [Bonagratia], according to the decisions of the Strassburg chapter, came to Paris in visiting and, collecting all those things in the doctrine of Brother Peter which seemed to ring poorly (*sonare male*), submitted them for determination and examination to Brothers Droco, minister of France, John Garau, Simon of Lens, and Arlotto of Prato, all masters of sacred theology, as well as Brothers Richard of Mediavilla, Giles of Bensa, and John of Murro, bachelors at Paris. After mature deliberation, these men agreed to reprove some of the things as dangerous and poorly stated (*male sonantia*). They sent this reproof to all the brothers in a letter under their seals called the *Letter of the Seven Seals*. With this letter the aforementioned minister general went to Avignon in order to suppress there those who ascribed to the reproved articles. And there, since he was gravely ill, he instructed his companion brother Gerard of Prato that, according to the decision made at Paris in the council of the aforesaid masters and bachelors, he should collect and interdict the books of the aforementioned Peter John and that no one should dare to say or hold anything contrary to the contents of the *Letter of the Seven Seals*.[45]

Olivi, in the *apologia* written to the Paris commission in 1285, says that passages from his writings were excerpted by the commission and collected in a *rotulus* with various judgments written in the margin. "Some were judged false, some heretical, some doubtful in the context of the faith, some dangerous to our order, some ignorant, some presumptuously stated, and some crucified as it were or marked with the sign of the cross."[46] To this *rotulus* they added a second document, the so-called *Letter of the Seven Seals*, in which they recorded a series of assertions opposed to Olivi's errors. Both the *rotulus* and the *Letter of the Seven Seals* were sent to all the convents in Olivi's province, where they were to be read before all the brothers. Olivi's writings were to be confiscated from anyone possessing them.

The basic pattern of events is plain enough, although certain details might be clearer. For example, it is hardly clear how Bonagratia was acting "in accordance with the decision (*definitionem*) of the Strassburg chapter." The *definitiones* of this chapter as we have them contain only one item which might be considered relevant: "The general chapter commands all ministers to notify the general minister if they have any brothers in their provinces who pertinaciously defend unsound opinions, also conveying the opinions and the arguments for them."[47] If this is the *definitio* in question, the terse phrase in the *Chronicle of the Twenty-four Generals* might be interpreted to mean that the decision of the chapter meeting in 1282 had spurred Olivi's provincial minister to provide the requested information and that Bonagratia was now acting upon it in 1283.

The most enticing alternative explanation would be that the *Chronicle* is simply incorrect. Writing a century after the event, the author merely drew the obvious conclusion from the *definitio* on the one hand and the process on the other. It would not necessarily follow that the chronicle was wrong in positing a connection between the general chapter and the Olivi process. It seems likely enough that the Olivi affair was discussed, and it is at least plausible that the decision to submit his writings to a Paris commission emerged from these discussions. It is even possible that the extant *definitio* was a result rather than a cause of the Olivi process, a general application of what had been decided in Olivi's particular case. Again, we simply do not know.

If the Paris commission was agreed upon at the Strassburg chapter, then we are left with the task of explaining a curious time lag. If the decision to investigate Olivi was made at Strassburg in the spring of 1282, why did Bonagratia wait until 1283 to set the commission in motion? Perhaps the delay is understandable when we consider that Bonagratia had to gather Olivi's writings and visit Paris before the commission could begin its work. Moreover, he did have other things to do besides harass Olivi.

Note that Olivi and the chronicle apparently disagree over what the commission examined. The chronicle seems to say that Bonagratia selected the questionable passages and submitted them to the commission, while Olivi gives the impression that the commission studied his works and made excerpts from them. Fortunately we possess three of the manuscripts used by the commission,[48] and these manuscripts encourage the suspicion that both views may be right to some extent. The commission studied whole questions rather than selected passages, and the *rotulus* contained excerpts drawn from these questions by the commission. Nevertheless, there is no reason to conclude that they examined all of Olivi's works. Thus it is possible that Bonagratia had effected a prior selection by deciding which questions were to be judged.

One more problem remains. How could Olivi's works have been confiscated in 1283 if, according to Koch's dating of the letter to R., they were already confiscated before the 1282 chapter? It seems unlikely that they were confiscated, returned, and confiscated

---

[45] *Chronica XXIV generalium*, pp. 374–376. John Garau is universally identified as John of Wales. John of Murro is now usually referred to as John of Murrovalle. Olivi, *Responsio* II, p. 130 provides essentially the same list of names, except that he alters one name slightly, referring to Giles of Baysi. Since he is writing in 1285, he can include Richard of Mediavilla among the masters.

[46] *Responsio* II, p. 132.

[47] Fussenegger, 1933: p. 137.

[48] They are MSS. Vat. Burgh. 46, 322 and 358. See Koch, 1930, "Verurteilung," p. 505 and Maier, 1951: p. 330.

again in that short time. Perhaps the answer lies in the fact that Olivi's letter says *he* is without his works, not that they have been confiscated throughout the order, whereas the commission demanded the latter.

The *rotulus* produced by the commission remains undiscovered, but Olivi's 1285 *apologia* and the three extant manuscripts used by the commission give us some idea of its form and content. Koch concludes from this evidence that it contained at least fifty articles. These articles consisted not merely of theses but excerpts from Olivi's writings. Each article included an indication of the work from which the excerpt had been made and a specific judgment on the article, such as "heretical," "dangerous," "presumptuous," or "false."[49] Koch regards the document as "a first-rate scientific job" and considers it an important step in the development of techniques for dealing with theological error.[50]

The second document mentioned in the sources, the *Letter of the Seven Seals*, is extant.[51] It consists of twenty-two articles, each consisting of a brief positive assertion stating the orthodox view in opposition to Olivi's purported errors. As Olivi indicates, this document was sent to the convents in his province along with the *rotulus*.

In the fall of 1283 Olivi was summoned to Avignon. There he was forced to assent to the *Letter of the Seven Seals* before a special council. The *Chronicle of the Twenty-four Generals*[52] and Raymond of Fronsac[53] both affirm that he did so. Olivi agrees, but with reservations. In his 1285 *apologia* he notes that the requirement placed him in an unfortunate predicament. *The Letter of the Seven Seals* was composed of positive statements written in opposition to Olivi's views as the commission interpreted them. Olivi saw that an endorsement of these statements would imply acceptance of the commission's judgment on his own works. Nevertheless he could not flatly refuse to endorse the statements, since he would thereby appear to deny the articles of faith contained therein. Thus, he says, he settled upon a third course, "confessing some simply and absolutely, . . . others under distinction," and offering no defense whatsoever concerning purely philosophical matters.[54] Such is more or less the course followed in his 1283 response to the *Letter of the Seven Seals* as it has come down to us.[55]

Bonagratia died in October, 1283. There is no reason to believe that his demise had anything to do with his role in Olivi's censure the same year, but at least one fourteenth-century writer thought the connection was more than coincidental. Angelo Clareno tells how Olivi, incensed at the persecution of the spirituals, came uninvited to Avignon and sought an audience with the general. Bonagratia decided to hear him out before an assembly of brothers, then impose a stiff penance on him for his flagrant disregard of the proper channels. The plan proved an unfortunate one for Bonagratia, who was so moved by Olivi's address that he was unable to impose the penance and, stricken to the heart, died a few days later along with two of Olivi's most prominent critics.[56]

Angelo's story stands in stark contrast to Olivi's actual fortunes after the censure. Far from journeying to Avignon uninvited, he was commanded to go there, and his mission was not to censure but to submit. Having done so, he might have hoped for an end to his difficulties, but none was in sight. The *Letter to the Seven Seals* was being publicized throughout his province. His own works were being confiscated. His reputation still stood under a cloud of suspicion.

Most important, Olivi himself was not through arguing. He considered his treatment unfair and wanted to complain to someone about it.[57] Having been censured without a hearing, he at least would have liked to confront his censors after the fact, and applied to his provincial minister for permission to go to Paris. Permission was denied. Granting the impossibility of direct contact, an epistolary confrontation would have offered some satisfaction, but Olivi found it impossible to accomplish even this much as long as he was deprived, not only of his writings, but of the *rotulus* as well. Thus for the time being he could only sit and store up grievances in southern France.

Then, sometime between January and May, 1285,[58] in a way unknown to us, Olivi gained access to the documents necessary for a decent defense. The result was his *apologia* addressed to the commission of seven, a work which provides invaluable evidence not only concerning the censure but also regarding Olivi's reaction to it. Various scholars have accused Olivi of excessive pride, self-abasement, duplicity or common pigheadedness on the basis of this document, but none of these characterizations really captures the spirit of the work. It is basically the protest of a man trying to safeguard his reputation and his humility at the same time, a difficult feat in any age but particularly taxing for a medieval Franciscan friar. Olivi valued humility and obedience, but he also disliked his new reputation as a purveyor of heterodox opinion. He felt that the commission had wronged him in its procedure as well as its conclusions, and wanted to tell them so respectfully but firmly.

---

[49] Koch, 1930, "Verurteilung," pp. 505 ff.
[50] *Ibid.*, pp. 506 f.; *idem*, 1930, "Philosophische," pp. 309–329.
[51] *Littera septem sigillarum*, edition cited in bibliography.
[52] *Chronica XXIV generalium*, p. 376.
[53] Raymundus de Fronciacho, 1887: p. 14.
[54] *Responsio* II, p. 134.
[55] *Responsio* I, pp. 126–130.
[56] Angelo Clareno, 1886: pp. 291 ff.
[57] The following information is based upon Olivi's comments in *Responsio* II, pp. 132–135.
[58] The date is determined by the fact that the resulting *apologia* is dated 1285 and is addressed to the seven censors, including Arlotto of Prato, whom it addresses as a master of theology. In May, 1285, the general chapter met at Milan and elected Arlotto minister general, a promotion Olivi would hardly have ignored had the *apologia* been written after May.

The work begins with a fullsome tribute to the obedience owed the Roman church on matters of faith. This tribute was easily rendered, since Olivi was not censured by the Roman church but rather by his own order. That, of course, is his point. The commission of seven has overstepped its authority.

> Thus, dearest fathers . . . although I am an abominable speck of a man, not only in respect of God, but also in respect to you, and although I am nothing or (if such can be said) less than nothing, nevertheless you should not demand such obedience from me or recommend that it be demanded, as if I should subject myself entirely to your opinions—however solemn and worthy of reverence they might be—as to the words of the Catholic faith or the holy scripture or to the determination of the Roman pontiff or a general council, unless it has been demonstrated that your opinion is that of the Catholic faith and sacred scripture.[59]

Olivi says he marvels at certain aspects of the affair. First, the commission made excerpts from certain questions which were secretly written by him for his own intellectual exercise and made public without his consent by confreres. These excerpts were then labeled with various judgments in such a way that the author was censured along with the writings. His questions were then confiscated and the judgment of the commission was ordered read through the order "as a sign of more evident and more horrible reprobation." Olivi wonders how such a "rigid, . . . solemn, unusual and defamatory process" should have been conducted without even asking him whether he wrote the passages or what he meant by them. Civil and canon law both demand that a criminal be heard before he is condemned. Such a requirement should be especially observed in cases where the issue is doctrinal truth and the defendant has always shown himself to be a fervid supporter of the faith, the church and the Franciscan rule.

Olivi also marvels at the way he was treated after the censure. He barely had time to read and ponder the *Letter of the Seven Seals* before he was asked to consent to it, "as if its contents were simply the faith or the authentic determination of a Roman pontiff or general council." Here Olivi recounts his perplexities concerning how to respond and his ultimate solution. He unconditionally accepted those aspects which represented indisputable assertions of the faith; conditionally accepted other aspects and affixed a brief explanation of the sense in which he ascribed to them; and, in the case of purely philosophical issues, he submitted without discussion to the commission, "partly because I disapprove of categorical statements on these matters (particularly stubborn ones) and partly because—as my customary way of handling philosophical questions clearly demonstrates—I neglect such statements more and value them less than many people believe."[60]

Finally, Olivi marvels that he was later accorded no way of replying to the commission, "particularly since no reason or authority was used to disprove my views, nor was it proved that I meant what they took me to mean." He then recounts the story of his frustrated efforts to answer his critics in person or in writing and alludes to the unforeseen circumstance which allowed him to compose the present letter.

Having offered his opinion of the commission's methodology, Olivi turns to specific issues. He first cites and responds to twenty of the articles from the *rotulus* which "touch the Catholic faith more directly." This part of the work offers an important insight into both the form and the content of the censure and shows us precisely how Olivi went about defending himself. He next mentions thirteen purely philosophical issues censured by the commission. Rather than defending them, he settles for a brief characterization of his *modus operandi* in such matters.

> I have recited various opinions, asserting none of them, except that sometimes I present a preponderance of arguments in favor of the opinion which contradicts the one common to certain masters, but I do not respond to these arguments. Thus I seem to imply that I approve of that part more, although in most of these cases I say that those opinions are to be examined with caution rather than asserted. I have recited those that seemed to present truly perplexing problems which I myself could not solve, and which seemed to me to be no less suitable for explaining and defending the faith than other views. On the other hand, I have been fearful that certain familiar philosophical opinions contain hidden snares and obscure, knotty dangers to the Catholic faith, and I have suspected (and still suspect) that these are henceforth to be promulgated by the sowers of error. If I am given an audience I shall be ready to explain these things, and even if the explanation seems ridiculous to the learned I am at least sure it will be clear to them that in holding these things I am motivated by zeal for the Catholic faith and Roman church. I am certain, however, that I do not lovingly adhere to philosophical views or human opinions, stubbornly insist on them, or value them as great things in themselves. On the contrary, I am appalled that the pagan Aristotle, the Saracen Averroes, and certain other heathen philosophers are held in such esteem, veneration, and authority by certain people, particularly in matters of sacred theology.[61]

---

[59] *Responsio* II, pp. 131–132: "Hinc est, carissimi patres, mihi valde venerabiles, et merito reverendi ac metuendi, quod quamvis ego abominandus homuncio, ne dicam, respectu Dei sed etiam respectu vestri, sim nihil et, se dici queat, minus quam nihil, ex hoc tamen a me obedientiam talem exigere aut exigendam consulere non debetis, ut dictis vestris, quamvis solemnibus, quamvis reverendis, tanquam catholicae fidei, aut velut Scripturae sacrae eloquiis, aut tanquam determinationi Romani Pontificis vel generalis concilii omnino debeam subdi, nisi enodatione luce clariori primitus innotescat vestrum dictum esse vere dictum catholicae fidei et Scripturae sacrae." Note the similar statement in *De obitu*, p. 269.

[60] *Responsio* II, p. 134.

[61] *Ibid.*, p. 405: "De omnibus enim praedictis et quibusdam consimilibus eis annexis, recitavi opiniones varias, nullam earum asserens, nisi quod ad illam partem, quae communi opinioni quarumdam repugnat, aliquando plures rationes adduco non respondens ad eas, in quo videor innuere quod illam partem plus approbo, quamvis in plerisque earum dicam eas esse cavendas et examinandas potius quam asserendas. Ego quidem idcirco recitavi eas, quia videbantur in se habere difficultates merito

Olivi comments briefly on two philosophical issues which, for some reason, he has seen fit to discuss separately, then closes with a plea that his judges repair the wrongs done to him or at least that they answer his letter. The work is dated 1285, and was written at Nîmes.

The *apologia* was completed, but apparently Olivi had not spoken his last word to the commission. We possess a lengthy defense of a single proposition regarding the divine nature. This document was apparently sent to the commission as a sort of appendix to the other one.[62]

There is no record of a reply and Olivi's reputation was not immediately cleared, but the letter may have had some effect. Before continuing the narrative of Olivi's fortunes, however, we must stop for a moment to examine the issues on which he was attacked by Brother Ar. and the commission.

VI. CONTROVERTED ISSUES: THEOLOGY

Having examined what little we know of the events surrounding Olivi's censure in 1283, we must now look for a moment at the issues on which he came to grief. Their sheer number makes this subject a complex one and precludes any exhaustive analysis, but an examination of certain key points will give at least the flavor of the process.

In the first place, between 1279 and 1283 Olivi was attacked on a series of theological issues including the nature and effects of grace and the virtues, the nature of the sacramental character, the relation of conservation to creation, the treatment of unbaptized children in limbo, the divine nature, divine knowledge, and the sacramentality of marriage. Four of these subjects seem to have caused special concern to men of his own time. Olivi was particularly attacked for his denial of the sacramentality of marriage, his understanding of sacramental grace and the sacramental character, and his view of the relationship between the divine essence and the persons of the trinity. We shall examine each of these in turn, starting with marriage.

MARRIAGE

Olivi's understanding of marriage is not mentioned in the letter to R., although a passing remark in 1283 shows that it was one of the issues raised as early as Jerome's generalate.[1] In the *Letter of the Seven Seals*, however, it is dealt with in the strongest terms used in that document: "That marriage is a sacrament of the new law which confers grace. To affirm the contrary is erroneous, to sustain it is heretical, to question it is illicit."[2] Other views are labeled "false," "erroneous," or even "dangerous," but this is the only one called "heretical."

In his *apologia* of 1285 Olivi tells us which of his writings was being judged and what aspect of it was considered unacceptable.

> Later . . . another view of mine from the question "whether virginity is better than matrimony" is cited. In the response to the twenty-fourth argument, where I prove that the sacrament of marriage "does not seem to be called a sacrament univocally with other sacraments of grace," . . . I say: "Therefore it does not seem to be any more of a sacrament than the bronze serpent, tabernacle or ark of Moses, and similar things, which, however, I do not assert at present."[3]

The work cited here is now thought of as question six of the *Questions on Evangelical Perfection*.[4] In it Olivi decides, of course, that virginity is better than marriage, but argues that such was not always the case. Before the fall marriage was superior, since there was no sin involved and offspring had to be produced in order to complete the number of the elect.[5] For Olivi the basic virtue to be considered here is not virginity but chastity, which is not simply identifiable with abstinence. In the proper circumstances both marriage and abstinence can become modes of chastity. In the state of innocence, when man's sexual desires were

---

dubitabiles et quas ego nescirem dissolvere, et videbantur mihi ad fidem nostram explicandam et defendendam non minus accommodae quam caeterae; et e contrario, in quibusdam opinionibus philosophicis usitatis occultos laqueos, et quaedam perplexa et nodosa pericula fidei catholicae timui, et vehementer suspicatus sum, et adhuc suspicor illa in posterum ab errorum seminatoribus propalanda. Et si daretur mihi audientia, paratus essem explicare illa, et esto quod a sapientibus pro ridiculo haberetur, ad minus certus sum quod nihilominus ipsismet appareret quod zelus fidei catholicae et Romanae ecclesiae me movit ad ista et ad alia plura non minora istis. Certus autem sum quod in talibus philosophicis aut in quibuscumque opinionibus humanis amore non inhaereo, nec pertinaciter illis insisto, nec eas secundum se velut res altas et magnas aestimo, quin potius vehementer detestor, quod Aristoteles paganus, et Averroes saracenus, et quidam alii infideles philosophi a quibusdam in tanta aestimatione et veneratione et in tanta auctoritate habentur, et praecipue in dictis et scriptis sacrae theologiae."

[62] *Amplior declaratio quinti articuli, qui est de divina essentia*, edition cited in bibliography.

[1] *Responsio* I, p. 127. The following comments are an abbreviated version of the discussion offered in Burr, 1972, "Olivi on Marriage." See also Emmen, 1967: pp. 11–57; Maier, 1951: pp. 326–339.

[2] *Littera septem sigillarum*, p. 51.

[3] *Responsio* II, p. 374: "Post hoc, bene infra, ponitur aliud dictum meum sumptum ex quaestione 'an virginitas sit melior matrimonio.' In responsione ad XXIV argumentum, ubi probo quod sacramentum matrimonii 'non videtur dici univoce sacramentum cum aliis sacramentis gratiae,' ubi, et post quasdam rationes, subdo: 'non ergo videtur habere aliam rationem sacramenti quam serpens aeneus vel tabernaculum seu arca Moysi, et consimilia, quod tamen ad praesens non assero'; et paulo post subditur: 'quid autem de hoc verum sit, alibi habet tradi.' Subditur autem, loco correctionis a latere, articulus magistralis litterae sigillatae, . . . 'cum matrimonium sit sacramentum novae legis et conferat gratiam, affirmare contrarium est erroneum, sustinere haereticum, dubitare illicitum.'"

[4] "An virginitas sit simpliciter melior matrimonio," edition cited in bibliography.

[5] *Ibid.*, p. 33.

thoroughly subjected to his higher powers, procreation could be both virtuous and thoroughly enjoyable.[6] With the fall, the situation changed abruptly. Because of the resulting *deordinatio* of man's powers, he is the victim of a "rebellion of the inferior appetite." The married man is now at the mercy of this inferior appetite and his *deordinatio* is exacerbated by its gratification. Thus marriage inevitably lures him from divine to worldly things, from contemplation to base pleasures.[7] In such circumstances, although it is "better to marry than to burn," those capable of following Paul's example had better do so. In short, *ordinatio* is best achieved by abstaining from sexual activity.

Olivi anticipates the objection that a sacramental state (like marriage) is worthier and more divine than a non-sacramental state (like virginity). He counters with two arguments, one of them safe enough. The things signified by a sacrament are more divine than the sacrament itself. It is the soul's union with God, not the act of marriage itself, which is the truly divine thing, and this union is encouraged more by virginity than by marriage.

Had Olivi rested his case at this point he would have been better off, but he apparently felt that the objection contained an element of truth which needed to be clarified. He himself thought it rather odd that marriage was a sacrament while an obviously superior state like virginity was not. Thus he took the fatal step and began to explain that the word "sacrament" does not mean quite the same thing in regard to marriage as it does in regard to baptism, penance, etc.

Most of Olivi's arguments in support of this assertion try to show how marriage differs from other sacraments in its institution, effects, significance, matter, form, and the like. In addition he argues that Ephesians 5:32, "it is a great *sacramentum*," cannot be used by his adversaries because Paul, in using the word *sacramentum*, simply wished to say that marriage is a sacred sign of a great thing. The same thing could be said of the adultery of Bathsheba.

Thus, in the words which stunned the commission, marriage "does not seem to be a sacrament in any way which could not be applied to the bronze serpent, tabernacle or ark of Moses, etc.; which, however, I do not assert at present."[8] Even if marriage is considered a sacrament of grace, it remains true that more grace is given to one who, properly disposed, chooses the state of virginity or monastic vows. If marriage is a sacrament, then these things seem to be greater and more divine sacraments.

Olivi returns to this line of thought in a later treatise dealing with the sacraments in general. There he asks whether marriage confers grace *ex vi sacramenti* and replies first with the arguments of "those who say that it does not do so."[9] The arguments actually contend that marriage is not a sacrament in the same sense as the others. Olivi then cites a second opinion according to which marriage is a mixture of carnal and spiritual. Insofar as it is spiritual, it confers grace through the special benediction of the minister and through that general and special assistance conferred upon all proper states instituted by Christ in his church. If one were to object that the same could be said of any virtuous state, work, or faith, it can be answered that the conjugal and regular states are unalterable except by Christ himself, have the force of sacramental institutions, and, besides the moral goodness they contain, have a special significance according to which they lead to a special sort of sacramental communion with God involving a special sort of help. Just as in the sacraments of baptism and confirmation one professes unalterable observance of the general precepts of Christ's law and receives sacramental grace for the proper observation of those general precepts, so in the profession of Christ's special states one professes unalterable observation of all things pertaining to the substance of those states and receives in return sacramental grace for their proper observance.

Olivi concludes by observing that he has spoken as well as possible for the latter position, although he has said elsewhere that the former one is not unarguable (*non improbabile*). The latter opinion, he says, would please him more if he could only be certain that the grace involved in such a profession is really sacramental in the sense that it is given *ex vi sacramenti* and not merely through equity or moral bounty (*ex vi equitatis et benignitatis moralis*) in the way Christ assists any virtuous act or state.

Thus Olivi has moderated his stand on marriage, but he has done so by allowing more room for the alternative offered in the conclusion of the question on virginity and marriage. If marriage is a sacrament, then so are virginity and monasticism. Olivi lumps them all together in speaking of "Christ's special states." This perspective is retained throughout the treatise on the sacraments. Thus when he asks which sacraments impart a character he considers not only baptism, confirmation and ordination but virginity and monasticism as well,[10] and when he finally lists the seven sacraments he speaks of the "states of living rightly under Christ" (*de statibus recte vivendi sub christo*) where one would expect to encounter marriage.[11]

This particular issue provides an interesting insight into Olivi's behavior in the face of opposition. In his response to the *Letter of the Seven Seals* he gingerly ascribes to the master's statement on marriage.

I accept the opinion in this respect, that it is a sacrament of the new law. I have never said the contrary, and if I did I recant. I also believe that grace is conferred, although I've

---

[6] *Ibid.*, pp. 44 f.
[7] *Ibid.*, pp. 43–45.
[8] *Ibid.*, p. 54.

[9] MS. Vat. lat. 4986, f. 135v.
[10] *Ibid.*, f. 137v.
[11] *Ibid.*, f. 140r.

sometimes recited without assertion the view that grace is not conferred and that it is not a sacrament in an entirely univocal sense. I satisfied lord Jerome on this score and, as far as I know, have said nothing about it since.[12]

By 1285 he was less wiling to be agreeable. In his *apologia* he says, "I never denied or doubted that it is a sacrament, . . . but only inquired whether it had full univocity with other sacraments and proved without assertion that it does not."[13] While he grants that it is heretical to deny that marriage is "a sacrament or sacramental state instituted by God," and in fact has never said otherwise, the commission is wrong in considering it equally heretical to deny that grace is conferred. Even if marriage does confer grace, the church does not demand belief on this point. Olivi cites passages from Peter Lombard and canon law explicitly denying that grace is conferred, all the while assuring his readers that he does so only to show that belief is not demanded and not because he himself denies it. In fact, he believes "that some grace is given by God to those entering that state in a proper way, . . . just as it is given to those properly assuming the state of virginity or religion."[14]

He does surrender on one point. His comparison of marriage with the bronze serpent, tabernacle, and ark of Moses was "too lax," for marriage is definitely a sacrament in a way these others are not. Olivi expresses his wonder at having made such a statement, but notes that "many things in my questions may be incorrect, since they were communicated by others against my wishes before I had subjected them to more diligent correction."

Thus Olivi acknowledges a bit of excess at one point but refuses to abandon his basic position. The same stance is apparent in his redaction of the offending question on virginity and matrimony, which we possess both in the form used by the commission and in a later, revised form. The revision is an exceedingly modest one. Olivi's only concession to the censure is an addition to the passage about the bronze serpent. In the revised version he says:

Therefore it does not seem to be a sacrament in any way which could not be applied to the bronze serpent, tabernacle, or ark of Moses, etc.; which, however, I do not assert at present. For it is too laxly stated, since marriage is a holy state of rational persons, divinely instituted for their good life and for propagating offspring for the worship of God. This description does not apply to the aforesaid examples.[15]

Thus Olivi preserves not only his basic attitude toward marriage but even his serpent image, simply qualifying it a bit more.

As to whether the position so tenaciously defended by Olivi was particularly unusual or dangerous, that question has been considered at length elsewhere and a brief summary of the matter will suffice here.[16] In denying that marriage confers grace Olivi was saying no more than what a whole series of twelfth- and thirteenth-century theologians had said before him. By his own time this view was certainly less popular, but even then Olivi was not the only one to hold it. In the early fourteenth century the Dominican scholar Durandus of S. Porciano could still consider it an open question.[17]

The other question, that of whether marriage has full univocity with the other sacraments, was intimately connected with the first by Olivi's time because his age generally accepted Peter Lombard's definition of a sacrament as both sign *and cause* of invisible grace.[18] Thus if one denied that marriage bestowed grace, one also had to deny its univocity with other sacraments. One had to argue, as Olivi does, that marriage is a sacrament in some sense but not in every sense.

Here again Olivi was not the only man to attempt such an argument. Durandus held the same opinion and Peter of Palude, while not endorsing it, still respected it enough to call it a *positio probabilis et subtilis*.[19] To be sure, Olivi and Durandus were swimming against the current of late medieval sacramental thought, but their position was hardly so odd as to deserve disciplinary action.

GRACE, BAPTISM, AND THE SACRAMENTAL CHARACTER

A second area of concern emerges from a group of censures dealing with grace, baptism, and the sacramental character.[20] In the letter to R., Olivi acknowledges four charges in this area. First, he is charged with saying that grace posits nothing in the soul absolutely, but only a relation to Christ's grace or a certain right to his merits, just as a monk has a right to the goods of his monastery. Olivi replies that he has never said anything like that but rather has written and taught the opposite. Nevertheless, sometimes in the past he has said that the opinion regarding baptized infants posited by Innocent III in his decretal cannot be re-

---

[12] *Responsio* I, p. 127: "Hanc sententiam accepto, quantum ad hoc quod sit sacramentum novae legis, et quantum ad hoc numquam dixi contrarium, et si dixi revoco. Credo etiam quod conferatur ibi gratia, licet aliquando recitatorie et absque assertione dixerim quod non confertur ibi gratia, et quod non sit sacramentum omnino univoce cum aliis, et de hoc domino Hieronymo satisfeci, et postea nihil horum dixi quod sciam."

[13] *Responsio* II, p. 374.

[14] *Ibid.*, p. 377.

[15] "An virginitas sit simpliciter melior matrimonio," p. 54: "Non ergo videtur habere aliam rationem sacramenti quam serpens aeneus vel tabernaculum seu archa Moysi, et consimilia; quod tamen ad praesens non assero. Est enim pro tanto nimis laxe dictum, quia coniugium est status personarum rationalium ad eorum bonam vitam et ad prolem propagandam ad Dei cultum divinitus institutus; quae praedictis exemplis non competunt."

[16] See Burr, 1972, "Olivi on Marriage," pp. 194–204.

[17] IV *Sent.*, d. 26, q. 3.

[18] IV *Sent.*, d. 1, c. 4.

[19] IV *Sent.*, d. 26, q. 4.

[20] The following comments represent an abbreviated version of the analysis offered in Burr, 1975. See also Emmen, 1962.

jected easily or with temerity, although Olivi himself has never asserted it.[21]

Second, he is accused of saying that informing grace is not necessary for the deletion of sin. Olivi says, "I hold the contrary." Third, he is said to teach that virtues are not given to infants in baptism. Olivi feels that some precision is required here.

> As I have said, there is nothing about this in my writings, nor have I ever asserted anything; but I said before the time of Brother Jerome that the opinion according to which such was not necessary for their salvation, or that commonly such did not occur, was to be given profound and solemn scrutiny and not temerariously rejected as heretical, for poison sometimes lurks where we expect to find honey and the reverse. Nevertheless, I have always held and continue to hold as the faith that they can never be saved without Christ's merit given to them *gratis,* which merit ought above all things to be called grace and virtue of virtues.[22]

Fourth, he is accused of saying that a character posits no more in the soul than dedication in a church. Olivi replies:

> I have written nothing of this, but sometimes I have recited, without assertion and among other opinions, a certain opinion explaining what is posited by the right of regal dominion in a king, the right to have property in one possessing it, the monastic profession in a monk (the will and life of whom have now strayed far from the vow), the bond of obligation in subordinates bound to the laws and mandates of their lords, and many other things similar to these which I do not care about. Nevertheless, I would like those who are upset by this opinion to show what is erroneous or heretical about it. I believe firmly and without doubt that the baptismal or sacerdotal character, whatever it involves, refers to something incomparably nobler than dedication of a material temple.[23]

However reasurring all this may have been to Olivi's friends, it hardly settled the problem. All of the charges reappeared in the *Letter of the Seven Seals.* Here again there are four relevant articles. Article seventeen states that "it is erroneous to say that grace involves nothing absolute in the soul but rather a relation to the grace of Christ or a certain right (*ius*) to Christ's merits, just as a monk has a right to the goods of the monastery, but not through something absolute." Article eighteen says, "It is an error to say that an infusion of grace informing the soul is not needed for the removal of guilt (*culpa*)." According to article nineteen, "it is an error to say that virtues are not given to infants in baptism." Finally, article twenty-one announces that "it is false to say that a character involves nothing more in the soul than does dedication in a church."[24]

In subscribing to the *Letter of the Seven Seals* in 1283, Olivi accepted all of these articles without acknowledging that they constituted any sort of problem for him. In fact, he lumped them all together and dismissed them with the comment that "they do not touch me, since I have always taught the contrary, following the common opinions. And I have always believed that grace posits something absolute in the soul."[25] His 1285 *apologia* shows even less interest in the problem, never mentioning these issues at all.

Fortunately there are extant sources which illuminate Olivi's position in these areas, although they may not be the ones actually used by the commission.[26] The best place to start is with Olivi's treatise on Christ's merit, in which he asks whether having a right to Christ's merit is the same as having a *habitus* of grace.[27] Here Olivi observes that some scholars argue for a distinction between the two by referring to infant baptism, but that there are two different opinions on this subject as well, both of them cited by Innocent III and Peter Lombard. According to one view the *habitus* of faith and charity are not commonly given to children in baptism. According to the other they are given *quo ad habitum* but not *quo ad usum.* Olivi acknowledges that the second view is more favored by the "modern masters," but he clearly prefers the first. He rejects the notion that a habit of grace is necessary to correct the deformity of sin and make the child acceptable to God.

---

[21] *Letter,* f. 51(63)v.

[22] *Ibid.*: "De hoc sicut iam dixi nihil est in scriptis meis; nihil etiam unquam asserui. Sed quod ex necessitate ad eorum salvationem hoc fieri non oporteat; aut quod communiter hoc non fiat; dixi ante tempora fratris Hieronymi esse opinionem profundo et solenni scrutinio discutiendam; et non temerarie tanquam hereticam a quolibet reprobandam; quia aliquando latet fel; ubi creditur esse mel et econverso; semper tamen tanquam fidem tenui; et teneo quod nunquam possunt saluari sine merito christi gratis sibi impenso; quod meritum super omnia gratia debet dici et virtus virtutum; qualiter autem fiat hoc; nostis forte melius quam ego."

[23] *Ibid.*: "Nihil de hoc scripsi quandam tamen opinionem sine assertione inter alias aliquando recitavi; in qua explicabatur quid ponat ius regalis dominii in rege aut ius proprietatis in habente proprium; aut quid ponat professio monachatus in monacho; cuius voluntas et vita iam penitus recessit a voto; aut quid ponit ius obligationis in subditis qui obligantur ad leges et mandata dominorum suorum; multaque alia his similia de quibus non curo. Vellem tamen quod huius dicti zelatores ostenderent quid erroris aut heresis contineat dictum illud. Ego enim sine dubitatione firmiter credo quod incomparabiliter nobilius quid dicit character baptismalis aut sacerdotalis; quam dedicatio templi materialis quicquid sit illud quod ponit."

[24] *Littera septem sigillorum,* f. 52 f.: "17. Item ceterum dicimus credimus et tenemus quod dicere, quod gratia nihil ponit in anima absolutum sed relationem ad gratiam Christi seu ius quoddam in meritis Christi, sicud monachus habet ius in bonis monasterii non per aliquid absolutum, est erroneum. 18. Item dicere quod ad deletionem culpe non exigitur infusio gratie animan informantis, error est. 19. Item dicere quod virtutes non dantur in baptismo parvulis, error est . . . 21. Item dicere quod caracter nihil plus ponit in anima quam dedicatio in ecclesia, falsum est."

[25] *Responsio* I, p. 130.

[26] See my comments in Burr, 1975: pp. 5–7 or Valens Heynck's in Heynck, 1964: pp. 344 ff.

[27] The entire question is found in Vat. Borgh. 173, ff. 54vb–60ra and Vat. Borgh. 54, ff. 133ra–137vb. The section dealing with infant baptism was published in Emmen, 1962. When dealing with the published part I shall cite Emmen's text.

In baptism the child is given a right to Christ's merit, and nothing more is either granted or required.

Nothing more is required because we are saved by Christ's merit, not by any qualitative change in us. Culpability and justification must be conceived primarily in terms of relationships. Olivi offers a series of suggestive analogies such as a king's gift of his kingdom to an infant or the pardon and ultimate adoption of a criminal by the king who had formerly condemned him. In each case the significant point is that the change rests primarily upon a new "relative and jurisdictional being" rather than a change on the individual's part.

Olivi's argument is based, not only upon his understanding of justification in terms of relationships, but also (albeit to a lesser extent) on his observation of Christian children, who simply do not act as if they had any special habit of grace denied to young Moslems. The assertion that they do have one exposes the Christian faith to the derision of nonbelievers, who marvel that the greatest and noblest habit should have so little effect.[28]

Olivi's formulation of the problem raises the question of whether a habit of grace is necessary for anyone, young or old. He replies that "although Christ's merit in itself is equally effective in those having the use of reason and in infants, God's justice nevertheless demands and ought to demand something more in the former than in the latter, something without which they are unfit for the merit of Christ." He who offends God in act cannot and should not be reconciled with him unless, through another act, he turns from his evil and adheres to God. Thus personal faith and contrition are required in adults.

Actually this statement does not quite answer the question. Much less does it say whether adult baptism differs from infant baptism in producing a *habitus* of grace. In this particular work Olivi does not speak to the question at all, nor does he have to, since the work is concerned with infant baptism.

In fact, the work actually makes no assertion about infant baptism either. No matter how clearly Olivi's own sentiments seem to show through, he stops short of an explicit statement of preference and concludes with an admonition to his readers that they should judge "soberly and with appropriate fear and trembling" which view is more consonant with the Christian fatih.

Olivi offers what looks very much like an answer in another work when he refers to three different senses of grace.[29] In one sense grace is the same as "the presence of uncreated charity to whoever is loved by it." In another sense it is the same as "jurisdictional possession or participation in Christ's merit," which can occur without the addition of any form. In the third sense it is the same as a "*habitus* of charity or grace really informing the mind." In infant baptism, grace in the first and second senses is given without any need for consent on the part of the recipient, while grace in the third sense is either not given at all or given in such a way that it can result in no act except through the addition of another *habitus* acquired through customary acts. Here Olivi is presenting both of the views discussed in the question on Christ's merit (which he cites at this point). In the sacraments in which consent is required, grace in the third sense is given *ex vi sacramenti* in proportion to the amount of cooperation shown by the recipient. If, as seems likely, Olivi would include adult baptism among the sacraments in which consent is required, this passage tells us not only that a *habitus* of grace is given in adult baptism but the terms on which it is given.

Olivi discusses baptism in still another work which brings some of the other censured articles into focus.[30] Here he raises the question of whether such notions as political or ecclesiastical authority, property rights, etc., posit any *res* besides the people or things involved. At the beginning of this work he notes that the problem is worth discussing because a difficulty of this sort is encountered in all *signa voluntaria et sacramentalia*, for it is often asked in a similar way whether the significations given by mere human decision to names and other utterances add anything to the words, decisions or intentions of the persons involved, or "whether the baptismal and sacramental character or consecration and the accompanying rights to receive or dispense the sacraments add any real essence beyond the persons baptized or ordained and the extrinsic signs and works of the sacraments."

Olivi concludes, "without prejudice to a better opinion, that one would seem to be able to say"—Olivi is claiming the opinion as his own, but in as nonassertive a form as possible—"that the aforesaid *habitudines* actually involve something real, but that they add no diverse essence really informing the subject of whom and in whom they are said to be." In the political realm, for example, legitimate authority rests upon the fact that God has designated someone to hold His place and commanded us to obey this person's laws as if they had been given by God himself. Thus such authority posits not only the persons involved but the divine will and the thing willed as it subsists in the divine will, as well as the means by which God wishes this authority to be realized, such as elections. In the course of the discussion Olivi finally turns to the sacraments.

The sacrament of baptism, insofar as it means that through which someone is baptized, includes in itself two most divine things: The signification of intention on the part of God . . . and the assistance of the divine will in con-

---

[28] *Ibid.*, p. 385 f.

[29] This is the treatise on the sacraments, Vat. lat. 4986, f. 136r. He offers a fourfold pattern in his commentary on the *Sentences*, MS. Padova, Univ. 2094, f. 180r.

[30] It is the question described by scholars as the *Quaestio de signis voluntariis* or the *Quaestio quid ponat ius vel dominium*, edition cited (under the latter title) in the bibliography.

ferring sanctification and grace justifying the one baptized. Insofar as it means the baptismal consecration which always remains in the baptized—even when he sins—and which is called a baptismal character, it includes two most divine things in itself. The first is the order of the divine will willing and decreeing that everyone rightly baptized is by that fact dedicated to the divine cultus.... The second is the order and assistance of the divine will in giving grace and consequently glory to the baptized unless he interposes an impediment through actual sin, and thus the baptismal character refers to a certain immobile right to obtain grace if the aforesaid impediment does not exist.[31]

Here again relationships are of central importance. The character is not a quality placed in man but rather an enduring relationship in which God commits himself to continuing assistance. The personal dimension of this relationship must not be obscured by the legal terminology Olivi often favors. The jurisdictional aspect is certainly present. Through baptism Christ's merit is applied to man and he is thus given the right to grace and glory. Nevertheless, this new legal relationship represents only part of the picture, since it marks the beginning of a new intimate relationship between God and man. In the question on Christ's merit, Olivi announces that such a relationship is far more important than any mere quality. In the case of ordination, for example, it "is no less divine, but rather far more divine" to claim that such ordination is the authority and power of Christ assisting the priest in all his sacerdotal functions than to say that "it is merely a created form informing some part or power of the priest," just as it is more divine to say that,

sacramental confirmation remaining permanently in the confirmed is a certain sublime assistance of divine virtue and might strengthening and arming one according to necessity in spiritual battles, or a jurisdictional condition (*habitudo*) through which such virtue is had in the aforesaid way with fuller right of participation in Christ's merit than was had through baptism alone, than to ascribe the entire force of confirmation to a certain characteristic *habitus*....[32]

The preceding comments, meager though they may be, give us some basis for evaluation of the accusations made against Olivi. First, he is accused of saying that "grace posits nothing absolutely in the soul, but rather a relation to Christ's grace or a certain right to his merits." He replies in the letter to R. that he has taught precisely the opposite. Here he is technically correct, since he speaks of grace in several senses, one of which (infused grace) does involve something in the soul.

Second, he is said to teach that informing grace is not necessary for the deletion of guilt. Olivi again replies that he believes the opposite, but it is hard to see how he can say it seriously. Certainly he does not grant any such necessity in the case of infants.

Third, he is accused of saying that the virtues are not given to infants in baptism. He replies in the letter to R. that there is nothing about this in his writings and that he has never asserted anything about it, although he has said that such a view should be given careful consideration. The first part of the statement may be true, although it raises some curious problems which need not be considered here.[33] The second part seems correct insofar as he does not actually assert the view in his extant writings, although he obviously favors it.

Fourth, Olivi is charged with saying that a character posits no more in the soul than dedication in a church. Olivi replies that he has written nothing about it but has recited such a view without asserting it. He emphasizes that baptism involves something incomparably nobler than dedication of a church. Here again, if we ignore the problem raised by the first part of the response, we can grant that Olivi's reply is substantially correct. Nevertheless, we might be tempted to guess that it would not have satisfied the commission, since the real issue was probably Olivi's refusal to think of the character as a quality placed in the soul.

In short, although the wording of the four charges allowed Olivi room to maneuver, they seem to have been aimed at two genuine aspects of his thought: His view of the character as a relationship and his denial that infants receive a habit of grace in baptism. We might ask how strange these views actually were in Olivi's time. In the first case, the answer is that Olivi's opinion was shared by others including Durandus of S. Porciano.[34] Within his own order most theologians tended to think of the character as a quality rather than a relation, but

---

[31] *Ibid.*, p. 325: "... sacramentum baptismi, prout dicit illud per quod aliquis baptizatur, includit in se duo divinissima, scilicet significationem seu intentionem Dei significantis et talem significationem instituentis et assistentiam divini velle ad conferendum sanctificationem et gratiam iustificantem ipsum baptizatum; in quantum autem per baptismum intelligitur baptismalis consecratio, que semper remanet in baptizato, etiam quando peccat, quam quidam baptismalem caracterem vocant, duo divinissima in se includit ad minus: primum est ordo divini voliti et ordo divini velle volentis et statuentis omnem baptizatum rite eo ipso esse divino cultui dedicatum et in sancto statu esse collocatum tanquam ipsius status ecclesiastici professorem et pro tanto acquisivisse statum ac professionem et obligationem divinam et a Deo volitam et statutam; secundum est ordo et assistentia divini velle ad dandum gratiam ac per consequens gloriam baptizato nisi ipse per actuale peccatum det vel dederit impedimentum, et pro tanto baptismalis caracter dicit quoddam immobile ius ad gratiam obtinendam non existente prefato impedimento."

[32] Emmen, 1962: p. 378: "Sic etiam divinius est quod confirmatio sacramentalis semper remanens in confirmato sit aut quaedam sublimis assistentia divinae virtutis et roboris ad ipsum in bellis spiritualibus, prout decet et expedit, roborandum et muniendum, aut iurisdictionalis habitudo, per quam talis virtus modo praedicto cum pleniori iure participationis meriti Christi, quam prius per solum Baptismum haberetur, quam absque his totam vim confirmationis adscribere cuidam habitui characterisco, cui ex vi suae naturae competat necessario disponere ad augmentum habitus caritatis necessario suscipiendum, si obstaculum peccati mortalis non adsit."

[33] See Burr, 1975: pp. 5–7 or Heynck, 1964: pp. 344 ff.

[34] IV *Sent.*, d. 4, q. 1.

Duns Scotus could still consider it to be a matter for varying opinions.[35]

As for the question of infant baptism, Olivi was right in believing that Peter Lombard and Innocent III both considered it to be an open question. Moreover, the essentially Thomist view that infants must receive grace in order to be acceptable to God would soon be undermined to some extent by Ockham and Scotus, who would argue that God could remit sin without giving grace, although he does not in fact do so.[36] Thus Olivi's position could be recognized as a theoretical possibility.

Nevertheless, it is a long way from theoretical possibility to fact. Ockham and Scotus agree with the Thomists of their day that in the present order of salvation justification is linked inseparably with infused grace, and in this respect they are in line with the major Franciscan theologians of the thirteenth century. Peter Lombard had bequeathed not only an openness on the effects of infant baptism but a general definition of the sacraments which, in making them the cause of invisible grace, seemed to demand that baptism be conceived as giving grace in some sense. By Olivi's time this definition was interpreted in terms of infused grace, which had come to play an important role in soteriology. Thus Olivi was again swimming against the theological current of his time. We shall see, however, that the question may have been considered an open one even by some theologians at the council of Vienne.

THE DIVINE ESSENCE

The censure of 1283 and the debate leading up to it involved several assertions regarding the divine nature, but one aspect of Olivi's thought received particular attention both then and thereafter. In the first proposition of the *Letter of the Seven Seals* the experts announce that "the divine essence is one in three *supposita*, in no way divided into three parts (*tripartita*), repeated (*geminata*), unfolded (*replicata*), repeatedly posited (*iterato posita*), or multiplied (*plurificata*)." The second proposition affirms that in speaking of God one should not speak of a producing and produced essence.[37]

In his reply to the *Letter of the Seven Seals* Olivi approves of the first proposition and says he never thought otherwise. If he has said otherwise—which he doubts—he withdraws it. If he has seemed to say the opposite at times, he has not meant to imply that this multiplication or repetition signifies anything in the divine essence except that multiplication of modes of being which the divine essence receives in the persons.

As to the second proposition, Olivi accepts it, "taking essence in the abstract according as it is common to the persons." He has, however, recited another opinion which states that the essence produces insofar as it is the essence of the father and is produced insofar as it is the essence of the son and holy spirit. This view, he believes, is neither erroneous nor contrary to the decretal by Innocent III.[38]

We are fortunate enough to have a good idea of what the commission's *rotulus* said on this score, since Olivi cites and discusses it at length in his 1285 *apologia*. The commission quoted a number of passages from Olivi's question on "whether there is personal production in God," a work which has survived the centuries and has even been published.[39] In the course of answering this question Olivi observes that there is disagreement on whether the divine essence is produced. "Certain people argue that essence is in no way produced, but only communicated or given." They say that it could not be produced without being distinct from the thing producing it. Others argue, however, that whatever is in the produced person is produced insofar as it is in the produced person and proper to him.[40]

Here again we find Olivi stating two positions and obviously agreeing with one of them without ever asserting it. In the lines that follow he lays down an argument for the second position which leaves the reader with little doubt as to his sympathies. In brief, his view is that "essence is not produced insofar as it is common to the produced and producing persons or to all the persons of the trinity, but insofar as it is proper to the person produced we can say that it is produced."[41] There is, then, a sense in which it is and a sense in which it is not.

Olivi goes on to show that he prefers this particular formulation because it allows him to reconcile what seems an awkward contradiction between two different sets of authorities. On the one hand Peter Lombard says that essence is not generated and Innocent III seems to agree with him. On the other hand a whole series of *sancti* seem to say the opposite. Olivi's solution is to assume that the two groups are using the word "essence" in different ways.

By employing this solution Olivi proposes to deliver the church from an awkward situation in which it had placed itself at the fourth Lateran council in 1215. At that time, Pope Innocent III tried to settle a debate which had been going on for some years. Peter Lombard had remained a controversial figure in the later twelfth century and at one point it had seemed at least possible that his *Sentences* would be condemned as heretical. His view of the trinity was an important element in this debate.

His most famous adversary regarding the trinity was Joachim of Fiore. Joachim's treatise *On the Unity and Essence of the Trinity* (now lost) attacked as heretical

---

[35] IV *Sent.*, d. 6, q. 10.
[36] Scotus, IV *Sent.*, d. 1, q. 6 and d. 3, q. 2; Ockham, IV *Sent.*, q. 3, in: *Opera Plurima* 4.
[37] *Littera septem sigillarum*, p. 51.
[38] *Responsio* I, 126.
[39] *Quaestio de trinitate*, edition cited in bibliography.
[40] *Ibid.*, p. 175.
[41] *Ibid.*, pp. 176 f.

the Lombard's assertion that "a certain greatest thing (*summa res*) is father, son and holy spirit, and that thing is neither generating, generated nor proceeding." Joachim felt that this formulation transformed the divine essence, the *summa res*, into a fourth thing existing alongside the three persons. The trinity thus became a quaternity.[42]

Joachim's polemic was written at a time when Peter Lombard was still fair game. By 1215, however, things were about to change. Innocent III, who had been educated at Paris, was a strong supporter of the Lombard. The decree produced by the council over which he presided defended Peter Lombard by name against the attack by Joachim, who was also named.[43] The council approved of precisely the assertion criticized by Joachim, adding that "distinctions should be in the persons and unity in the nature."

It is hard to say precisely why Joachim attacked the Lombard's view or precisely what he intended to put in its place. It is clear at least in general why he disapproved of the Lombard's formulation. He felt that in separating the divine essence from generation the Lombard had made it a discrete entity. Perhaps Marjorie Reeves is correct in suggesting that "the intensity of his opposition derives from the peculiar integration of his trinitarian doctrine with his understanding of history," since the resulting synthesis provides no room for the Lombard's *summa res non generans*, which in Joachim's view stands "aloof from history and unable to enter into it."[44] The various realms of Joachim's thought are so interrelated that it would be hard to imagine him considering one aspect abstracted from the rest. Nevertheless, it would be a mistake to assume that Joachim's criticism depended upon his theology of history. His primary criticism of the Lombard's view was not that it contradicted his view of history but that it contradicted the Christian understanding of God's triune nature.

Joachim's own understanding of the trinity is unclear. Medieval critics felt that in rejecting the Lombard's *summa res* he had compromised God's unity and moved toward tritheism. Since those who followed Peter Lombard tried to protect God's unity and trinity by balancing the single essence against the three persons without any great effort to show how the two were related to one another, it is easy to see how Joachim's assault would have been taken for an attack on the divine unity whether it was such or not. Nevertheless the decree of 1215 offers examples from Joachim's missing treatise which seem to suggest that he offered a unity which was "not true and proper but, as it were, collective and analogous (*similitudinariam*)," comparing the divine nature with many men who are one people and many faithful who are one church. Thus several modern scholars have concluded that Joachim was heavily influenced by the Greek approach to the trinity, which emphasized the three persons. More recently, however, some historians have argued persuasively that Joachim was misunderstood by medieval and modern interpreters alike and that he actually placed heavy stress on the divine unity, although in his own way.[45]

At any rate, by Olivi's time Innocent's decree had worked its effect upon theologians and Peter Lombard's distinction between essence and the persons was accepted. This left them with the problem of dealing with the *sancti*, who had persisted in ignoring such a distinction. We are now in a somewhat better position to see, not only the dynamics of Olivi's view, but also the dynamics of the reaction against that view. The excerpts from the *rotulus* provided by Olivi in his 1285 *apologia* show that the commission disapproved of those statements which compromised what they considered to be the inviolable distinction between essence or nature on the one hand and the three persons on the other. Thus they objected to a series of statements in which words like *replicata, iterata,* and *producta* were used in connection with the essence.[46]

We have seen that Olivi's submission to the *Letter of the Seven Seals* was less than complete on this particular issue. While agreeing that their denial of a produced or producing essence is true in one sense, he insists that there is another sense in which one can use such words. His reaction in 1285 was even stronger. He not only included a spirited defense of his position in the *apologia* but added an appendix aimed at precisely this question.

A good deal of Olivi's counterattack on the commission centers about the subject of *auctoritates*. He marshals an impressive number of them to show that the *sancti* in all ages have been much more flexible on this matter than the commission is.[47] While some of his authorities are of at least questionable value—he even tries to recruit Peter Lombard for his cause at one point[48]—many others offer evidence that Olivi had done his homework well. There was, of course, the problem of authorities pointing in the wrong direction. As far as Olivi was concerned only one needed serious attention, and that was Innocent's decree. Even here the problem was surmountable. Olivi argues that his view does not contradict the decree because the latter refers to essence as it applies to all three persons and comprehends all three together, not as it applies to each of the persons separately.[49] He stoutly denies that he is

---

[42] For Joachim's view see Reeves and Hirsch-Reich, 1972: part 3, ch. 13.

[43] The decree is published in *Corpus iuris canonici* 3: pp. 6 f.

[44] Reeves, 1969: p. 31. A similar explanation is offered in Reeves and Hirsch-Reich, 1972: p. 219.

[45] For citations see Reeves and Hirsch-Reich, 1972: pp. 220–223.

[46] *Responsio* II, pp. 141 f., 147 f.

[47] *Responsio* II, pp. 143–146, 149–152; *Amplior declaratio*, pp. 99–131.

[48] *Responsio* II, pp. 150 f.

[49] *Amplior declaratio*, pp. 368–371.

a defender of the error which Innocent attributes to Joachim, "namely that in the divine persons there is no unity of essence *secundum rem et naturam*, but only *secundum concordiam voluntatis*." His works demonstrate, he says, that he is a stout defender of the divine unity.[50]

In short, Olivi argues that his view "does not go against the words of Innocent III . . . but rather harmonizes (*concordat*) the words of the *sancti* with those of the decretal, removing the apparent contradiction between the two by means of a certain distinction." That distinction is, of course, the one between "essence as it is common to all three persons and comprehends all three in itself" and "essence insofar as it is proper to this or that person." In the former case essence is not produced or producing, in the latter it is. Innocent speaks of it in the first sense, while many of the *sancti* speak of it in the second.[51]

Olivi's argument against the commission contains a number of other facets, some of them worth at least a passing comment. First, he is conscious that the rational difficulties cited against his own view must be judged in the light of the rational limitations of trinitarian doctrine itself. "If someone should criticize this view by asking how the essence of the father can produce entirely the same essence in the son, I ask them how the father can produce a son who is the same essence as he and entirely the same as he. One is as hard to believe and understand as the other." Olivi cites other trinitarian assertions which tax credulity and intelligence in the same way and yet are accepted as true.[52]

Second, Olivi emphasizes the insufficiency of his contemporaries' attempt to explain away the sayings of the *sancti* by assigning them some meaning other than the obvious one. Granting that a few statements can be explained in that way, most of them cannot. Olivi observes that it would be odd (*mirabile est et valde stupendum*) if so many people spoke in such roundabout fashion so commonly without even bothering to note that the most obvious meaning of their statements was heretical.[53]

Finally, Olivi again questions the commission's *modus operandi* in much the same way he had done at the beginning of the *apologia*. He points to the danger of deciding such matters authoritatively and punishing dissenters without any word from the Roman pontiff and the universal church, especially since the view in question was recited without assertion.[54]

It is noteworthy that Olivi, like Joachim, should have been accused of weakening the divine unity. The parallel reminds us to ask whether Olivi's trinitarian views were connected in any significant way with his theology of history. If they were, Olivi is silent about it. One might argue, as others do for Joachim, that Olivi's position on the trinity offers a much more satisfactory basis for his trinitarian theology of history than would the Lombard's view. Perhaps it does, but Olivi does not say so. Least of all does he identify himself with Joachim of Fiore. Although it is possible to argue that Olivi corrects Peter Lombard in Joachim's direction by reintegrating the divine essence with the persons in such a way as to escape any implication of quaternity, in the 1285 *apologia* he neither defends Joachim nor explicity attacks the Lombard, and in any case the discussion moves entirely on the level of trinitarian theology without involving history in any way. There may be more here than meets the eye, but until it does meet the eye little can be said about it.

VII. CONTROVERTED ISSUES: PHILOSOPHY

Between 1279 and 1283 Olivi was attacked for a series of philosophical assertions involving the predicaments, universals, *rationes seminales*, the nature of human knowledge, the impossibility of matter without form, the relation of the soul to its powers, the relation of the virtues to the powers of the soul, the relation of existence to essence, and the soul as form of the body. His thoughts on the first and last of these issues seem to have played an especially important role and have received a notably greater share of attention from modern scholars. We will look at both, starting with the last.

THE SOUL AS FORM OF THE BODY

In his letter to R., Olivi lists among the disputed issues his assertion "that the intellectual soul does not inform the body except through the sensitive soul." He acknowledges that

> in two questions I have written that the rational soul really informs the body and is really the form of the body, although its intellectual part is not the form of the body. It is nonetheless consubstantially conjoined in one whole, in one *suppositum*, and in one total or complete nature. You can read what moved me to say this in the question "whether a man's sensitive soul is from the one begetting him," for it seems to me that there lurks in this matter the danger of destroying his immortality, freedom, and intellectuality.[1]

---

[50] *Responsio* II, pp. 146 f.
[51] *Ibid.*, p. 148.
[52] *Amplior declaratio*, pp. 373, 377.
[53] *Ibid.*, pp. 381–383.
[54] *Ibid.*, p. 99.

[1] *Letter*, f. 51(63)v: "Quot anima intellectualis non informet corpus sed tantum per sensitivam. De hoc in duabus questionibus scripsi quod anima rationalis vere informat corpus et vere est forma corporis quamvis eius pars intellectiva corporis non sit forma; sit tamen nihilominus consubstantialiter coniuncta in uno toto et in uno supposito; et in una natura totali seu completa; quid autem ad hoc me moverit potestis legere in questione an sensitiva hominis sit a generante; videtur enim mihi quod ibi sit periculum destructionis sue immortalitatis; et sue libertatis; et sue intellectualitatis; et ceterorum inconvenientium que ibidem qualitercunque tetigi."

The *Letter of the Seven Seals* takes up the same theme when it asserts that "the rational soul, insofar as it is rational, is form of the human body, nor does it follow from this that it is not substance or that it is extended or mortal."[2] In ascribing to it Olivi says, "I accept this opinion *ratione essentiae* of the rational soul, but not *ratione potentiae*."[3]

In his 1285 *apologia* Olivi provides a clearer insight into the nature and sources of the problem. He says that the *rotulus* contains excerpts from his questions "whether infants, sleepers and madmen can exercise free will" and "whether the sensitive power in man is from the one generating him or from the creator alone."

There I say that the intellective part of the soul is not united to the body as form, although it is united to it substantially. I also say there that the rational soul is form of the body in such a way that it is not such through all the parts of its essence, hence not through matter or the material part, nor through the intellective part, but only through its sensitive part.[4]

Olivi observes that the masters have described this view as a "notably dangerous error," yet "I would really like to be instructed by you or others as to what is so dangerous about it and why." He knows, he says, that "it is dangerous to say the intellective part of the rational soul is not the form of man or does not constitute one being and one substance with the human body." Fortunately he has not said anything of the kind. He thought he had shown clearly enough that these two truths can be safeguarded without saying that the intellective part is the form of the body, as long as one supposes two things, namely "that the sensitive part is essentially rooted (*radicata*) in the substance or matter of the intellective soul and that the substantial forms of the soul's powers are formal and substantial parts of the soul." He will be happy to acquiesce if shown the dangers of his position. In the meantime, however, the dangers of the opposing view are considerable.

The two questions mentioned by Olivi are extant and have been published by Jansen.[5] These and other questions give us a very satisfactory idea of what the controversy was about. Moreover, the matter has been illuminated by a number of modern historians, particularly Efrem Bettoni and Theodor Schneider.[6] Schneider's work is particularly valuable in showing how the issue in question was related to the ongoing battle between Thomists and various Franciscans over the unity or plurality of forms in the human soul.

According to Schneider, Olivi found himself unable to accept the Thomist affirmation of a single form because, like other Franciscans, he thought such a position compromised Christian dogma. If the intellectual soul is the form of the body in the strong Aristotelian sense of "form," then either the soul is mortal or the body is immortal.[7] Here Olivi was not only voicing a criticism which might be launched against the Thomist view from the Franciscan pluralistic perspective, but was pointing to a much wider problem encountered by all who thought seriously about Christian anthropology in Aristotelian terms.[8] Thus, against Thomas, he wanted to formulate a view which avoided too intimate a unity between the human body and the intellectual soul.

On the other hand it was necessary to guard the unity of the soul. A simple juxatposition of intellective, sensitive, and vegetative forms was unacceptable. One widely accepted Franciscan answer to the problem was an essential subordination of the lower forms to the higher, but Olivi could not ascribe to this view because, with Thomas and Aristotle, he rejected the notion that one form could be in potency to another, thus becoming, in effect, its "matter."[9]

Thus Olivi pioneered his own solution. Like other Franciscans he accepted the notion of a spiritual matter in the soul, yet he utilized this notion in a strikingly different way. In Olivi's solution the intellective, sensitive, and vegetative forms become "formal parts" of the rational soul. Each formal part, upon informing its spiritual matter, disposes it to be informed by the next higher formal part. These formal parts or formal *rationes* would be forms by themselves, but when informing the same matter they must be considered formal parts. The final form is the form of the whole. It and no other can be said to give being *per se*.[10]

The preceding description is perhaps too lucid. As Schneider and Bettoni both recognize, it is not always clear whether the form of the whole is to be thought of as the last of the series of forms or as the sum of all previous forms.[11] It would seem, however, that the former is more in line with Olivi's meaning. As Bettoni suggests, the preceding forms can be considered parts of the form of the whole "not in a rigorous sense, but only insofar as they are subordinated to it and place themselves, so to speak, at its service."[12]

Thus the three formal parts of the soul are related to one another insofar as they inform the same spiritual matter, each preparing it to receive the next higher formal part. One more ingredient must now be added: the body. Olivi must relate the soul and body in such

---

[2] *Littera septem sigillarum*, p. 52.
[3] *Responsio* I, p. 128.
[4] *Responsio* II, p. 155: "Ibi enim dico quod pars animae intellectiva non unitur corpori ut forma, quamvis uniatur ei substantialiter; ibi etiam dico quod anima rationalis sic est forma corporis quod tamen non est hoc per omnes partes suae essentiae, utpote non per materiam seu per partem materialem, nec per partem intellectivam sed solum per partem eius sensitivam."
[5] II *Sent.*, q. 51 (II, 101 ff.) and q. 59 (II, 518 ff.).
[6] Bettoni, 1959; Schneider, 1973.

[7] II *Sent.*, q. 50 (II, 77).
[8] Bettoni, 1959: pp. 369 f. and Schneider, 1973: pp. 243 f. recognize the parallels between Olivi and Siger of Brabant in this respect.
[9] II *Sent.*, q. 51 (II, 142). See Schneider, 1973: p. 229.
[10] II *Sent.*, q. 50 (II, 35 ff.).
[11] Schneider, 1973: p. 230; Bettoni, 1959: p. 310.
[12] Bettoni, 1959: p. 310. See II *Sent.*, q. 50 (II, 38).

a way that the soul is the form of the body and yet the body is not directly informed by the intellective part. He does so by assuming that the vegetative and sensitive parts inform the corporeal matter of the body as well as the spiritual matter of the soul.[13] Thus the direct link between soul and body is by way of the sensitive and vegetative parts.

This is not to say that the intellective part is entirely unconnected. A form has a certain "substantial inclination" to its matter. If the matter is in turn inclined to something else, the form will be inclined to that something else as well. The formal relationship between the vegetative and sensitive parts on the one hand and corporeal matter on the other produces an inclination on the part of the spiritual matter informed by these parts. Since the intellective part informs that same spiritual matter, it participates in the inclination.[14] All the formal parts, then, are inclined to the corporeal matter, although not in the same way. The rational soul, which is made up of intellective, sensitive, and vegetative parts, is form of the body through the sensitive rather than the intellective part, yet the entire rational soul can be designated as the form of the body, just as a man rather than his tongue is said to speak, even though he speaks only by means of his tongue.[15]

Thus Olivi's comments in the letter to R., the reply to the *Letter of the Seven Seals*, and the 1285 *apologia* actually do portray the essence of his thought. Moreover, one can see why Franciscan scholars like Richard of Mediavilla were uneasy. Olivi shared their objections to the Thomistic view, yet he joined with the Thomists in denouncing their own solution as an "irrational evasion."[16] Having abandoned the apparently respectable notion of an essential subordination, he opted for an alternative view which seemed to stretch the unity of man dangerously thin. Man's body was related to his intellective part by a tortuously indirect connection.

Nevertheless, there is room for question as to whether his censors were justified in considering his position any more problematic than their own. Schneider comments that in Olivi's formulation "the (only) substantial and not (strictly) formal unity of *pars intellectiva* and body became significantly apparent and thus irritated the other pluralists, in whom this pitfall was still deeper but remained verbally concealed."[17] Moreover, both Schneider and Bettoni recognize that Olivi's formulation is not so strikingly different from Thomas Aquinas's as one might at first imagine. Thomas, distinguishing between the soul and its powers, argues that the soul is the form of the body, but not *secundum intellectivam potentiam*.[18] Olivi, who speaks of the intellective, sensitive, and vegetative *parts* of the soul, says that the soul is the form of the body, but not *ratione partis intellectivae*. Bettoni goes so far as to suggest that "the Olivian solution of the fundamental psychological problem differs from the Thomist solution only in this: That it is expressed in such a way as to be completely consistent with the doctrines of universal hylomorphism and the plurality of forms."[19]

We have not heard the last of this problem. Long after Olivi's death his view of the soul would return to haunt his supporters at the council of Vienne.

THE PREDICAMENTS

Olivi's understanding of the predicaments comprises a second area which seems to have excited considerable interest in his time as well as ours.[20] In the letter to R. he defends himself against four charges on this score. First, he is accused of having taught that "quantity and substantial form . . . are the same in essence, since quantity does not differ in essence from the quantified thing." Olivi denies the accusation.

> I am amazed that this view should be assigned to me, since I simply recited it in order to consider more deeply the subtleties of metaphysical principles. Indeed, it is not at all stated as it is here, but in a much different context, as you can see in the question "whether the will is an active power" and much more fully in the explication of those things which I wrote against Brother Ar. . . . In reciting such views I intended above all to keep people from adhering too securely to Aristotle's views as if they were inerrant principles. I intended them to notice that in the most difficult and obscure matters Aristotle says, without any proof or discussion of opposing arguments, many things which are today held as first principles or rather as the true faith.[21]

Olivi is also accused of saying "that *locus* is nothing more than the form of the ambient body." He protests that

> I have never said or written anything about this, and if I did I would say that one must speak in one way of a mathematical *locus*, in another of a natural *locus*. In the first case I would say that a *locus* is the same as the surface of an ambient body, differing only in *ratio*. In the second

---

[13] II *Sent.*, q. 51 (II, 123).
[14] II *Sent.*, q. 51 (II, 117).
[15] *Ibid.*, p. 144.
[16] *Ibid.*, p. 110.
[17] Schneider, 1973: p. 237.
[18] *De unitate intellectus*, cap. 3.
[19] Bettoni, 1959: p. 376.
[20] For modern treatments see especially Maier, 1955: pp. 159–175; idem, 1964/67: 1: pp. 175–208; Bettoni, 1959: pp. 201–215.
[21] *Letter*, f. 52(64)v: "Quot quantitas et forma substantialis et accidentalis sint idem per essentiam, quia quantitas non differt per essentiam a re quanta. Miror quod hoc mihi imponitur, cum ego solum recitatorie ad subtilitates principiorum methaphysicalum profundius intuendas dixerim; non quidem omnino ita sicut in hoc articulo ponitur, sed sub aliis circumstantiis; sicut in questione an voluntas sit potentia activa intueri potestis, et multo plenius in explicatione illorum que scripsi contra fratrem Ar., sed illud credo quod non habetis. In talibus autem recitationibus hoc super omnia intendebam, quod non nimis secure inheret homo dictis Aristotelis quasi principiis inerrabilibus, sed potius averteret quod in rebus difficillimis nimisque perplexis sine omni ratione et contrarietatum discussione plura dixit que hodie tanquam prima principia immo tanquam vera fides tenentur."

case I would say that it adds a definite *situs* and a definite correlation of principal wordly bodies.[22]

Third, Olivi is accused of saying "that *ubi* is nothing more than *locus*." He replies that "this is asinine, since *ubi* is the same as being in a *locus*, and being in a place pertains to the located thing rather than the *locus*." [23]

Fourth, he is accused of claiming that "*quando* is nothing more than time, and universally that the predicaments do not differ *in re* but *in ratione*, except for substance, quality and *actio*." He replies,

I have never either asserted or recited such a thing. It is true that in a certain question regarding *motus* I find it opportune to recite various opinions concerning the distinction of predicaments without asserting any of them. In one of these opinions it is said that *tempus* and *quando* differ no more than *tempus* and "being-in-time" or than time taken in the abstract and in the concrete. In the same opinion it is said that the distinction of predicaments is not always based upon a real or essential diversity, but sometimes on a mere diversity of *rationes reales*.[24]

It is not stated, however, that only the aforementioned predicaments differ *in re*. On the contrary, it is said there "that *ubi* differs from its substance, though not entirely from *situs*." In the final analysis,

I do not care much what the truth of the matter might be, for I have sometimes recited these things in order to prevent excessive adherence to any merely human opinion (the examination and critique of opposing arguments being helpful in this respect) and in order to show what falsehoods and dangers might be contained in these various opinions by relating them to truths of our faith in the explication and defense of which they are more frequently advanced.[25]

The *Letter of the Seven Seals* offers a single comment on this matter: "To say that the predicaments are not really distinct is contrary to the philosopher and especially dangerous in the cases of relation and quantity." [26] Behind that comment, however, lies a whole series of charges contained in the missing *rotulus*. We know that such is the case because Olivi's 1285 *apologia* lists the troublesome areas without discussing them. He acknowledges there that the censure deals not only with theological matters but with philosophical questions as well, "such as whether a distinction of predicaments always necessarily involves an essential difference or sometimes merely involves a difference of *rationes reales*." He then cites a number of specific problem areas arising from the application of this general question to motion, action, passion, quantity, etc. He observes that in all these cases,

I have recited various opinions, asserting none of them, except that I sometimes offer (without responding to them) several arguments for the position opposed to the common opinion of some. Thus I seem to suggest that I approve more of that position, even though in most of these cases I say that the position is to be examined carefully and cautiously rather than asserted. I recited those positions which seemed to contain difficulties I would not have known how to settle. These were positions which seemed to me no less suitable for explaining and defending our faith than other views. On the other hand, I feared and strongly suspected that certain accepted philosophical opinions contain hidden snares and obscure, knotty dangers to the Catholic faith.[27]

Our sources for a reconstruction of Olivi's position on the predicaments are, happily, rather good. They show, among other things, that the nature of quantity played an especially important role in Olivi's debate with Brother Ar. and his supporters. His polemic against Brother Ar. closes with a long appendix of sorts in which Olivi switches from an offensive to a defensive posture, noting that,

since, in reference to a certain opinion regarding quantity which I have recited without assertion on occasion along with other opinions, this man and his supporters accuse me of reciting ridiculous and dangerous opinions, leaving the arguments for these opinions unrefuted, and thus seem-

---

[22] *Ibid.*, f. 52(64)v: "Quod locus nihil aliud est quam forma corporis ambientis. De hoc nunquam aliquid dixi vel scripsi, et si inde aliquid loquerer dicerem quod aliter est loquendum de loco mathematice accepto, aliter do loco naturali. Primo modo credo quod est idem quod superficies corporis ambientis sola ratione differens. Secundo modo credo quod ultra hoc addat certum situm certamque correlationem principalium corporum mundanorum."

[23] *Ibid.*, f. 52(64)v.

[24] *Ibid.*, f. 52(64)v: "Quod quando nihil aliud est quam tempus, et universaliter quod predicamenta non different re, sed ratione, preter substantiam, qualitatem et actionem. Nec assertorie nec recitatorie omnina tale quid dixi. Verum est quod in quadam questione de motu ex quadam occasione recito opiniones diversas de distinctione predicamentorum nullam penitus asserendo. In quarum quadam dicitur quod tempus et quando non plus different quam tempus et esse in tempore aut quam tempus sumptum in abstracto et sumptum in concreto, et in eadem dicitur quod distinctio predicamentorum non semper sumitur a diversitate reali seu essentiali sed aliquando a sola diversitate rationum realium."

[25] *Ibid.*: "Quid igitur veritas de hoc habeat non magno opere curo. Ad hoc enim ista aliquando recitavi ne nimium inhereretur humano cuicunque dicto, ad quod quidem valet contrarietatum excogitatio varia et animadversio, et ut averteretur in opinionum diversitatibus quid falsi quid periculi contineri posset, conferendo eas ad multiplices veritates fidei nostre ad quarum explicationem et defensionem sepius adducuntur."

[26] *Littera septem sigillarum*, p. 52.

[27] *Responsio* II, p. 405: "De omnibus enim praedictis et quibusdam consimilibus eis annexis, recitavi opiniones varias, nullam earum asserens, nisi quod ad illam partem, quae communi opinioni quorumdam repugnat, aliquando plures rationes adduco non respondens ad eas, in quo videor innuere quod illam partem plus approbo, quamvis in plerisque earum dicam eas esse cavendas et examinandas potius quam asserendas. Ego quidem idcirco recitavi eas, quia videbantur in se habere difficultates merito dubitabiles et quas ego nescirem dissolvere, et videbantur mihi ad fidem nostram explicandam et defendendam non minus accommodae quam caeterae; et e contrario, in quibusdam opinionibus philosophicis usitatis occultos laqueos, et quaedam perplexa et nodosa pericula fidei catholicae timui, et vehementer suspicatus sum, et adhuc suspicor illa in posterum ab errorum seminatoribus propalanda. Et si daretur mihi audientia, paratus essem explicare illa, et esto quod a sapientibus pro ridiculo haberetur, ad minus certus sum quod nihilominus ipsismet appareret quod zelus fidei catholicae et Romanae ecclesiae me movit ad ista et ad alia plura non minora istis."

ing to suggest hidden approval of these opinions—even though the accusation touches very few aspects of my teaching and these aspects consist of philosophical questions which involve no hidden dangers to the faith—I intend to present a fuller exposition of this opinion, showing as far as possible all of the dangers and philosophical difficulties which might be involved, so that it will be clear whether it was harmful for me to recite it. Christ is my witness that whatever I did or said was done through zeal for the faith of the Roman church and not in order to hide or secretly disseminate any poisonous and erroneous dogma. My failure to refute the arguments for the aforesaid opinion was due to the fact that I did not (and still do not) know how to do so although I thought it useful to present these arguments.[28]

The opinion in question is that "quantity means nothing other than the parts of quantified things extrinsically related (*coordinatas*) to one another with *situs* and *positio*." Thus the quantity of a thing "adds nothing to it except position of parts." It is not an entity distinct from the thing itself.

In the course of the discussion Olivi catalogs and counters seventeen objections against his own view and launches twenty-five objections against the opposing position. Most of the debate is purely philosophical, suggesting no obvious dangers to the faith. An examination of the first two objections against Olivi's position will suggest the essential nature of the argument.

First, it is claimed that the opinion destroys the predicament of quantity. If quantity were not *per se realiter distinctum* from other predicaments, then it would not refer *per se* to some essence which properly and determinately belongs to the genus of quantity. Moreover, a question regarding the quantity of a thing (*quantus est*) would not differ from a question regarding what the thing is (*quid est*). Thus in reply to the question, "how big is it?" one can reply "a rock." Olivi replies that real and essential diversity is not always necessary for a distinction of predicaments. According to Aristotle *actio* and *passio* are the same *secundum rem*, even though they belong in different predicaments. Moreover, our doctors say that many relations are substantial to these things in which they exist, and yet *relatio* is a predicament. Thus a diversity of *rationes* from which follows a diversity in modes of predication (*modorum predicandi*) seems to suffice for the distinction of predicaments. Otherwise our diverse modes of predication concerning God would imply an essential diversity.

Second, quantity would be equivalent to the essences of several other predicaments, for the quantity of whiteness would be the same as whiteness, that of a body the same as a body, etc. Thus the same quantity would be in diverse predicaments *per se*, so that it would be substance and various qualities. Olivi replies that the position in question does not imply a single quantity for the substance and various accidents. On the contrary, it affirms that there are diverse quantities of the substance and particular accidents. Moreover, even if the distinction of predicaments is sometimes taken from a distinction of *rationes* and *modi predicandi* rather than a distinction of really separable essences, and quantity is thus essentially identical with things in diverse predicaments, it does not thereby follow that quantity can be reduced to other predicaments according to that *ratio* through which it is distinguished from the *rationes* of those predicaments. It is this difference in *rationes*, not an essential difference, which allows us to place quantity in a separate predicament. Things apprehended by the intellect in a single such *ratio* can be assigned to a single predicament even if they are essentially different. Conversely, things apprehended through diverse *rationes* can be placed in different predicaments even if they are essentially identical.

In the course of this response Olivi turns briefly to the problem of whether Aristotle was correct in accepting no more and no less than ten predicaments. While he offers no real discussion of the matter, Olivi does note that "it has not as yet been proved that there can be no more predicaments than the ten posited by Aristotle, the god of this age." He emphasizes that views like the one in question are advanced by him in order that their truth or falsity can be established.[29]

And so it goes. Objection follows objection, response follows response, as the basic philosophical issues are hunted down and examined. Not until the fourteenth objection do we find a theological danger cited against Olivi's view. Here it is argued that, according to the Olivian position, in the eucharistic conversion the quantity of the bread would be converted into Christ's body. It would then follow that the remaining accidents, having no quantity, would not be subjected in anything, since, according to the masters, quantity is the only subject of the eucharistic species and of the changes undergone by them until their destruction. Moreover, since quantity is commonly considered to be an accident, Olivi's view would imply that an accident is converted into Christ's body.

The fifteenth objection develops the eucharistic implications in a different way, arguing that according to

---

[28] *Quodlibeta*, f. 49v: "Quoniam autem ex quadam opinione quam de quantitate inter ceteras aliquando recitavi absque tamen assertione aliqua, imponitur mihi ab isto et ab eius consentaneis quod ego opiniones aliquas ridiculosas et periculosas recito dimittendo rationes earum insolutas, ex quo videor occulte eas approbare, quamvis in paucis locis hoc mihi contingerit, et solum in talibus in quibus nullum periculum fidei de facili latere posset utpote in quibus materiis philosophicis et naturalibus, idcirco opinionem istam intendo hic plenius recitare, ostendo proposse omnia pericula et inconvenientia que materiam istam contingere possunt, ut ex omnium adunata collectione possit plenius apparere an damnosum fuerit me recitasse eam. Testis enim est mihi Christus quod zelo fidei romane ecclesie feci quecumque ibi huius per me sunt facta aut dicta, non intentione occultandi aut occulte disseminandi aliquid venenatum et erroneum dogma. Quod autem non respondi ad rationes opinionum talium causa fuit quia nescivi nec adhuc scio et nihilominus videbatur utile mihi conscribere ipsas."

[29] *Ibid.*, f. 51v.

Olivi's view the quantity of Christ's body would be present through conversion rather than through concomitance. Thus the body could not be entirely in every part of the host and in fact could not be present at all if, as some say, Christ can be present in the eucharist only because he is *per se et directe* there according as he is substance (*secundum hoc quod est substantia*) rather than according as he is quantified, since substance *as* substance does not involve *situs* (*substantia inquantum substantia non determinat sibi situm*).

It is not hard to recognize behind these objections an understanding of eucharistic presence generally similar to the one developed by Thomas Aquinas, for whom substantial conversion or transubstantiation provides the key to the problem. "Nothing," Thomas says, "can be where it formerly was not except through change of place (*loci mutationem*) or conversion of something else into itself."[30] Local motion is impossible in the case of eucharistic presence, so we are left with conversion as the only alternative. Once accepted, substantial conversion offers the answer to a whole series of thorny problems. As to the question of how Christ can be present on several altars at once and in each part of every broken host, Thomas answers that presence in the manner of substance allows such phenomena, while presence in the manner of dimensive quantity does not. In the eucharist the substance of the bread is changed into the substance of Christ's body through the power of the sacrament (*ex vi sacramenti*). Christ's divinity, soul, and accidents are thereby present, but only by natural concomitance. Thus they are there in the manner of substance rather than in their own manner. In short, Christ's quantity is present, but not in the manner of quantity. Thus he is present in each part of the host and in several hosts at once, cannot be seen or felt, etc.

While the accidents of Christ's body exist in the eucharist in the manner of substance, the accidents of the bread remain without any substance whatsoever. Thus one still encounters what looks, feels, and tastes like bread. This assertion called for some explanation by Thomas and others, since philosophers in the later thirteenth century were divided on the question of whether it was possible for accidents to exist without a subject.[31] Thomas's solution to the problem is that of all accidents only quantity can subsist as a particular, individuated accident without any subject. Other accidents are related to their subject through the mediation of dimensive quantity. Thus when the substance is removed these accidents can remain subjected in dimensive quantity, which in turn subsists by divine power without any subject whatsoever.[32]

Thomas has been cited here because he is the man with whom this view has become popularly identified. In reality many aspects of the Thomist view were the common property of several theologians in his time, some of them Franciscans. Bonaventure, for example, suggests that transubstantiation is the only rationally satisfying explanation of eucharistic presence and asserts that all other accidents are subjected in quantity.[33] Many of his confreres agreed. Thus Olivi's view of quantity, if accepted, would have necessitated a basic reconsideration of eucharistic presence not only by Dominicans but by many of his fellow Franciscans.

The two objections just cited show how unwelcome such a reconsideration was to Olivi's opponents. The fourteenth, which asserts that Olivi's view would imply the conversion of an accident into Christ's body, rests upon an acceptance of the essentially Thomist position and a misinterpretation of Olivi's. Olivi recognizes as much, noting that in his view the accidents will have their own quantity (i.e. their own parts spatially related to one another) just as substance does. Thus the quantity of the accidents will remain after conversion. The quantity of the substance will, in a sense, be converted into Christ's body, but such is the case only because this quantity is not really distinct from the substance itself.

The fifteenth objection largely presupposes the Thomist position in arguing that the quantity of Christ's body could not be entirely present in every part of the host or on several altars at once unless it is present according as it is substance rather than according as it is quantified. This presupposition clearly rankles Olivi, who replies that any view according to which God cannot convert something into the quantity of Christ's body or into that body insofar as it is quantified, or any view according to which God cannot make the whole quantity of Christ's body be present in each part of the host through conversion, "does not seem safe and, in fact, I believe it to be heretical." Olivi then asks precisely what the scholars of his day mean when they say that the body of Christ is present "according as it is substance but not according as it is quantified except *per accidens*" or that quantity is there only "according as it is being (*ens*)" but not "according as it is quantified except *per accidens*." If they mean that the body is not present "in a local or dimensional manner (*secundum modum localem et dimensivum*)" so that its diverse parts are commensurate with the diverse parts of the *locus*, then what they say is true but their way of saying it is highly improper (*valde impropria nec bene sonans*). If, on the other hand, they mean to say that "the *ratio* of quantity is not present according as it is quantity, but only according as it is being (*ens*)," then their statement "is not only unsafe but unintelligible, since the *ratio* through which it is being is not really distinct from the *ratio*

---

[30] *Summa theologiae*, III, q. 75, a. 2.
[31] See, for example, articles 138–141 of the 219 articles condemned by Bishop Stephen Tempier in 1277, found in *Chartularium universitatis parisiensis* 1: p. 551.
[32] *Summa theologiae*, III, q. 77, a. 2.

[33] IV *Sent.*, d. 11, p. 1, a. 1, qq. 1 and 3; d. 12, p. 1, a. 2, q. 3; both are in *Opera* 4.

through which it is quantity. In fact, they are entirely the same." Furthermore, when they say that the body of Christ is present according as it is substance but not as it is quantified except *per accidens*,

do they mean by this that the parts of the body are not present as situated outside one another and continuous with one another in the body, but rather that they are, as it were, present all together and without one another, constituting, as it were, a simple body? Perish the thought! Thus I would like to ask precisely what they do mean by these statements, since I do not understand them.[34]

Olivi confesses the same sort of bewilderment about the idea of quantity being present only *per accidens*.

The presentation of objections closes with a brief statement of purpose which serves as an introduction to his attack on the opposing view.

Behold, then, all the difficulties I was able to hear from others or discover on my own regarding the aforesaid position. We shall now offer whatever can be said convincingly in its favor so that, once the arguments are stated, it can be left to the judgment of the wise and of my superiors which view is more rational or irrational, which more consonant with and suitable for the faith, which more contrary to and dangerous for it.[35]

Olivi's critique of the opposing view is both philosophical and theological. Here again a summary of the first few objections will give the flavor of the philosophical arguments. In the first place, he says, it seems to follow from the opposing opinion that essential parts of corporeal matter or corporeal forms are not really such at all, since what is not divisible *per se* has no parts. Thus if (as the other position holds) only quantity is *per se* divisible, then the whiteness extended throughout the surface of a wall will not have substantial parts extended outside one another into which it can be divided. It will follow that the whiteness in one part of the wall will not be substantial but rather accidental to the total whiteness of that wall. The same will follow, not only for the parts of any extended form, but also for the parts of extended matter.

Second, it seems to follow from the other position that every corporeal essence except quantity is in itself (*de se*) simple and intellectual, since no such essence is quantified or extended in itself, nor does it have in itself quantified or extended parts. It would seem to be simple, not as a point is simple (since that simplicity belongs to the genus of quantity), but as an intellectual being is simple. If this argument is countered with the assertion that such essences are neither quantified nor simple in themselves, it can be answered that simplicity and extension are contradictory in the sense that every being which is not one must necessarily be the other.

Third, it seems to follow from the other position that it is at least possible for God to make such essences simple and intellectual merely by separating them from quantity and that such an act would not alter their species. It would then follow that every corporeal essence is *per se* intellectual in species. If it should be suggested that a form without quantity is indivisible merely through the privation of divisibility rather than through the positive attribute of simplicity, it can be replied that such a position is nonsensical, involving the contradiction that a thing is indivisible yet not simple. Of equally little value is the evasion that God can take away any particular quantity but not all quantity, for there is no compelling reason for such an assertion.

Fourth, it seems to follow from the other position that simplicity would be as accidental to an angel as quantity is to a corporeal thing. Thus God could take away an angel's simplicity and quantify him.

With the seventeenth, eighteenth, and nineteenth objections Olivi launches a counterattack on the eucharistic front. According to the seventeenth, if all the accidents in the sacrament are extended by a single accidental quantity it would seem to follow that God could not separate them so that the parts of each accident are continuous and ordered to one another as they were before the separation. Who would dare to say that God could not do so? According to the eighteenth, it seems to follow that the body of Christ is not in each part of the host (or even in the host at all) by virtue of the eucharistic conversion (*ex vi conversionis*), for if the substance of bread insofar as it is abstracted from all *situs, positio, continuatio*, and *extensio* is converted into Christ's body, it is not clear why, through this conversion, the body should be more in one place than in another. To restate the argument as it applies to the parts: Since the parts of the bread insofar as they are parts of a substance abstracted from all *situs* or *positio* are converted into Christ's body, there is no reason why, through his conversion, Christ should be in the *situs* of each of these parts.

According to the nineteenth objection, it seems to follow that God could not make the quantity of Christ's body be present in the eucharist *per se* and directly as the substance is. Thus he could not convert the bread into the quantity of Christ's body. If there is any truth in the position of those who say that the body of Christ is not present *per se* and directly insofar as it is quantified, but rather insofar as it is substance, and that quantity insofar as it is quantity could not be in each part of the host *primo et per se* but only concomitantly and insofar as it is rooted (*radicata*) in the substance (or else

---

[34] *Quodlibeta*, f. 52r: "Nunquid per hoc intendunt quod partes corporis non sint ibi secundum quod sunt in corpore extra se invicem situate et sibi invicem continuate, sed potius quod ibi sint quasi intra se invicem ut omnes simul coexistentes, et quasi unum simplex corpus constituentes? Absit hoc sentire. Quero igitur quid per hoc intendunt quia non clare intelligo."

[35] *Ibid.*, f. 50r: "Ecco omnia inconvenientia quae contra positionem predictam potui ab aliis audire, vel per me investigare. Referamus igitur quicquid pro ea probabiliter potest dici, ut relatione facta sapientum et maiorum meorum iudicio relinquetur quae pars sit ratioabilior et quae irrationabilior. Aut quae earum sit fidei magis consona et accomoda et que magis contraria et nociva."

it would be there in a local and dimensional manner), then God certainly could not cause quantity to be present *primo et per se*. "The Catholic should, however, be careful in deciding whether it is safe to say such a thing, for it seems to me to be very dangerous and to detract from God's power and perhaps from the sacrament of the altar."[36]

Olivi concludes his treatise on quantity with a remark meant to clarify his intentions.

These are the arguments which I have encountered so far in favor of the opinion in question. I am not concerned about whether the opinion is accepted, except insofar as I am unwilling to see either myself or anyone else drawn into accepting either side of the controversy without careful thought, for I do not want to see those things which do not directly affect the articles of our faith treated or held as if they were themselves articles of faith. Such things should rather be treated as ancillary to it. That is the reason why I sometimes recite diverse opinions and theories regarding such questions. In such matters no single opinion should be advanced as the faith, for unless I am mistaken about such matters (which I do not believe) dangers of the highest order lurk in such an assertion and in reliance upon the support of human opinions, be they of Aristotle, Averroes, or anyone else except the holy doctors authoritatively received and approved by the Roman church.[37]

The treatise on quantity is, as we have seen, a sort of appendix to the polemic against Brother Ar. Another passage in the body of the polemic also alludes explicitly to the body of Christ and implicitly to eucharistic thought in connection with the issue of quantity. Olivi protrays his adversary as saying that God can make Christ's body exist alive yet unquantified. Olivi objects that such a view is against the common opinion and cites Bonaventure to the effect that, although a substance can exist without quantity, it cannot so exist and still be living and organic. A being which exists entirely in a single point and is thus indivisible cannot be organic because, in order to be such, it must have *situatio* of organs and organic parts. In the case of Christ's body, can one imagine it alive and functioning without the heart, head, and other principal members being related to one another in the necessary way? How, for example, would the sensitive powers operate in such a being? Again, would such a body be simple in the sense that a point is simple or in the sense that an intellectual being is simple? It cannot be the former, since a point belongs to the genus of quantity, nor can it be the latter, since Christ's body would then not be a body at all, but rather a spiritual being.

Brother Ar.'s view has other dangerous theological implications. The church has condemned as heretical those who held that man will rise again *in corpore aereo* and those who claimed that Christ came in a celestial body rather than one composed of the elements. Both groups denied the reality (*veritatem*) of the human body, one in the final resurrection and the other in the incarnation. Brother Ar.'s view does the same, for if the species of our body is not violated by existence in a single point it necessarily follows that all the things which cannot be present in this form are accidental to the body. Olivi recalls Christ's invitation to his disciples to verify the reality of his resurrected body by touching it. This invitation presupposes that a real body has density, something which a point lacks.

Olivi notes in passing that he has discussed this problem in a certain article, giving the arguments for each of the opposing views "so that we should not support either view pertinaciously as if it were an article of the faith, for the danger of error and heresy generally lurks where one does not expect it."[38]

Olivi also takes issue with Brother Ar.'s belief that God can cause a thing to exist without any measure of its duration, so that it is not in time. Ar.'s argument is the same as in the previous matter, stating in the minor premise that time or duration is an accident. Olivi notes that Ar.'s position is against the common opinion, which holds that there can be no motion without time or aeviternity without constant duration. It also seems to be against the faith, since it apparently follows that all created things can exist from eternity. If a thing can receive actual being from God without duration, this actual being has nothing in itself through which it is present at one moment rather than another. If one thinks carefully through the implications of this position he will discover not only the possibility of eternity in created things but an actually realized eternity in things existing without any temporal or aeviternal duration.

In the course of the works cited so far, Olivi mentions a number of other writings by him which touch upon the predicaments. As a matter of fact, a substantial number of his questions do bear upon the problem. There is neither space nor reason to examine them all here, but it will be helpful to sketch at least the outlines of his position as it appears in some of the most significant questions.

One discussion of the matter is found in a question dealing with which predicaments can be the terms of change (*motus*).[39] Olivi comments that, in order to answer the question, "one need only see which predicaments refer in themselves to distinct essences and which

---

[36] *Ibid.*, f. 51r.

[37] *Ibid.*, f. 53r: "Haec sunt quae pro parte ista ad presens occurunt de eius approbatione non aliter curans, nisi quod nollem in alteram partium me vel alium leviter precipitari de hiis enim quae directe non spectant ad intrinseca fidei nostre, vellem quod nunquam tractarentur aut tenerentur tanquam dicta fidei, sed solum tanquam ancillaria eius, et hoc est causa quare in talibus aliquando opiniones et excogitationes diversas recito, nec alteri partium tanquam fidei insistatur nisi enim simplicis fidei me nimium decipiat, quod non credo, pro maxima pericula videntur mihi latere in tanta assertione, et autenticatione humanorum opinionum sive sint Artist. sive Averroys, sive quorumcumque aliorum preter doctores sacros a romana ecclesia autentice receptos et solemnizatos."

[38] *Ibid.*, f. 42r.

[39] II *Sent.*, q. 28 (I, 482 ff.).

refer only to *rationes* founded (*fundatus*) upon the essences of others without any real diversity." Since, however, there are diverse opinions on the matter, he proposes to recite them without personally asserting any particular view.

Some followers of Aristotle, believing that Aristotle intended the ten predicaments to be ten genera of things essentially distinct from one another, accept this view as if it were a first principle, even though Aristotle is not found to have said much about their always necessarily referring to diverse essences. Much less did he ever present any necessary or probable argument for the distinction and number of the predicaments.[40]

Some Aristotelians, wishing to defend the number of predicaments postulated by Aristotle, argue that the distinction of predicaments is founded upon a diversity in ways of being and that these ways of being are proportionate to our ways of speaking about being (*modi autem essendi sunt proportionales modis praedicandi*). Thus the ten predicaments reflect ten distinct genera of being.[41] Others would disagree sharply with this position, insisting that "our way of speaking about things follows our way of understanding them rather than their way of being."[42]

Olivi presents arguments for the various positions, yet refuses to present any definite conclusion. "Having recited the views of various persons as faithfully as possible," he says, "I leave the task of judgment to the wise."[43]

Another question, this time on whether unity adds anything to being,[44] eventually gets around to the issue of the predicaments by noting that one of the several views on unity and being is held by those who "say that the distinction of predicaments was not made on the basis of an essential diversity or according to a diversity of understanding (*intellectus*) alone, but rather on the basis of a diversity of *rationes reales*." He announces that he has recited the rationale for this position elsewhere. Olivi's brief examination of the matter is crowned with a rather noncommittal conclusion in which he announces that he will leave judgment to his betters.

The fullest consideration of quantity outside of the polemic against Brother Ar. is found in a question dealing with the problem of whether free will is an active or passive power.[45] Here Olivi announces a distinction between those who see quantity as a separate form and those who argue that "quantity or extension really adds nothing to quantified matter or extended and quantified forms except perhaps *unio* and *situs* and *positio* of their parts."[46] Here again there is no explicit statement of preference on Olivi's part, but his own sentiments are strongly suggested by the fact that one view is given nine lines while the other is accorded almost nine full pages. The arguments are largely the same as those found in the polemic against Brother Ar. In the course of the discussion Olivi suggests, among other things, that the opposing view leads to the idea of a single intellect in all men.

Here too the problem of Aristotle and the predicaments is raised and disposed of. Olivi asserts that neither Aristotle nor anyone else has proved the number of the predicaments or the ways in which they are distinguished from one another. Aristotle himself does not argue that they all represent distinct essences. In fact, he says in one place that *agere* and *pati* are the same *secundum rem*, differing only *secundum rationem*.

All in all, it is somewhat easier to describe what Olivi is against than what he is for. Despite his dedication to the principle of nonassertion, his own opinion regarding quantity seems clear enough. Nevertheless, his view of the predicaments in general is less so, and it is hard to see how we can really understand the former without understanding the latter as well. Certainly Olivi rejects the notion of the predicaments as ten metaphysical building blocks from which the world is constructed. There is, incidentally, nothing unique about such a rejection for Olivi's time. The real question is what sort of view he did espouse, and here Olivi's position is not so clear as one might at first imagine.

If Olivi does not accept the aforementioned view of the predicaments, neither does he usually regard them as nothing more than conceptual tools employed by us to describe the construction and behavior of particular things. His reference to *rationes reales* suggests a third possibility, for Olivi does not consign these *rationes reales* to the conceptual realm alone but speaks of them as existing *in things*.[47] Thus "quantity" and "substance" are different concepts which derive their validity from the very structure of created being, even though they do not refer to distinct essences.

Unfortunately Olivi's *rationes reales* cannot be described as easily as one might wish. He seems to be close to other philosophers of his time who tried to mediate between extreme realism and extreme nominalism by employing a distinction somewhere between the two. One recalls Henry of Ghent's intentional distinction, Aquinas's logical distinction *cum fundamento in re*, and Scotus's formal distinction. Precisely how Olivi's view is related to each of these distinctions is hard to say, perhaps even impossible. Perhaps Bettoni is cor-

---

[40] *Ibid.*, p. 483: "Quidam enim sequaces Aristotelis credentes quod Aristoteles voluerit decem praedicamenta esse decem genera rerum inter se essentialiter distinctarum acceperunt quasi pro primo principio quod hoc ita se habeat, quamquam Aristoteles non inveniatur multum expressisse quod dicant semper necessario diversas essentias et multo minus inveniatur aliquam rationem sive necessariam sive probabilem ad distinctionem et numerum praedicamentorum probandum alicubi adduxisse."

[41] *Ibid.*, p. 484. Bettoni, 1959: p. 202 notes that the view described here resembles Henry of Ghent's position.

[42] *Ibid.*, p. 486.

[43] *Ibid.*, p. 498.

[44] II *Sent.*, q. 14 (I, 256 ff.).

[45] II *Sent.*, q. 58 (II, 394 ff.).

[46] *Ibid.*, p. 440.

[47] II *Sent.*, q. 13 (I, 134 f.).

rect in suggesting that Olivi's view is itself confused and thus "his distinction of *rationes reales* is not philosophically vital."[48]

At any rate, Olivi's opponents did not call for censure and suppression of his opinion simply because it was unclear. While the battle was fought mainly on philosophical grounds, it also involved theological issues. Olivi in turn sought to show that his opponents' position challenged Christian doctrine at a number of points. We have seen him claim that their view compromises divine omnipotence, eucharistic presence, and the importance of the body in Christian thought while opening the door to the eternity of created things and a single intellect in all men. His opponents were more conservative, choosing to single out the area of eucharistic presence as the theological Achilles' heel of Olivi's opinion.[49]

Thus the most important question regarding Olivi's view of quantity is whether it does inevitably lead to a heterodox view of eucharistic presence. The question needs more discussion than it can receive here and, as a matter of fact, it has received such attention elsewhere.[50] At this time it will suffice to note that Olivi's formulation of eucharistic presence, although hardly well developed, seems to avoid the whole question of quantity by developing a view of presence similar to Scotus's *respectus extrinsecus adveniens*.[51] His formulation is not without its difficulties, but these are hardly obvious enough to place him in a special category and they are not in any case immediately related to his view of quantity. Thus it is difficult to agree with the commission in viewing this aspect of his thought as especially dangerous.

VIII. CONTROVERTED ISSUES: POVERTY

The letter to R. does not discuss any charges connected with Franciscan poverty. Perhaps R. and his friends were in accord with Olivi on this matter and needed no reassurance. Certainly poverty was an issue at this stage, since Olivi's polemic against Brother Ar. begins with a reference to it.

At any rate, the commission of Parisian scholars was quite interested in the subject. The *Letter of the Seven Seals* devotes four articles to it, and we can see from the 1285 *apologia* that the *rotulus* went even farther. The commission attacked Olivi's general view of *usus pauper* and its relation to the Franciscan vow, as well as his ideas on a number of specific practices within the order.

---

[48] Bettoni, 1959: pp. 237–243.
[49] The same charge is made by Richard of Mediavilla, one member of the commission, in his *Quodlibeta*, II, a. 2, q. 2.
[50] See Burr, 1974.
[51] For an examination of Scotus's formulation see Burr, 1972, "Scotus and Transubstantiation."

USUS PAUPER AND THE VOW

We can start with the issue of *usus pauper* and its relation to the Franciscan vow. The *Letter of the Seven Seals* announces that

usus pauper, insofar as it includes extreme necessity (meaning manifestly existing or imminent need of such a sort that the proper state of one's body or person cannot be maintained without its satisfaction) is in no way included in the vow of evangelical poverty, and to say the contrary is erroneous.[1]

In his reply to the *Letter of the Seven Seals* Olivi says,

I accept this view if "extreme necessity" is taken to mean extreme deprivation (*penuria*), as the masters seem to take it. I do not believe I have said the opposite, and if I did I recant. Nevertheless, taking "extreme" for the mean of virtue, not as an indivisible point (*pro medio virtutis non in puncto indivisibili*), but with the required latitude and in a way befitting status and offices, I have said that it is included in the view of evangelical poverty.[2]

In his 1285 *apologia*[3] Olivi notes that the commission has singled out the following statements from his question on whether *usus pauper* is included in the vow of evangelical poverty (i.e., the ninth of the *Questions on Evangelical Perfection*):

1) It is so solidly and clearly true that *usus pauper* is substantially included in the Franciscan vow that this point follows unquestionably from all things said in the preceding question in order to show that poverty is one of the principal councils of evangelical perfection. In fact, *usus pauper* follows more directly than renunciation of common possessions or jurisdiction.

2) It is not only false but heretical to say that some poverty is more perfect than evangelical poverty; yet a poverty which included the vow of *usus pauper* would be more perfect than one which did not. Therefore, etc. ...

3) Since *usus pauper* falls under the vow indeterminately, not every deviation from it involves mortal sin, but only such a deviation as, all things considered, should be regarded as rich rather than poor use.

4) Extreme necessity, taken strictly so that death is immediately imminent unless help is given, does not necessarily fall under the profession of *usus pauper*. Extreme necessity as it falls under the vow means manifestly existing or imminent need of such a sort that the proper state of one's body or person cannot be maintained without its satisfaction, although even necessity of this sort falls under the vow only indeterminately.

---

[1] *Littera septem sigillarum*, p. 52: "Item usus pauper rerum prout in se claudit extremam necessitatem, que dicit indigentiam manifeste existentem vel de proximo imminentem et talem quod debitus status corporis sui vel persone Deo servientis, nisi sibi succurratur, stare non potest, nullo modo includitur in voto evangelice paupertatis; et contrarium dicere est erroneum."

[2] *Responsio* I, p. 129: "Hanc sententiam accepto, sumendo li extremam necessitatem pro extrema penuria, sicut magistri hic accipere videntur; et sub hoc sensu non credo me dixisse contrarium, et si dixi revoco. Sumendo autem li extremam pro medio virtutis non in puncto indivisibili, sed in latitudine debita, et convenienti statui et officiis, sic dixi quod includitur in voto evangelicae paupertatis.

[3] *Responsio* II, p. 381–386.

In the margin the commission has written, "Commonly false and dangerous to our state." The word "state" refers, of course, to the Franciscan mode or state of being, while the "commonly" seems to indicate that the commission as a whole agreed on the verdict.

Olivi wonders whether this judgment refers to all that is said in the excerpts or only to some part of them. He gathers from the *Letter of the Seven Seals* that it is aimed more strongly against the final statement. He also wonders whether they intend to disassociate *usus pauper* entirely from the vow, or only *usus pauper* taken in the aforesaid way. If the former, why not say it clearly, and while they are at it why not censure Bonaventure, Pecham, Hugh of Digne, and Nicholas III? If the latter, and their target is extreme necessity, they should realize that extreme necessity can be taken in two ways. Here Olivi returns to the familiar explanation, this time explicitly citing Aristotle in connection with his own view. He adds a list of quotations from his own writings intended to show his moderation on the subject of *usus pauper*.

Olivi acknowledges that there may also be a difference of opinion regarding the way in which such things are included in the vow. Perhaps his censors feel that a vow should deal with precisely determinable conduct. If such is the case, then Olivi refers them to what he has written elsewhere on the subject of how certain things can be included in a vow indeterminately.

Anyone reading only the *Letter of the Seven Seals* might be tempted to suspect that the objection to Olivi's thought on *usus pauper* rested upon a misunderstanding of "extreme necessity" as he employs the term. After seeing the passages cited by the *rotulus*, however, one is inclined to believe that the commission knew what it was talking about. The difference of opinion was a real one, with the commission defending a position roughly similar to the one attacked by Olivi in the treatise *Quoniam contra paupertatem evangelicam*. The dispute was now raging within the order, and at the moment Olivi was losing it.

Olivi later returns in the 1285 *apologia* to still another censure directed at his understanding of the rule. This one is aimed at a passage from his question on whether one vowing the gospel or some rule simply and without determination is required to observe all things contained in it.[4] The commission has taken note of a statement that in the Franciscan rule those things at least can be considered councils in which the words "I counsel," "I admonish" or something similar are used; or where it is a question of license, concession or something similar; or where it is a question of things having less perfection or utility. In the margin the commission has written, "Commonly poorly stated, not knowing how to distinguish between that which is counseled and that which is conceded." One censor has added a longer comment elaborating upon the criticism and citing St. Jerome in the process.

Olivi replies that he does know Jerome's distinction and in fact has quoted it in another question. In the present case, however, he uses the word "councils" in a somewhat larger sense to signify all that does not fall under the category of precept. The commission may accuse him of using a word improperly, but not of speaking falsehood.

FRANCISCAN BISHOPS AND POOR USE

The commission also attacked a series of propositions concerning the practice of poverty within the order. In the first place, the *Letter of the Seven Seals* says, "It is false and erroneous to say that those of the evangelical state who assume episcopal office are more fully obliged to *usus pauper* than before, and that there can be no dispensation from this obligation."[5] In his reply to the letter Olivi concedes that they are not held to it more than before in areas where such observance would impede their duties. Moreover, he has not claimed that they are so obliged in all cases, but only under certain conditions. Again, the "more than before" is meant not *simpliciter* but *secundum quid*, according to congruity of status. He has always said and written that they can be excused from the obligation in some way during that period. Although he has written this, he has not said it in the schools and is not pleased that his statement has been spread about.[6]

In the 1285 *apologia* Olivi observes that the commission attacked two statements on this matter taken from his works.[7] In one case he is merely quoting another Franciscan scholar, but the committee nonetheless pronounced the view "commonly false." In the other case the view expressed is pure Olivi and is important enough to merit close examination.

Olivi is quoted as saying of Franciscan bishops, "It is to be held without doubt that they are bound to observe *usus pauper*, in some way even more than before." He asks whether he has been censured because he said that Franciscan bishops were obliged to *usus pauper*, because he said they were obliged more than before, or because he said there could be no dispensation. If the first, then what we known as evangelical poverty is not the highest state, our beliefs about Christ and the apostles are wrong, and the Franciscan order is built upon sand. If the second, then it should be made clear that the phrase "more than before" is to be taken not *simpliciter* but *secundum quid*, meaning "more in some way." If the third, it should be

---

[4] *Responsio* II, p. 394. It is question seventeen of the *Quaestiones de perfectione evangelica*, edition cited in the bibliography.

[5] *Littera septem sigillarum*, p. 52.
[6] *Responsio* I, p. 129.
[7] *Responsio* II, p. 386–390. Both statements are from what is now considered question nine of the *Questiones de perfectione evangelica*. The first occurs in the context of Olivi's consideration of clothing, the second in his comments on whether Franciscan bishops are dispensed from poor use.

understood that this does not rule out whatever behavior may be useful or necessary for the rule of souls, for the vow itself is never to be considered prejudicial to perfection, necessity, and spiritual utility. In other words, the vow itself provides the flexibility needed in such cases, and thus no dispensation is necessary.

Although these remarks offer a good summary of Olivi's position, it would be illuminating to look rather closely at the question in which the censured statement occurs. It is addressed explicitly to the issue of whether Franciscans who become bishops are dispensed from *usus pauper*, and the assertion which so offended the commission is actually the first thing Olivi says in responding to the question. He goes on to say that they cannot be dispensed because there is, in fact, no reason why any man should be dispensed from evangelical vows.[8] Even if there should be situations in which such a dispensation was called for, certainly such would not be the case in this situation, since the episcopal status "demands evangelical perfection in the highest way in those things which belong to it, so much so that the status is never achieved in full decency and perfection unless evangelical perfection is observed along with it." As a sign of this fact Christ imposed evangelical perfection, especially *usus pauper*, on his apostles when he sent them out to preach and later when he appointed them to the apostolate.

Let us imagine, Olivi says, what the world would be like if all bishops today lived as the apostles did, especially in regard to *usus pauper*. The goods of the church would be expended for the poor, faithful and responsible stewards would supervise the use of such temporal possessions according to canon law, and the bishops would give themselves over to prayer, preaching, spiritual guidance, and the example of a holy life. Would not the faithful and even the infidel be drawn incomparably more to God if such were the case? Olivi obviously has little doubt that his question rates an affirmative answer.

Such, unhappily, is not the case in the church of Olivi's time. Instead, he says, not only secular bishops but those who have vowed some rule (in Olivi's terms, *religiosi*) want to travel by horse with a crowd of overdressed retainers, dine splendidly, personally supervise the use of temporal possessions, etc. Thus "they provide as scandalous an example to their subordinates as other prelates do." All these abuses are rooted in weatlh and the love of wealth. Thus it follows that the episcopal office, far from requiring a dispensation from *usus pauper*, demands its observance in even fuller measure.

Olivi's handling of objections to his position bears some examination, since it sheds light on his own view and on some of the reasons why opponents thought dispensation was in order. He cites a number of objections, but most of them can be reduced to three basic arguments. First, dispensation is necessary for the sake of a more effective ministry. The simple believer, who does not appreciate inner virtue, will look upon *usus pauper* as contemptible and his contempt will extend to episcopal authority itself. "As the vulgar proverb says, familiarity breeds contempt." Dispensation will also aid an effective ministry by providing the bishop with adequate resources to perform his function. A horse and other amenities will help him to get around and do the things required by his flock.

Second, dispensation is possible because the episcopal status is higher than that of a simple monk or friar. It is more perfect than these, and the things it entails are more important. It is an accepted axiom that a lesser vow can be commuted to a better one and a less perfect status can be commuted to a more perfect one.

Third, *usus pauper* could not be required of bishops because the church has not required it in the past and does not require it now. In fact, it encourages the opposite behavior. If it were not more useful and rational to use horses and go about in decent magnificence, why would so many bishops do so? Why would the church approve of their doing so? Certainly one should not believe that the church is in error.

Olivi's answer to the first sort of objection is a flat denial that a more effective ministry will be gained by dispensation. There are two different types of reverence, one based on the recognition of sanctity and the other on the recognition of temporal magnificence. The first is derived from the exterior and exemplary perfection of bishops and is in itself holier than the second, inflaming the faithful to love both virtue and the bishops themselves. The second is more inclined to induce fear of doing evil and also of the bishops. Certainly too much familiarity breeds contempt, but a dedicated observer of evangelical perfection will hardly strike the average Christian as a familiar sight. Such bishops will be separated from others by their virtue and the faithful will regard them as they would Christ himself.

As to the matter of providing the bishop with adequate means to do his job, that really depends on what job he is expected to do. Dispensation may aid the bishop in accomplishing things which are useful in a temporal sense. He may be able to gain more wealth for the church and increase its worldy power. In the spiritual realm, however, there will be a net loss. Olivi even wonders whether episcopal poverty might be more useful in a temporal sense, since the bishops' flock would be less burdened with expenses and ecclesiastical resources could be spent on the poor as they ought to be.

The second sort of objection leads Olivi into a tortuous jungle of distinctions which often serve to confuse the issue rather than clarify it. At times, however,

---

[8] *De perf.*, q. 9, f. 74ra. At this point he refers ahead to his question regarding the dispensation of vows, which is now considered to be the fourteenth of his *Questiones de perfectione evangelica*. The *responsio* section dealing with Franciscan bishops in q. 9 runs from 74ra to 74vb. The reply to objections is at 74vb–76va, while the objections themselves are at 55vb–56ra.

the issue emerges with crystal clarity. In a sense the episcopal status is indeed higher than that of the simple monk or friar, but that is because the former status calls for all the perfections of the latter status and more besides. There is, Olivi says, a type of perfection which necessarily presupposes another to which it is added and which serves as its foundation. There is another type which is the foundation and presupposes no other. Again, some states are said to be perfect because they are perfectly ordained to perfecting others, while some states are called perfect because they are perfectly ordained to perfecting oneself. The episcopal state is the former sort in both senses. It is ordained to perfecting others and presupposes another sort of perfection as its foundation. Conversely, *perfectio personalis seu religionis* is ordained to perfecting oneself and presupposes no other foundation. It follows that episcopal perfection is rooted in personal perfection and necessarily demands it. In fact, this status "demands, presupposes, and binds one *de congruo* to the perfection of *religio* and also to all perfection of this life." Thus, although the episcopal status may be more perfect that that of *religio* (meaning, of course, that of a monk or friar), it does not dispense one from the latter but rather adds to it. It is not as if a less perfect state were commuted to a more perfect one incompatible with the first, as when a married man takes a vow of chastity.

The third sort of objection is answered in various ways. Olivi notes that, while the example of the *sancti* is to be followed, that of Christ and his disciples is especially authoritative. At one point he alludes very obliquely to the various *status ecclesie*, an apparent reference to the progress of the church through various periods. Again, in an intriguing passage which closes the question, he denies any implication that the church is in error and offers a lengthy report on Cyprian and the issue of whether heretics should be rebaptized when they enter the Catholic Church. His point is that, since this matter was not yet definitively settled by a general council, Cyprian was not heretical in defending what proved to be the wrong view. The immediate application is that, whatever the practice has been to date, the matter of Franciscan bishops is still open to dispute because there has been no determination by the church.

There are two sides to Olivi's argument. On the one hand, he argues forcefully that a Franciscan bishop must observe *usus pauper* because it is included in his vow. There can be no dispensation from this vow, even by the pope himself. Here Olivi's position is related to what we saw in an earlier chapter to be his attitude towards vows, and the difference between him and his opponents on the present issue is not unrelated to the difference acknowledged there regarding *usus pauper* as a part of the vow. Olivi's somewhat more flexible notion of the obligations incurred in a vow allows him to envisage a situation in which a Franciscan bishop is held to his vow of *usus pauper* and yet is left free to partake of worldly pleasures from time to time when the situation demands it.

Nevertheless, in the present instance it is not simply a question of whether Franciscan bishops can be dispensed from their vows. It is not even simply a question of Franciscan bishops. That is where the matter begins, but not where it ends. In the course of his answer Olivi argues that all bishops should practice *usus pauper*.

Olivi's attitude is comprehensible only when it is viewed in the light of his theology of history, which is seen only fragmentarily in the course of this particular question. Certainly he indicates clearly enough that the apostles, who were the original bishops, practiced *usus pauper*. He is less clear about what happened next, alluding to it only in his unexplained reference to the *status ecclesie*. If forced to elaborate, he might have used roughly the same explanation he would employ nearly two decades later in the Revelation commentary, where he remarks that, although the apostles practiced evangelical poverty, the pontificate "was usefully and rationally commuted to a state possessing temporals from the time of Constantine until the end of the fifth period," although many of the popes in the intervening centuries were *regulares* and preferred poverty to temporal possessions.[9] Thus the possession of temporals by ecclesiastical leaders was introduced well after apostolic times and has continued to the present day. It was not evil in itself but rather was just and proper *for its own time*.

Nevertheless, times change. The passage in the Revelation commentary predicts that in the end the pontificate will return to its original state. This development will be encouraged by the great imperfection in possession and dispensation of ecclesiastical possessions as well as the pride, luxury, simony, fraud, etc., accompanying these possessions. These ills have become so widespread that "around the end of the fifth period practically the whole church is infected, disordered, and made like a new Babylon from top to bottom."

Certainly the negative part of this appraisal is strongly suggested in the question on dispensation. It is impossible to read through the question without noticing that Olivi has a very low opinion of bishops in his time. The positive aspect is less obvious. Olivi makes it clear that Franciscan bishops will do a better job than the others if they stick to their vows, but he does not announce that a new day is dawning in which leadership will be exercised by devotees of evangelical perfection. Never-

---

[9] *Apoc.*, ff. 6va–7rb, where the passage is written at the bottom of these pages, having been omitted from the body of the text. Other manuscripts include it in the proper place. Note that the basic outlines of this view are at least suggested by Olivi's comments in *De perf.*, q. 9, f. 75a, where Olivi says "habendo interius habitum paupertatis pro tempore secundum conformitatem statuum ecclesie potuit hoc perfecte fieri, quamvis multi anachoritarum et multi circa tempora beati benedicti in paupere usu quam plurimum habundarent."

theless, this thought is probably lurking in the background.

Thus the basic issues involved in this question are more important than one might at first suppose. How important they really are will be seen in the final chapter when we examine the condemnation of the Revelation commentary. For the moment we can only observe that the disturbing implications of Olivi's argument concerning Franciscan bishops should have been more evident to a pope John XXII in 1318 than to a Franciscan theologian in 1283. When we turn to the condemnation of 1318–1326 it will be obvious what John XXII would have found objectionable about Olivi's thoughts on episcopal *usus pauper*. It is less obvious why the masters objected to them in 1283. It is a shame they did not supply Olivi with the explanation he desired, since it would be interesting to know precisely how they would have justified their censure.

BURIAL

Olivi was also attacked on the issue of Franciscan involvement in the burial of laymen. The *Letter of the Seven Seals* announces that "burying the dead is a work of mercy, spiritual and in no way out of harmony with evangelical perfection." Another article adds that "having the right to bury is not contrary to the highest poverty." [10] In ascribing to these propositions Olivi agrees with the first proposition as long as the burial "is not under unworthy or imperfect circumstances, such as for reasons of cupidity or with impediment to some worthier actions." As to the second proposition, he grants that having the right of burial is not contrary to evangelical poverty if one is speaking of a spiritual right regarding the body, but is such if one speaks of a right regarding burial fees or the place of burial.[11]

In his 1285 work Olivi elaborates upon his position in the process of citing and then defending the brief comment under attack by the commission.[12] In the disputed statement Olivi asserts that having a right to the body which is to be buried and having a right to retrieve that body if it is taken away by someone else "is not directly repugnant to the highest poverty," except perhaps insofar as the right to retrieve something which is not directly spiritual seems contrary to it and insofar as the act of burial, being the lowest and least perfect of spiritual acts, does not accord well with the perfection found in such poverty. He goes on to say that there is great imperfection in the execution of the office of burial, except in case of necessity. There is such because the act is of little utility or spirituality, involves a rather unspiritual matter, and impedes the performance of more perfect acts and occupations. Baptizing is certainly more spiritual than burying, yet even here Paul told the Corinthians that he was sent to preach and not to baptize. Christ, wishing to remove this impediment to more spiritual acts, told the man, "Let the dead bury the dead, you go and announce the kingdom of God."

The commission has written in the margin that Olivi's view is "very false and dangerous." This remark spurs Olivi to provide in the 1285 *apologia* a further explanation which more or less follows the outline of his original question. He affirms that jurisdiction in this area can cover the place of burial, the body to be buried, and the receipt of burial fees. The first and third can be held only by those having private or common property. The second is a spiritual act and is not directly contrary to the highest poverty, but it is a relatively imperfect act except in case of necessity, having little utility or spirituality and impeding more perfect acts and occupations. The fulfillment of this office carries with it a danger of cupidity, simony, and evil example; particularly when the clergy are scandalized, there is appearance of cupidity, or litigation results.

Here Olivi is dealing with one of the main bones of contention between secular clergy and mendicants during the later thirteenth century. By burying laymen in their churchyards the mendicants were impinging upon clerical perquisites and thereby upon clerical revenues. By the end of the century the practice had become an equally sensitive issue within the order, since rigorists felt that it provided an all-too-seductive invitation to greed.

PROCURATORS

One final issue is unmentioned in the *Letter of the Seven Seals* but emerges in the 1285 *apologia*. Olivi announces that the commission has cited in the *rotulus* a passage from his question on whether observers of evangelical poverty can have procurators who will collect what is willed or given to the order and carry on legal processes against debtors.[13] In the passage, which is taken from the ninth of his *Questions on Evangelical Perfection*, Olivi argues that some things are licit because of the perfection of one's status and others because of concession to the weak, lest they do worse. Again, one can have such procurators in two ways. Either one gives them authority and jurisdiction or one simply selects a person who is given authority by others. The first alternative is impossible for Franciscans, since they have no authority and jurisdiction to surrender. The second cannot be in accordance with the perfection of the Franciscan state, much less can such procurators be encouraged to bring others to judgment except as a concession to the weak. The commission labeled this view "commonly false." Olivi protests that his statement seems moderate enough and asks precisely what part of it is false. A brief defense of each part is appended.

---

[10] *Littera septem sigillarum*, p. 52.

[11] *Responsio* I, p. 129.

[12] *Responsio* II, pp. 378 f. The commission's target is the reply to the thirty-seventh objection in question eight of Olivi's *Quaestiones de perfectione evangelica*, f. 52ra-rc.

[13] *Responsio* II, pp. 390–394.

Here again Olivi and his censors were coming into conflict over an issue which divided Franciscans of the later thirteenth century. Even in Francis's time the friars had been allowed recourse to a "spiritual friend" (as the rule of 1223 describes him) who could use money to buy clothes and to care for ailing brothers.[14] After 1230 and *Quo elongati* they could avail themselves of a *nuntius*, who was viewed as the representative of the almsgiver and therefore not under the Franciscans' control. Such an arrangement had proved increasingly handier as members of the order ceased to engage in manual labor outside the convent and came to rely entirely on contributions for their support. Thus it is hardly surprising that the papal bulls *Ordinem vestrum* (1245) and *Quanto studiosus* (1247) significantly amplified the role which could be played by such intermediaries and the control which could be exercised over them by the Franciscans themselves. The procurator, who acted as a representative of the papacy yet was appointed and largely controlled by the friars, made his appearance in *Quanto studiosus*.

The dangers of this legislation were noticed by the Franciscans themselves, and under the generalates of John of Parma and Bonaventure an effort was made to suspend the privileges extended by *Ordinem vestrum* and *Quanto studiosus*. This program was undoubtedly unpopular with a segment of the order and was in any case frustrated by subsequent papal bulls. *Exiit qui seminat* (1279) had little impact in this respect, since it recognized the legitimacy of procurators without specifying how they were to be used, but *Exultantes in domino* (1283) allowed the friars to appoint procurators and exercise ample authority over them. The chapter general at Milan in 1285 acknowledged and accepted this state of affairs.

Thus the official position of the order on procurators was in a state of flux when Olivi penned the censured comment sometime before the promulgation of *Exiit qui seminat*, and was such even when he wrote his *apologia* in early 1285, prior to the Milan chapter. Nevertheless, by the latter date a line of development had been suggested by *Exultantes in domino*. Olivi certainly was not in harmony with this line of development, although his objections to it, far from branding him as a rebel, would seem to place him in a hitherto respectable tradition within his own order. He did not reject the institution of procurators. In the passage censured by the commission he attacks, not procurators in general, but certain views on how they are chosen and controlled and what they can do. Within the same question, in a section dealing with the use of money, he acknowledges that, while its use is entirely prohibited to Franciscans, it is nonetheless possible for them to receive from *dispensatores* items which were purchased with money. Such middlemen are under the command of the lords who give the money, not of the Franciscans. Thus the prohibition against possession of money is safeguarded even while the brothers are benefiting from momentary donations.[15]

Other examples could be cited. In the sixteenth of the *Questions on Evangelical Poverty* Olivi accepts the institution of procurators but suggests that certain conditions be met. First, the money should be kept only for present or imminent necessities. Second, the brothers should scrutinize their own attitudes toward this money, being sure that they regard it as something which belongs entirely to the giver and not to them. There should be no assumption that the procurator is obliged to spend this money for their necessities. Olivi feels that in imposing these conditions he is walking shoulder-to-shoulder with Gregory IX and Nicholas III, both of whom are cited in the course of his comments.[16]

In his commentary on the Franciscan rule, probably written in late 1288, Olivi says that the passage allowing the spending of money through *amici spirituales* applies not only to the two specific cases mentioned (illness and clothing) but to similar matters as well.[17] These two are mentioned because they occur more frequently and are *minus dissona paupertati*, since the getting and spending of money for buildings, books and the like, though sometimes necessary, can more easily lead to abuse. The brothers should become involved in such financial transactions only *mediate et absque omni dominio vel auctoritate*, in the way outlined by Popes Gregory and Nicholas. Thus Olivi implicitly takes his stand with *Quo elongati*, prudently ignoring *Ordinem vestrum*, *Quanto studiosus*, and *Exultantes in domino*. The question of procurators will arise again in the next chapter in connection with Olivi's letter to Conrad of Offida, and further comment on it can be reserved for that time.

Thus in the period between 1279 and 1283 Olivi was attacked for his views on philosophy, theology, and Franciscan poverty. Note that one other area is significantly absent. Nothing is said in the *Letter of the Seven Seals* (or, apparently, in the *rotulus*) about his apocalyptic views, nor is this matter among the nineteen articles discussed in the letter to R. The only indication that anyone took notice of Olivi's apocalyptic speculation is provided by the closing comments to R., in which, after disposing of the nineteen articles, he defends himself against the charge of following "fantastic visions" and predicting future events.[18] Someone seems to have worried about such things, but not the Paris commission and perhaps not Brother Ar. either.

---

[14] For the following see Lambert, 1961: pp. 84–88, 96–102, 106, 110, 116, 120 ff., 161 f.

[15] *De perf.*, q. 9, ff. 67rb, 69vb–71rb.

[16] *De perf.*, q. 16, f. 101r–v.

[17] *Rule Commentary*, pp. 142 f. For the dating see Flood's introduction, p. 69.

[18] *Letter*, f. 53(63)r. See ch. 5 above.

IX. REHABILITATION AND LATER LIFE

Four chapters ago we left Olivi penning his *apologia* to the commission. The year was 1285, and Olivi was not the only one writing at that time. Raymond of Fronsac tells us that in that year Arnold of Roquefeuil, minister of Provence, and thirty-five other Franciscans from that province composed a petition in which Olivi was described as the head of a superstitious sect as well as a sower of discord and error.[1] Thus the Olivi affair remained an important issue in his own territory. He still had a following and he was still being attacked.

If the petition was written in the early months of 1285, it may have been part of a campaign to gain further action against Olivi at the general chapter meeting, which was to be held in Milan. If so, the effort was in vain. When Olivi's case was discussed at the chapter the result was nothing more than a temporary endorsement of the previous decisions. The general chapter commanded the ministers to inquire diligently in their provinces as to whether any brother had questions or other writings by Olivi. If so, they were to seize these documents and permit no one to use them until the minister general ordered otherwise.[2]

Like other important issues during the period 1283–1285, the problem of what to do with Olivi's writings had remained in Limbo while the order was waiting to choose a new minister general. Now the brothers assembled at Milan were selecting the man who would act upon such questions. That man was Arlotto of Prato, a member of the commission which had censured Olivi two years earlier. Ominous as this selection might sound for Olivi's future, it may have worked to his advantage. Perhaps Olivi's *apologia* had impressed Arlotto, or perhaps he simply felt that the time had come to explore the matter further. In any case, the *Chronicle of the Twenty-four Generals* announces that Arlotto "summoned Olivi to Paris so that he could respond personally."[3]

The result of this measure is unknown to us. The chronicle laconically reports that Arlotto died after a year in office "and thus the aforementioned affair remained undiscussed." Undiscussed by whom? Did anything at all happen? It is interesting that Ubertino of Casale names Arlotto along with Matthew of Aquasparta and Raymond Gaufredi as one of the ministers who rescinded the measures against Olivi.[4]

Angelo Clareno, of course, provides a complete scenario according to which Olivi went to Paris and explained his view of the divine nature in the presence of Arlotto, Richard of Mediavilla, and John of Murrovalle. When he had finished, Arlotto, smiling, invited the other two masters to respond and found that neither was willing to do so. Olivi then discussed other questions with the same result, "for they could not resist the wisdom and spirit which spoke in him."[5]

There is no other evidence that such an interview took place, and one's faith in Angelo is not reinforced by the fact that his brief description of Olivi's argument on the divine nature is strangely reminiscent of the defense on that subject written in early 1285 as an appendix to the *apologia*. Nevertheless, it is possible that the narrative contains a grain of historical truth.

In any case, Olivi was soon rehabilitated. Another general chapter meeting was held at Montpellier in 1287. Olivi attended and was allowed to clarify his view of *usus pauper*, perhaps of other things as well. We know only about his comments on *usus pauper*.[6] There is little need to present them here, since they reflect basically the same position defended by Olivi before the censure.

This time, however, Olivi's views were accepted as orthodox. Not only was he freed from the stigma of heterodoxy, but the new minister general, Matthew of Aquasparta, appointed him *lector* in the order *studium* at the convent of Santa Croce in Florence. Ubertino of Casale suggests that the appointment was made at the suggestion of Olivi's old minister Jerome of Ascoli, now Pope Nicholas IV.[7]

Scholars differ as to why Olivi, once rehabilitated, was sent to Florence rather than kept at a *studium* in southern France. Tocco[8] asserts that the assignment represented an effort to defuse the spiritual movement in southern France by sending its leader where he could no longer exert influence over his followers. This view is a hard one to defend. If the minister general did not want Olivi to consort with the more radical proponents

---

[1] Raymundus de Fronciacho, 1887: p. 14. See also Ubertino da Casale, 1886: p. 388. Ubertino suggests that the "error" in question concerned Franciscan poverty. Arnold is also mentioned in Raymundus de Fronciacho and Bonagratia de Bergamo, 1887: p. 144.

[2] Callebaut, 1929: p. 289.

[3] *Chronica XXIV generalium*, p. 382.

[4] Ubertino da Casale, 1886: p. 387.

[5] Angelo Clareno, 1886: pp. 295 ff.

[6] Ubertino da Casale, 1886: pp. 400 f. claims to report Olivi's comments on this occasion. It is also at least possible that the confession published by Heysse, 1918: pp. 264–267 dates from this chapter, since in MS. Florence, Bibl. Laur. S. Croce Plut. 31 sin. cod. 3, ff. 174vb–175ra (the manuscript used by Heysse) it is described as having been delivered "in general chapter," while in MS. Pistoia, Fort. D298, f. 251v it is explicitly said to have been delivered before Matthew of Aquasparta at the 1287 chapter meeting in Montpellier. Unfortunately, the passage given by Ubertino is not found in the confession published by Heysse. Thus, if the excerpt provided by Ubertino is genuine and he is correct in ascribing it to the Montpellier chapter meeting, the confession edited by Heysse may have been offered at some other chapter, although it is hard to find a likely occasion for it. Part of the other confession published by Heysse, 1918: pp. 267–269, which purports to have been delivered by Olivi on his deathbed, may date from the period just before the Milan chapter of 1285, since, as we shall see, the Florentine manuscript of that confession identifies Martin IV, who died in March, 1285, as the current pope.

[7] Ubertino da Casale, 1887: p. 400.

[8] Tocco, 1909: pp. 370 ff., cited and criticized by Jarraux, 1933: pp. 151 f.

of Franciscan poverty, Italy was hardly the place to send him. Indeed, if he was that worried about Olivi's views and influence, he need not have sent him anywhere at all as a *lector*. Other historians seem more correct in suggesting that, if Olivi was being separated from anyone, it was from his enemies rather than his friends.[9]

Olivi taught at Santa Croce for only two years, but this brief Florentine interlude probably had an important effect upon his stature as a leader of the more zealous wing in the order. There is no evidence that he was widely known in Italy before that time. The Italian spirituals had their own heroes and hardly needed to look to France for inspiration. In Florence, however, Olivi met two of the people whom we identify most closely with him, Petrus de Trabibus and the oft-mentioned Ubertino. The former was probably an established teacher when Olivi arrived, but after hearing what the new arrival had to say he accepted it so completely that he eventually became Olivi's most zealous disciple in theological matters.[10] Ubertino was an important leader in his own right and later, at the council of Vienne, would be careful to emphasize that he was no servile follower of Olivi's views; yet he was nonetheless deeply influenced by Olivi and that influence must have been due in large part to the impression made by Olivi when they were together at Florence. Ubertino would be Olivi's chief defender at Vienne.

It is possible to overstate Olivi's impact on the Italian spirituals. He probably never exerted the influence there that he had in southern France. Nevertheless, the extant manuscript evidence suggests an effect that was impressive both in degree and in duration, and his teaching at Santa Croce must have been instrumental in creating that effect.

Olivi's Italian duties ended in 1289 when the new minister general, Raymond Gaufredi, transferred him back to the *studium* at Montpellier.[11] Olivi was home again, and probably stayed in southern France for most of the decade he still had to live. We cannot follow his precise movements during these years, but Ubertino of Casale assures us that he kept teaching up to the time of his death without any further censures.[12] Thus his rehabilitation as a theologian seems to have been complete and unreversed from 1287 through 1298.

The war continued on the poverty front, and Olivi seems to have been in the thick of it. In fact, it escalated after 1289. While Olivi's return may have contributed to that escalation, it can hardly be considered the principal cause. His transfer and the increasing agitation within the more rigorous wing of the order may have been due to the same factor, the election of Raymond Gaufredi. Angelo Clareno, who calls Raymond a *vir mansuetus et pius*, describes how he went visiting the provinces and discovered the rigorists of Ancona languishing in captivity. When he asked their offense and was told it was excessive observance of poverty, he publically wished that the whole order were guilty of the same crime and ordered them released. They were eventually sent by him as missionaries to Armenia.[13]

The main point is that Raymond's obvious sympathy for the zealous proponents of *usus pauper* may have encouraged the latter to stand by their guns and make new demands, thus causing an equally vigorous reaction by their opponents. The result was an altercation serious enough to attract the pope's attention, and according to the *Chronicle of the Twenty-four Generals* Nicholas IV wrote to Raymond in 1290 demanding an investigation of "certain brothers who seemed to introduce schism into the province of Provence, condemning the state of the other brethren and considering themselves to be more spiritual than the others." The chronicle notes that the investigation was completed and Raymond submitted the result to the general chapter meeting at Paris in 1292. Certain Provençal brothers found guilty of sowing schism were punished for their activities.[14]

It is not clear how deeply Olivi himself was involved in these difficulties. The *Chronicle of the Twenty-four Generals* describes the disciplined friars as Olivi's followers and says that Olivi defended his view of *usus pauper* at the general chapter meeting; yet it also observes that Olivi himself was not implicated. He had, it says, many indiscreet followers who created scandal in the name of devotion. At least one polemic directed at the spirituals in the early fourteenth century is content to take roughly the same position,[15] but others go a great deal farther. Raymond of Fronsac, a leader of the fourteenth-century conventual assault on Olivi's memory, says that one of the pope's letters was aimed at Olivi personally,[16] that Olivi was forced to recant his view of *usus pauper*,[17] and that Nicholas IV "punished brother Peter John for his excesses."[18]

Ubertino of Casale counterattacks with the claim that Nicholas, far from attacking Olivi's view, personally approved of it and denied in Ubertino's presence that his letter had been written with Olivi in mind. It was directed instead at other friars who were "stirring up the province with their bad examples, words, and superstitious doctrines."[19] Moreover, according to Ubertino, Olivi simply repeated at Paris essentially the same ex-

---

[9] See Gratien de Paris, 1928: p. 382.
[10] See Heynck, 1956: pp. 371–398.
[11] Ubertino da Casale, 1887: p. 389.
[12] *Ibid.*, p. 381.

[13] Angelo Clareno, 1886: pp. 305 f. Angelo is a relatively good source for this anecdote, since he was a member of the group in question.
[14] *Chronica XXIV generalium*, pp. 420–422.
[15] Amorós, 1931: p. 504.
[16] Raymundus de Fronciacho, 1887: pp. 14 f.
[17] *Ibid.*
[18] Raymundus de Fronciacho and Bonagratia de Bergamo, 1887: p. 157.
[19] Ubertino da Casale, 1886: p. 389.

planation of *usus pauper* already given five years earlier at Montpellier.[20]

The pope's letter would go a long way toward settling the matter, but time has denied us the luxury of such a simple solution. Lacking the key letter, one is tempted to guess that Ubertino is right in claiming that it "makes no mention" of Olivi,[21] particularly since Raymond of Fronsac himself describes it as condemning Olivi's doctrine "in general terms" and leans heavily upon rather circumstantial evidence in arguing that the letter was directed at Olivi in any way whatsoever.[22]

As to the matter of Olivi's clarification before the chapter, it has not survived, but the *Chronicle of the Twenty-four Generals* probably provides us with an accurate description of its contents. According to the chronicle, Olivi presented essentially the same explanation accepted at Montpellier, but with an addition which the chronicler obligingly includes. In this addendum Olivi affirms that Franciscans are bound to no way of life except that defined by *Exiit qui seminat* and observed and understood by "the community of the order of professors." Olivi goes on to claim that he has never said anything different and, if he has, recants it.[23]

The basic question, then, seems to be whether Ubertino was correct in claiming that Olivi's position remained unchanged. The key assertion was probably the one affirming unanimity with the community. Raymond of Fronsac and others may have interpreted it as a major concession on Olivi's part. Nevertheless, the concession was probably more apparent than real, since Olivi had previously argued that his view of *usus pauper* was implied in the accepted practices of the order.[24] The community envisaged by Olivi in his declaration is not exactly identifiable with the community represented at Vienne by Raymond of Fronsac.

In short, Olivi seems to have been involved only peripherally in the disciplinary action of 1292. The targets of that action were so close to Olivi's view that everyone from Ubertino to the *Chronicle of the Twenty-four Generals* noted the resemblance, and they were so close that Olivi himself was called in to underline the difference. Underline it he did, however, and the censure fell elsewhere this time. It is hardly surprising that the chapter should have acted in this way. The rigorist group in Provence was not a disciplined secret society but a relatively unstructured movement which, in time, produced its own left wing and moderates.

The Paris chapter meeting hardly put an end to rigorist hopes. After all, Raymond Gaufredi was still minister general and Pope Nicholas IV died in 1292.

After a two-year vacancy the papal chair was filled by a man who seemed to surpass the spirituals' wildest hopes, the hermit Peter Morrone. Once Peter became Pope Celestine V, he soon showed his sympathy with spiritual aims by absolving a group of Italian zealots from obedience to their superiors and allowing them to observe the rule as rigorously as they wished. The spirituals were encouraged to believe that a new era of Franciscan observance was at hand.

The new era was of brief duration. Celestine, having reconsidered his position, resigned after four months and was succeeded by a radically different type of man, Boniface VIII. Boniface soon canceled the exemption granted by his predecessor and, in October, 1295, removed Raymond Gaufredi from office. The following spring John of Murrovalle, friend of Boniface and member of the commission which had censured Olivi in 1283, became the new minister general.

In the meantime opposition to Boniface was developing inside and outside the Franciscan order. Boniface was engaged in political infighting in Italy and his opponents were quick to seize upon the unusual circumstances of his election to argue that his succession was invalid since his predecessor could not legally resign. This argument sounded very good to a number of Italian spirituals, particularly those whose exemption had been revoked. Thus the battle over Franciscan poverty became entwined with a very worldly struggle for power between Boniface and his enemies.

Olivi's reaction to this situation shows his basic aversion to positions which would challenge established ecclesiastical authority. His response took two forms, a question on papal resignation and a letter to Conrad of Offida assailing Franciscan rebels against Boniface. Both were written after Boniface was elected but before he deposed Raymond Gaufredi. The first document, composed in the summer of 1295, examines the question in scholarly fashion and concludes that the pope has the right to abdicate with the consent of the cardinals when it is to the advantage of the church that he do so, just as he can be removed if he is incompetent, heretical, or insane.[25] In the course of the argument Olivi speaks frequently and with feeling of papal authority but works hard to bring it in line with a second factor, the well-being of the church. Papal power can be taken away because one can imagine situations in which it *must* be taken away or the church will be injured. In the case of a criminal pope the cardinals must somehow be able to get rid of him. Nevertheless, Olivi ultimately shrinks from the implication of superior authority contained in this situation and remarks that the pope has, in effect, deposed himself through his own criminality and thus the deposition is more of a renunciation than

---

[20] *Ibid.*, p. 400. See also *ibid.*, p. 191, which seems to say that the ban on Olivi's work was lifted at the Paris general chapter.
[21] *Ibid.*, p. 389.
[22] Raymundus de Fronciacho, 1887: pp. 14 f.
[23] *Chronica XXIV generalium*, pp. 421 f.
[24] See, for example, *Quoniam contra paupertatem evangelicam*, f. 56v.

[25] *An papa possit renuntiare papatui*, edition cited in bibliography as *De perf.*, q. 13.

a judicial condemnation. The cardinals' role, then, is more or less declaratory.²⁶

Here as elsewhere Olivi argues that the papal and episcopal offices combine two different types of power: The power of sacerdotal and episcopal order which enables one to celebrate mass or confer orders, and the jurisdictional power through which one exercises authority over the faithful. The first involves an indelible character, the second does not. Thus the second, unlike the first, can be renounced.

The letter to Conrad of Offida, a leader of the Italian spirituals, shows what Olivi thought was at stake in the debate over Boniface VIII and why he was so adamant about supporting Boniface's claim. Some Italian spirituals were claiming that Celestine was still pope because he could not resign. Moreover, they were claiming that the papal constitutions *Quo elongati* and *Exiit qui seminat* had violated the rule by permitting the use of money through procurators and by granting that friars could have more than two tunics. Finally, they were citing the text from Revelation, "come out of her, my people," as a call to rebellion, urging the spirituals to separate themselves from the carnal leadership of church and order.

Olivi, writing in September, 1295, was genuinely appalled. As he observes in the letter, these spirituals and their ignorant, misguided followers were playing into the hands of those who opposed evangelical perfection. Critics outside the order could take their interpretation of the rule as evidence that it was impossible to observe and therefore injurious, while the lax within the order could cite their views as proof that the rigorists (or, as Olivi would say, "the spiritual professors of the rule") advocated extreme, immoderate practices.²⁷

Olivi disposes of the arguments against papal resignation much as he does in the question on that subject. As to the matter of the papal constitutions, he accuses his opponents of a simple-minded literalism which, if carried to its logical extreme, would force them to tear out an offending eye. Moreover, he stands squarely with the popes in denying that Francis's testament is binding upon the order as the rule is.

On the particular subject of procurators, he agrees with the pope that the purity of the rule is not compromised if money entrusted to them is expended for the necessities of the brethren, since "it is clear to all except the insane" that no right to the money is thereby exercised by the brothers themselves.²⁸ After all, Paul himself sanctioned collections of money for the holy poor, as Olivi himself has explained elsewhere.

The matter of tunics is dealt with in an equally forceful manner. Olivi feels that he is supported by reason and by the rule itself, since the rule expressly states that ministers and custodians shall provide for the brothers according to the exigencies of time and place.

The final question, that of whether the pure should escape the corrupt society which surrounds them, is settled by an appeal to holy Franciscans of the past. Did Brother Leo leave the order? No indeed! Then why should a few Italian spirituals do so? Olivi closes with the observation that, although he feels scorn for the stiff-necked and pertinacious in the group, he sympathizes with the well-meaning but simple followers who are deluded by a specious appeal to Franciscan poverty.²⁹

The letter to Conrad of Offida has had a profound effect upon historians, many of whom suspect that it shows Olivi chasing his own tail, assailing a position uncomfortably similar to his own. Ehrle takes the letter as an indication that Olivi "was no longer lord of the spirits he . . . had conjured up" and suggests that it shows the suppleness with which Olivi could avert attack through a subtle shift of his own argument.³⁰ Livarius Oliger seems shocked by Olivi's conduct. "Who will not be amazed," he says, "to hear Olivi speaking thus and rebuking the spirituals with such harsh words? Did he not disseminate similar and worse views in his own writings?"³¹

These judgments are not entirely fair to Olivi. In the first place, he did not "conjure up" the Italian spirituals, or the French spirituals either for that matter. He was one important figure within a general movement, not the creator of that movement. Moreover, there is no reason to accept Ehrle's insinuation that the letter was written to protect Olivi from official sanctions. If that had been his aim, he should have conveyed his thoughts to the minister general, not Conrad of Offida. In reality, the destination and content of the letter show that Olivi did intend to protect a reputation, but not his own. He attacked the Italian rebels because they threatened not Peter John Olivi but the Franciscan rule and its rigorous observance.

The most interesting question is whether Oliger is right in protesting that Olivi himself advanced similar and worse views. Here the issue is clouded by the fact that most of Olivi's works are written in opposition to a radically different position than the one countered in the letter to Conrad of Offida. In the *Questions on Evangelical Poverty*, where one would expect to find Olivi's thoughts on procurators and tunics, he constantly defends *usus pauper* against those advocating greater laxity. This basic orientation conditions not only his answers but the very questions he asks. Thus, when he turns to the subject of procurators in the ninth question, he asks whether Franciscans can institute procurators to collect things given to them, bring debtors to

---

²⁶ *Ibid.*, p. 358. Brian Tierney, 1972: p. 114 notes that Olivi follows the doctrine of the canonist Huguccio in this respect.
²⁷ *Epistola ad Conradum de Offida*, p. 372.
²⁸ *Ibid.*, p. 371.

²⁹ *Ibid.*, p. 273.
³⁰ Ehrle, 1887: p. 438.
³¹ Oliger, 1918: p. 335.

judgment, etc. He more or less denies that they can do so, but it is important to recognize that it is the entire question he is denying. This and not the basic issue of procurators is the matter being considered, and even here Olivi's disapproval does not extend to a complete rejection, since he grants the possibility that such activities may be allowed as a concession to the imperfection of weaker brothers in order to prevent worse from occurring.[32] When he discusses procurators elsewhere, it is clear that he accepts the basic institution as long as certain limitations are placed on their activity in order to avoid abuses.[33]

The same thing could be said about the matter of tunics. In the ninth of the *Questions on Evangelical Perfection* Olivi is arguing against a position which would compromise the obligation to practice *usus pauper* in this regard.[34] Thus the emphasis is entirely different there from that found in the letter to Conrad of Offida and might obscure the basic consistency of the two documents. In reality Olivi is satisfied that the ministers have authority to exercise discretion on the number of tunics allowed, as is clear from his commentary on the rule.[35]

Thus on the specific issues of procurators and tunics Olivi is quite consistent. The letter to Conrad of Offida cannot be construed as an abandonment of earlier, more radical views. The matter is not thereby settled, however. There are other areas in which Olivi's connection with the Italian spirituals bears examination. For example, in the letter Olivi castigates the spirituals for placing St. Francis's testament on a level with the rule, and yet in the sixteenth of the *Questions on Evangelical Perfection* he seems to do the same thing. In reply to the argument that the pope has authority to alter the practices of the order as he sees fit, Olivi argues that "no one of sound mind would deny the pope authority to ordain that which is truly better and more expedient at a given time, or deny that these ordinations or decrees should be obeyed with the greatest humility." Nevertheless,

where (let it never occur!) he audaciously and pertinaciously wishes to introduce some profane novelty in opposition to the counsels and examples of Christ and the apostles, in opposition to *fidae dignissima testimonia et regularia statuta docmata exempla* of the angelic man Francis who is sealed in christiform fashion with the sacred stigmata, and in subversion of the whole evangelical state, then in this case he would not act as the vicar of Christ but as the noonday devil and he should by no means be obeyed but rather resisted with all one's powers as Lucifer and the noonday devil.[36]

---

[32] *De perf.*, q. 9, ff. 78d–79c.

[33] *De perf.*, q. 9, ff. 67rb, 69vb–rb; q. 16, f. 101r–v. See my comments in chapter 8 above.

[34] *De perf.*, q. 9, f. 72ra–vb.

[35] *Rule Commentary*, p. 132.

[36] *De perf.*, q. 16, f. 103r: ". . . ubi quod absit contra Christi et apostolorum consilia et exempla et contra angelici viri Francisci sacris stigmatibus christiformiter signati fide dignissima testimonia et regularia statuta docmata exempla in sub-

Olivi goes on to say that those resisting such an impious decree should consider any excommunication incurred in the process to be worthless in the eyes of God.

Two observations are in order. First, it might be noted that the phrase given in Latin above lacks the precision one might hope to encounter in a discussion of this magnitude. Olivi is talking about the gravest sort of defiance and it seems only proper to define as carefully as possible the conditions under which such defiance should be practiced. Olivi does not do so. Thus, while a passage of this sort does not explicitly espouse the position held by the Italian rebels, it is vague enough to encourage such a position.

The second observation to be made here is that Olivi, like the Italian rebels, foresees a point beyond which obedience cannot and should not go. Moreover, we have seen that despite the pious "may it never occur!" Olivi's apocalyptic preoccupations remove such a situation from the realm of theoretical possibility and promote it to the status of the anticipated future occurrence. Both Olivi and the Italian rebels envisage a pseudopope who will invite Franciscans to commit apostasy. Both agree that the resulting temptation will be a cunning one causing even the elect to experience great perplexity. The difference is that for the Italian rebels the future is now. They believe that these events are occurring, while Olivi still places them in the future. They see Boniface as the pseudopope, while Olivi sees him as legitimate. The apocalyptic scenario is strikingly similar, but the time and cast of characters are different.

What was the basic difference between Olivi and the Italian spirituals which kept Olivi within the institution? Was it simply a matter of good sense triumphing over apocalyptic doctrine? To some extent this is perhaps the case, but there is more involved. The contrast is also due to the fact that, despite Olivi's frequent handwringing over current laxity, he was much more attuned to the accepted practices of church and order in his time than the Italian rebels were. Because he was more attuned to these practices he drew the line in a different place. He drew it this side of *Quo elongati* and *Exiit qui seminat* and thus allowed himself the pleasure of fidelity to Franciscan practice as defined by at least some of the popes through 1279.

There is more to it than that. Olivi accepted papal authority because he ascribed to Franciscan life as the popes defined it, but the reverse is also true. He accepted papal authority because the popes ascribed to Franciscan life as he defined it. Here we return to a subject already mentioned in an earlier chapter, the importance of papal authority for Olivi and other Franciscans of his time. Whenever Franciscan scholars of Olivi's generation were tempted to defend the Francis-

---

versionem totius evangelici status audaciter et pertinaciter vellet aliquid acceptare et tam profanam novitatem inducere quia in hoc casu non ut Christi vicarius sed ut demon meredianus procederet nequaquam esset sibi obediendum immo tanquam Lucifero et meridiano demoni totis viribus resistendum."

can rule and life against papal encroachments, they had to consider the fact that their defense of the Franciscan order in the face of hostile churchmen was based partly upon an appeal to papal authority. Thus, as Brian Tierney has shown, defense of the rule was closely related to defense of papal power, a fact which might be expected to exert some effect upon Olivi's stance.

This is to say that Olivi's position was more complex because, as a well-educated Franciscan scholar, he had more factors to consider. Other elements could be cited, not the least of which is the evidence from the Bible. As an expositor of scripture, Olivi was quite aware that the evidence was confusing to the untrained mind and called for a great deal of explanation. Thus his allusion to the collection of money in the early church is more than a desperate debating gambit seized upon in his quarrel with the Italian rebels. It is one of the many Biblical examples with which he continually wrestles throughout his writings.[37] Olivi's effort to come to terms with the Biblical and patristic evidence resulted in a nuanced view of poverty which allowed for a variety of practices in different situations, recognizing that even the use of money might be expedient under certain conditions.

Whatever Olivi's ideological ties with the rebellious element may have been, there is no evidence that he was treated as a part of it by either the pope or his superiors. We have no reason to doubt Ubertino's assertion that he lived out his final years as a respected member of the order. Perhaps "respected" is too weak. Clearly he was venerated by many.

The only other letter by Olivi surviving from this period suggests the importance he had assumed as a spiritual leader inside and outside the order. The letter, written in May, 1295, is addressed to the three sons of King Charles of Naples.[38] The three, one of whom was the future king Robert of Naples and another the future St. Louis of Toulouse, were being held as hostages in Catalonia.

Olivi, writing from Narbonne, acknowledges their letters requesting that he visit or write them. He protests that he has not failed to do so because of any lack of desire or love, but rather through a series of considerations including their father's fear that he might "beguinize" (*inbeguiniri*) them, an early use of what would become the standard term for lay supporters of the spiritual Franciscans in southern France. Olivi is, he says, still ready to come and has his minister general's permission to do so if the proper conditions are met. In fact, the letter closes with an odd and rather ominous announcement that "if I do not come to you I may have to hurry off to another place." Is this an indication that Olivi was still under attack and contemplated the possibility that things might yet get too hot for him in Narbonne? We do not know. In the letter personal notices are kept to a minimum, and Olivi devotes most of his energy to a consolatory message which depicts suffering, death, and captivity as essential elements in all progress, spiritual and otherwise.

The proposed trip apparently never occurred. Olivi stayed on at Narbonne and was still there at the time of his death in 1298. He seems to have remained active until the end. We know that he was writing his Revelation commentary in 1297[39] and may even have worked on other commentaries after that date.[40]

Olivi's decision to ponder the book of Revelation in his twilight years has excited comment from various scholars. Some see it as an indication of profound disenchantment with the church and the Franciscan order, others as evidence that Olivi had turned from his former scholarly pursuits to engage in a different sort of intellectual activity. We have seen that such views have their limitations, since Olivi remained interested in both the *Sentences* and apocalyptic speculation throughout his life and the pattern of history contemplated in his earlier apocalyptic speculations is similar to that found in the Revelation commentary, although less detailed. Nevertheless, there is still at least some question as to whether Olivi's opinions were undergoing a degree of change in his final years, and some scholars have seriously suggested that in 1297 Olivi was finally ready to suspect that the heralded apocalyptic pseudopope had arrived in the person of Boniface VIII.[41]

Such a change on Olivi's part is not impossible. While he supported Boniface as late as September, 1295, it is not unthinkable that he was more taken by the Italian rebels' arguments than he cared to acknowledge and finally came around to their view after seeing Raymond Gaufredi removed in October and John of Murrovalle substituted for him the following spring. All of this is possible, but there is no real evidence for it. Olivi refers to "the novelty of the election of Pope Celestine and his successor and other presently worsening matters,"[42] raises the possibility that the pseudopope will be such partly because he is schismatically rather than canonically elected, and credits him with a number

---

[37] See for example *De perf.*, q. 9, f. 64b.

[38] *Epistola ad regis Sicilie filios*, edition cited in bibliography. The letter is discussed at length by Benz, 1964: pp. 258–265 and by Manselli, 1955: pp. 167–172. Benz considers it one of the most significant works for Olivi's spiritualist understanding of history and the church, while Manselli rightly deemphasizes its importance in this respect.

[39] *Apoc.*, f. 84ra says only three years remain in the thirteenth century.

[40] See Pacetti, 1954: p. 21*.

[41] The most recent defense of this view is found in Warren Lewis's edition of the Revelation commentary, a Tübingen dissertation which will soon be published. Lewis alludes several times to Olivi's identification of Boniface VIII with the heretical pseudopope and Antichrist, sometimes affirming that Olivi saw it as a possibility and sometimes suggesting that Olivi was more or less committed to this interpretation but hesitated to announce it in clear, unequivocal terms.

[42] *Apoc.*, f. 84ra.

of practices which might well call Boniface to mind; yet none of these things adds up to a strong case for the purported identification. Moreover, against such suggestive passages one must balance the fact that Olivi closes his Revelation commentary by submitting it to the Roman church for correction and that according to Ubertino he surrendered all of his works to the supreme pontiff for judgment one year later on his deathbed. It is rather unlikely that Olivi remained so eager to avoid trouble that even in the hour of death he feigned allegiance to a man he considered to be the Antichrist. It might be argued that his submissions were directed to the *real* supreme pontiff and not to the schismatically elected pseudopope Boniface, but there is no compelling reason to resort to such a hypothesis and it is in any case hard to imagine whom Olivi might have considered the true pope to be in 1298, since Celestine had died in May, 1296. Perhaps he was submitting to the next true pope who happened to appear, but here too the probability is a rather slender one. Thus if Olivi was at all open to assigning Boniface that unflattering apocalyptic role, he would seem to have considered it a vague possibility at best.

Most of our knowledge concerning Olivi's death rests upon a report preserved and frequently recited by the Beguines. This report has come down to us in two different versions, one provided by Bernard Gui and the other, longer one published by Albanus Heysse.[43] The latter version may well be a conflation of two different documents, since most of it is a confession in which Olivi restates his views on Franciscan poverty and, in the oldest extant manuscript, announces his adherence to the holy scriptures, Catholic faith and Roman church, "the governor of which is now Pope Martin."[44] Martin IV died in 1285. Nevertheless, the Gui version is certainly part of a longer work which at one time may have contained an expression of allegiance to papal authority, since Ubertino of Casale asserts that on his deathbed Olivi submitted his works to the judgment of the supreme pontiff.[45] Both versions agree that Olivi died on Friday, March 14, 1298, in the convent at Narbonne at the age of fifty, and that he told the brothers who were present at his death that he had received all his knowledge from God at Paris when he was illumined by Christ in the third hour.

What does one do with a statement like that? One solution is to attribute it to his followers. It is, after all, a natural idea for them to fall upon, particularly since, as we shall see, some of them eventually came to regard his writings as unquestionable revealed truth.

Perhaps the story is not completely baseless. It is not beyond belief that, while he was at Paris, Olivi was suddenly struck, not with *all* his knowledge, but with some central insight which seemed to allow him to make sense of everything else. One is reminded of Luther's narrative of the experience he underwent in the process of composing a commentary on Hebrews [46] and Joachim of Fiore's narrative concerning his illumination in the process of composing a commentary on Revelation.[47]

The hardest explanation to accept would be that Olivi said precisely what the confession says he did. If he did say it, it would mean that his view of his own intellectual credentials at the time of his death was strikingly at variance with the attitude shown by him throughout his life. Perhaps in his final hours he did seriously believe that all his knowledge had been revealed at once in Paris, but one can certainly be allowed to hope not.

X. OLIVI AND THE COUNCIL OF VIENNE

Olivi's death marked the beginning of a new period in the extended battle over his orthodoxy. The reverence shown him in his later years was intensified and centered about the Franciscan church in Narbonne, where Olivi was buried in the middle of the choir.[1] Angelo Clareno says that on the anniversary of Olivi's death the crowds at his grave rivaled those at the Portiuncula.[2] This popular Olivi cult might have led in time to canonization if other factors had not entered into the picture.

At the same time, Olivi's writings were being treated with respect not only among Franciscans but by pious laymen as well. Some of them were translated into the

---

[43] The former version is found in Bernardus Guidonis, 1886: p. 287, and is quoted in chapter one, footnote one above. The latter version is published by Heysse, 1918: pp. 267–269. See also the edition offered by Wadding, 1931: ann. 1297, n. 33, which differs notably from the one offered by Heysse; and the excerpt provided by Ubertino da Casale, 1886: pp. 411 f.

[44] Heysse, 1918: p. 269. Heysse's edition is based on MS. Florence, Bibl. Laur. S. Croce Plut. 31 sin. cod. 3, f. 175ra–rb. MS. Pistoia, Fort. D298, ff. 253v–255v contains essentially the same text but prudently leaves a blank space where the pope's name should appear. In the version printed by Wadding, the name given is "Boniface" rather than "Martin." The excerpt provided by Ubertino lists Martin as the present pope, but Ubertino does not say that the confession was delivered on Olivi's deathbed. In fact, he seems to assume that it was presented earlier.

[45] Ubertino da Casale, 1886: p. 383 f. and 411. *Chronica XXIV generalium,* p. 458, says the same thing. Heysse, 1918: p. 264, offers two possible explanations, the less likely of which is that Olivi repeated on his deathbed the confession he had delivered over a decade earlier. The other is that the version published by Heysse was inspired by Ubertino da Casale, 1886: p. 411, since Ubertino alludes to Olivi's deathbed submission and immediately thereafter offers an excerpt from "a certain confession" by Olivi which turns out to be the same one presented in the Florentine and Pistoian manuscripts. Someone, taking his cue from Ubertino, combined this confession with a brief notice of Olivi's death, thus producing the version found in the Florentine and Pistoian manuscripts.

[46] See Luther's preface to the 1545 edition of his Latin writings in *Werke* **54**: pp. 179–187 and his comments in *Tischreden,* no. 3232c, 4007.

[47] *Expositio in Apocalypsim,* f. 39r–v.

[1] Bernardus Guidonis, 1886: p. 287.

[2] Angelo Clareno, 1885, *Fratribus universis,* p. 544.

vulgar tongue. It seems to have been his devotional works which were first translated and widely circulated. Raoul Manselli suggests that, although the developing movement was characterized by a lively eschatological expectation, the Revelation commentary was relatively unknown in the early stages; yet evidence for the latter statement seems rather thin at best. Certainly the Revelation commentary was gaining some notariety among Franciscans within a decade after Olivi's death.[3]

The eschatological expectation did not at first produce any general tendency to rebel against ecclesiastical authority. The Beguines—a name applied to the group of pious laymen in whose ranks Olivi's writings and memory were preserved—excited ecclesiastical concern almost immediately, but most of them probably adhered faithfully to the Roman church.

To be sure, Olivi's name was soon connected with some disturbing phenomena, such as the appearance of Jerome of Catalonia in Venice around 1301. Jerome, who traveled with a group of women, came bearing some books which, as he told Angelo Clareno and his associates, were sent to them by Olivi himself. Angelo was warned to be extremely cautious with this new arrival, and the advice proved solid enough, since Jerome eventually reversed himself and attacked Angelo's group. Angelo says he later learned that the books were stolen.[4]

Mention of Angelo brings us to one of the main roadblocks on the way to Olivi's canonization: The battle over Franciscan poverty within the order continued to escalate after 1298. The story of this battle has been told skillfully and at length by other writers,[5] and thus it can be treated in cursory fashion here. The main point to be grasped is that the battle over poverty shaped the context in which the "Olivi question" would be considered for the next few years. After Olivi's death, when the order was split by debate over the practice of poverty, the proponents of a more relaxed observance tried to attack the spirituals by impugning the orthodoxy of their recently deceased hero. They did so by citing his purported heterodoxy not only on the issue of Franciscan poverty but on a variety of theological and philosophical subjects as well. Thus Olivi was criticized on a number of issues, but the attacks were largely inspired by the poverty controversy.

The assault on Olivi's orthodoxy began almost immediately after his death and involved the highest levels of the Franciscan order. At the general chapter meeting of 1299 the minister general, John of Murrovalle, apparently led the attack on Olivi's views, which were again examined and condemned.[6] John then proceeded to circulate a series of letters which called for the confiscation and incineration of Olivi's works, punishment of those who refused to surrender them, the extinction of the *secta fratris Petri Johannis*, and the dispersal of his *sectatores* even outside the province.[7] When the spirituals appealed to Boniface VIII the pope ordered an investigation which led to further punishment for the protesters.[8]

In 1304 John of Murrovalle, who had since become a cardinal, was replaced as minister general by Gonsalvo of Valboa, who observed the same policy toward Olivi and the spirituals. Ubertino of Casale and Angelo Clareno both describe in graphic terms the travails visited upon those who defended Olivi's view and reputation.[9] Ubertino cites the case of a brother named Ponce who was imprisoned for saying that, although he had no writings by Olivi, if he had any he would surrender them for correction only to the pope. Angelo says that the unfortunate Ponce was thrown into prison so tightly fettered that he sat ill in his own urine and excrement and, when he finally died, those who came to bury him found that his body was largely eaten away by worms from the loins down.

Olivi's supporters reacted in a number of ways, but two basic tendencies can be recognized. On the one hand, certain exponents of the Olivi cult soon began to elevate their idol to the status of an apocalyptic figure and to regard attacks on him as the work of the Old Deceiver. Thus a document produced by Olivi's detractors in 1311 complains that according to some of his supporters Olivi's doctrine was revealed to him by the holy spirit and his views are to be defended as articles of faith.[10] Once Olivi was seen in this light it was only natural that any institutional censure of his doctrine should be regarded as evidence that the era of extreme eschatological tribulation was at hand, with all the revolutionary implications following therefrom. This approach was to have a real future, as we shall see.

A second, more sober type of reaction to attacks on Olivi chose to defend his general orthodoxy and virtue while dissociating the defenders from any errors that might actually be included in Olivi's writings. Here it was Olivi the intelligent but fallible scholar who was at issue, not Olivi the cultic hero. This is the approach which dominated the defense accorded to Olivi by leaders of the spiritual faction up to and during the

---

[3] For this and much of what follows see the generally excellent discussion by Manselli, 1959: pp. 36ff.

[4] Angelo Clareno, 1885, *Epistola excusatoria*, p. 528.

[5] See especially Lambert, 1961: ch. 7–9.

[6] Amorós, 1931: p. 504. This document says that John gathered a general chapter meeting at Paris. Amorós, the editor, assumes that this is a mistake and the 1299 meeting at Lyons is actually meant.

[7] Raymundus de Fronciacho, 1887: pp. 15 f. For reference to John of Murrovalle's activity see also Raymundus de Fronciacho and Bonagratia de Bergamo, 1887: p. 157; Angelo Clareno, 1886: pp. 311 f.; and Ubertino da Casale, 1886: pp. 38 ff.

[8] Amorós, 1931: pp. 504 f.

[9] Ubertino da Casale, 1886: pp. 384–387; Angelo Clareno, 1886: pp. 300 f.

[10] Raymundus de Fronciacho and Bonagratia de Bergamo, 1886: p. 371. A milder version of Olivi as apocalyptic figure is offered by Angelo Clareno, 1886: p. 289.

council of Vienne. Ubertino is the prime example. While emphasizing his own freedom from any servile reliance upon Olivi and his willingness to see any possible errors condemned by the pope,[11] he argues that such errors, if indeed they exist at all, represent no more than a handful of assertions in a vast body of otherwise sound doctrine and that the opposition to Olivi is inspired by a desire to compromise true Franciscan poverty by discrediting one of its ablest proponents.

The charges launched against Olivi by his critics—we can now call them "the community" as modern historians are wont to do—are partly the same ones debated in his own lifetime, but there are some new items as well. Ubertino cites a letter by John of Murrovalle which seems to pinpoint as the major error of Olivi's supporters the notion that *usus pauper* is a substantial part of the Franciscan vow.[12] Raymond of Fronsac sheds a bit more light on the matter by citing a letter from the minister of the province of Aragon implying that at this stage the order concentrated on two other issues besides *usus pauper*. On the one hand, the brothers were constrained to cease venerating an uncanonized dead man (i.e. Olivi). On the other, they were to hold the orthodox opinion on the wound in Christ's side.[13] Here we encounter a whole new issue which, although unexplained in this document, will become clearer in a moment.

The scope of the attack on Olivi is best seen in the documents emanating from the confrontation between community and spirituals orchestrated by Pope Clement V between 1309 and 1312. During this period Clement, having been approached from several sides on the subject, decided to intervene in the intraorder dispute and end it with an authoritative decision based upon careful examination of the issues. The process began in late 1309 when he appointed a commission of cardinals to investigate four basic issues, one of them the question of Olivi's orthodoxy. Both sides eventually participated in the investigation and the result was a flood of polemical writings in which spirituals and conventuals alike tried to put the best possible face on their actions.

Olivi is often mentioned in these writings, but few documents spend much time trying to establish his guilt or innocence. The most illuminating exchange in this respect took place in 1311. In March of that year Raymond of Fronsac and Bonagratia of Bergamo, who were now spearheading the conventual attack, produced a document arguing that the spirituals were supporters of heresy because they ascribed to Olivi's views. A list of Olivi's errors was provided.[14] This list makes interesting reading because it shows what aspects of the 1283 censure the community thought damning enough to be repeated. In the philosophical and theological areas these are Olivi's teaching on the divine nature, marriage, infant baptism, the sacramental character, and the rational soul as the form of the body. On the subject of poverty, Raymond and Bonagratia list the assertion that Franciscans who become bishops are in some way more bound to observe *usus pauper* than they were before, that *usus pauper* is a substantial part of the Franciscan life and profession; and that burial of the dead is not a work of mercy except in case of necessity.

In addition to these old chestnuts, the new accusation regarding Christ's side wound is included. Olivi is said to teach that it does not contradict the text of John 19 to say that Christ was alive when his side was opened by the lance, but that such an assertion is in fact quite consonant with the mysteries of the church. The authors view this opinion as an assault upon gospel truth.

Last, and almost as an afterthought, the authors accuse Olivi of disseminating "false and fantastic prophecies concerning the church" in his writings and especially in his Revelation commentary, "calling the church a great whore and dogmatizing many other things in disparagement of the church."

It is no excuse, Raymond and Bonagratia say, to argue that Olivi offered these views as opinions without asserting them, for it is heresy to call into doubt that which the church has defined. Nor is it any excuse to argue that in the end Olivi submitted his works to the holy see for correction. The person (and not his doctrine) is excused from the taint of heresy when his works contain elements of doubtful orthodoxy and he *physically* submits these works to the apostolic seat for examination and correction. Such is not applicable to Olivi's case. He did not actually submit them in that way. Moreover, his works do not merely contain doubtful elements but openly contradict established truths defined by holy councils and the universal church. Raymond and Bonagratia argue that all the aforesaid opinions *and books* by Olivi were justly condemned by the Franciscan order and apostolic authority and by the advice of Parisian masters, both because the heresies contained in them were so dangerous and because the errors were so thoroughly dispersed throughout the works that it would be neither possible nor useful to separate the true from the false.

Raymond and Bonagratia then turn from Olivi to his *sectatores*, providing a fascinating excursus on the developing eschatological excesses within that group.[15] As we have seen, some of the group say that Olivi's views were revealed to him by the holy spirit and are to be accepted as gospel truth. He himself is viewed as an apocalyptic figure predicted in Revelation, being specifically identified as the angel who comes after the angel

---

[11] See Ubertino da Casale, 1886: p. 406 and *idem*, 1887, *Sanctitas vestra*, p. 88.

[12] Ubertino da Casale, 1886: pp. 385 ff.

[13] Raymundus de Fronciacho, 1887: p. 17.

[14] Raymundus de Fronciacho and Bonagratia de Bergamo, 1886: pp. 367–370.

[15] *Ibid.*, p. 371.

with the sign of the living God. Some of his followers say that marriage is nothing more than a disguised brothel. Some say that an angel took the pontifical authority from Nicholas III because of his iniquities and gave it to certain brothers and their followers who observe the spirit of evangelical poverty. From that time on no valid pope has been elected by the cardinals and only those who have the spirit of poverty are true priests. Some members of this group have elected their own pope or rector. Some say that a reformation of the church should occur in Constantinople. Despite ecclesiastical prohibition Olivi is venerated as a saint by this group.

Several comments are in order. In the first place, something must finally be said about the business of the side wound. The censured view is indeed Olivi's, and is found in some but not all manuscripts of his commentary on the gospel of John.[16] Here Olivi observes that while the opposite order of events is commonly accepted he has heard "a certain most holy person" accustomed to divine revelations say that Christ had revealed to him that he was living when pierced by the lance. Olivi was at first astonished, he says, but soon he began to consider whether this view accorded with the words of scripture and found that it apparently did. He cites two other cases in which a gospel seems to narrate events out of their actual sequence, then cites the testimony of still another holy person subject to frequent mystical experiences who has informed Olivi that her visions often included Christ dying *after* infliction of the side wound.

The bulk of the passage is given over to an examination of the mystical meanings to be derived from this sequence of events. Olivi endeavors to show in this way that his view is consonant with the mysteries of the Christian faith. In the process Francis and his stigmata are introduced in a characteristically Olivian manner. Since John was the disciple singularly identified with love and was given over to Mary as her son at the cross, it is fitting that he should have been chosen to reveal certain more secret aspects of Christ's love such as the washing of the feet, Christ's words at the last supper, Christ's final arrangement regarding his mother, and "this wound, which is mentioned by none of the others." Thus the side wound seems to signify the ineffable secret of love in a special manner. As a sign of this fact St. Francis's side wound was revealed to fewer people and more secretly than his other stigmata during his lifetime[17] and gave Francis more pain than the others. And perhaps it is possible that, just as this was finally written only by John of the contemplative order and love, so "its proper interpretation was reserved for the final order which was reinitiated by the wounded Francis and is to be more fully propagated and born in the final passions of the church."

Tempting as this new interpretation might be, Olivi does not insist on it. In the end he is content to say that he speaks "without temerity of assertion, since it is not our place to define this matter. Hence these things are to be left to that secret which no one knows unless he receives it."[18]

Olivi was hardly the only man in his time to wonder whether the spear wound preceded Christ's death. In a confession written between 1299 and 1304, Matthew of Bouzigues cites Olivi with approval on this matter.[19] It seems that Bernard Délicieux also found his theory attractive.[20] Moreover, a notarized statement by four Franciscans from Marseilles in 1300 cites an old document in a Marseilles library in an effort to show that the gospel of Matthew as St. Jerome knew it included the story of the spear wound and placed it before Christ's death.[21] As we shall see, Ubertino of Casale claims to have seen the same thing in an old manuscript.[22] Neither claim is astonishing, since modern Bible scholars have identified several manuscripts containing such an interpolation.[23]

Nevertheless, it is impossible to deduce from this fact that Olivi was victimized by a variant reading. Others might cite the interpolation in Matthew, but Olivi does not. He assumes that only John tells about the side wound. Thus he proceeds on the assumption that the letter of scripture is against him and must somehow be explained away. Supporting evidence is sought elsewhere, in mystical visions and mystical meanings.

A second aspect of Raymond and Bonagratia's work is noteworthy. Their reference to Olivi's "false and fantastic prophecies" shows that Olivi's apocalyptic chickens were finally coming home to roost. It was hardly the first time anyone had noticed that particular side of Olivi. As we have seen, the letter to R. shows that his apocalyptic interests were an issue before the censure of 1283.[24] Nevertheless, they played no obvious role in the debates about Olivi's orthodoxy during the 1280's and 1290's.

It is understandable why serious interest in Olivi's apocalyptic thought developed at this particular stage. One reason for its late appearance may lie in the fact that the Revelation commentary was not written until

---

[16] E. g. the passage in question is found in MS. Rome, Ottob. lat. 3302, but not in MS. Florence, Laurenziana Plut. 10 dext. 8. It was first noticed by Victorinus Doucet in MS. Padua, Univ. 1540, and is published as it appears in that manuscript in Doucet, 1935: pp. 436–441.

[17] Olivi is echoing Bonaventure, *Legenda maior*, XIII, in: *Opera* 8.

[18] Olivi is citing Rev. 2:17.

[19] See Manselli, 1959: pp. 42–44.

[20] See Dmitrewski, 1924: p. 464.

[21] The document is published by Doucet, 1935: pp. 441 f. The date of this document is hardly surprising when we remember that Olivi's view on the matter was one of the opinions particularly combated under John of Murrovalle.

[22] Ubertino da Casale, 1886: pp. 404 f.

[23] See Burkitt, 1922: pp. 186–188.

[24] *Letter*, f. 53(65)r.

the end of Olivi's life. Although, as we have seen, it is not Olivi's only apocalyptic offering, the Revelation commentary presents his apocalyptic program in greater detail and more striking fashion than the other works. Thus it is natural that its circulation should have caused new interest in Olivi's apocalyptic thought. Boniface VIII certainly noticed it and asked Aegidius Romanus to produce a work evaluating it (or perhaps simply refuting it). Aegidius complied, but the work is no longer extant and no action seems to have followed from it anyway.[25]

The other reason lies in what Raymond and Bonagratia have to say about Olivi's *sectatores*. Their description need not be accepted as unquestionable truth. Since they are guilty of gross exaggeration in arguing that Olivi's views are explicitly contrary to the faith as defined by councils and the universal church, they may also be guilty of exaggeration in depicting the more exotic beliefs of his admirers. Nevertheless, our knowledge of later events makes it easy to believe that their description contains a hard core of truth. If some of Olivi's followers were already threatening the authority of the ecclesiastical hierarchy it is understandable that the order might have thought it was time to take a hard look at the Revelation commentary.

The attack by Raymond and Bonagratia was soon answered by Ubertino of Casale.[26] Ubertino observes that, if the spirituals commit heresy by accepting Olivi's teachings, they are at least in good company, since during his lifetime he was appointed to important teaching positions by his ministers and commended by Pope Nicholas III.[27] Moreover, when the present minister general was a scholar at Paris he defended as probable the same opinion on the divine essence which his procurator Raymond of Fronsac now condemns as heretical.[28] The real reason for the attack on Olivi is clearly not his theology but the forceful manner in which he exposed contemporary relaxations of the rule.[29]

Nevertheless, Ubertino descends to particulars, cataloging the points at which the community has falsified the state of Christian doctrine in order to injure Olivi. No council has decreed that the divine essence as it is in the father and identical with the father cannot be generating.[30] Olivi has shown on numerous occasions how his own view agrees with the Nicaean council, the decretal of Innocent III, and the holy fathers. Several quotations from Olivi are offered to demonstrate this fact.[31]

As for the view attributed to Olivi that marriage is no more a sacrament than the serpent, tabernacle, or ark of Moses, that it is not a sacrament univocally with the other sacraments of the new law, and that it confers no grace, Olivi clearly asserts that marriage is a sacrament of the new law and that it is a sacrament in a different sense from the serpent, tabernacle, and ark. He does show that it differs in many ways from other sacraments of the new law, a point made in even stronger fashion by Peter Lombard, Hostiensis, and others. Ubertino brandishes a series of quotations by established authorities stating that grace is not conferred in marriage.[32]

Olivi is charged with saying that grace and the virtues are not conferred to infants in baptism. Such is not the case, Ubertino says, for Olivi expressly says that infants are given grace through which they are cleansed of original sin and made worthy of eternal life. He does offer without assertion two different opinions on whether such grace necessarily includes a *habitus* of virtues. The negative opinion on this subject seems to reflect the views of Peter Lombard, Gratien, Augustine, Anselm, and others, while Innocent III cites both views without rejecting either.[33] Thus the question is clearly an open one.

Olivi is accused of saying that the rational soul is not the form of the human body, yet he expressly asserts the opposite. Having accepted this much, which is a matter of faith, he recites a certain purely philosophical opinion on the composition of the soul. Such philosophical views recited in nonassertive fashion by catholic authors are not considered errors in faith unless their authors are malevolent or the view obviously vitiates some dogma. As far as the actual content of Olivi's view is concerned, those doctors who distinguish between the essence and powers of the soul commonly say that it informs the body through the former and not through the latter. In his reply to the *Letter of the Seven Seals* Olivi offers a similar view.[34]

Olivi's opponents charge him with saying that a character posits nothing more in the soul than does dedication in a church. On the contrary, Ubertino says, Olivi argues that a character posits three or four most divine things. Orthodoxy demands no more, for the church has not determined precisely what a character is.[35]

On the subject of Franciscans appointed to bishoprics, Olivi does say that they cannot be absolved from their vows and in fact should not be, since in their new positions they should provide an example of the more spiritual and perfect life. Nevertheless, Olivi says that they can use costly things when it is necessary for the performance of their duties. Bonaventure and Pecham both speak more strictly on this subject than Olivi does.

As for the idea that Olivi erred in saying that *usus pauper* is a substantial part of the vow, in reality it is

---

[25] See Edith Pásztor, 1958: p. 371 and Amorós, 1934: p. 403.
[26] Ubertino da Casale, 1886: p. 382.
[27] *Ibid.*, p. 389.
[28] *Ibid.*, p. 383.
[29] *Ibid.*, pp. 384–388.
[30] *Ibid.*, p. 389.
[31] *Ibid.*, pp. 392 f.

[32] *Ibid.*, pp. 393–395.
[33] *Ibid.*, pp. 395 f.
[34] *Ibid.*, pp. 396 f.
[35] *Ibid.*, pp. 397 f.

an error to deny this assertion. Ubertino asserts that Olivi's view was accepted at the general chapter meetings of Montpellier and Paris and is substantially the same view propounded by the former minister general Bonagratia, whose words, ironically enough, are explicitly accepted by the same procurator who seeks to condemn that view in Olivi's writings.[36]

Olivi is charged with saying that burial of the dead is not an act of piety except in case of necessity. He never said anything of the sort, although he does argue that the involvement of Franciscans in the business of burials detracts from the highest poverty and perfection if it involves cupidity, scandal to the clergy, and a bad example for the people.[37]

Next Olivi is accused of saying that the lance wound was inflicted before Christ died. In fact, Ubertino says, Olivi explicitly holds and teaches the contrary view in one of his questions and in his commentary on John, although in the latter work he does examine without assertion the question of whether the opposite order could be accepted.[38] Ubertino notes that the incident of the side wound is inserted before Christ's death in several copies of the gospel of Matthew, while he himself has seen such an interpolation in one old book which presents that gospel as corrected by Jerome himself, strong evidence that Matthew originally contained the passage. Moreover, the same order of events is found in the gospel of Nicodemus.[39]

Finally, there is the charge that Olivi attacks the church in his Revelation commentary. Ubertino characterizes this charge as *mendacissimum*, since Olivi always reverently defends the authority of the Roman pontiff and church. A medley of quotations is offered to demonstrate Olivi's submission to papal authority.[40]

In reply to the accusation that Olivi's writings as a whole must be suppressed because his manifold errors are spread throughout his works, Ubertino observes that the community has isolated only eight questionable views. To the accusation that Olivi's works were never physically handed over to the pope for correction, Ubertino replies that Olivi offered his writings for papal correction on his deathbed and all the brothers who have since wished to submit them to the pope have been imprisoned. The case of the unfortunate Ponce is again cited at this point.[41]

As to the matter of Olivi's *sectatores*, Ubertino prefers to concentrate not on the existence of such a group but on the connection between Olivi and the heretical views cited by the community. His point is that if such a group exists its beliefs are not supported by Olivi's writings. Ubertino pays almost no attention to the question of whether the community is describing an actual phenomenon. He simply says that "although we do not know that such heresies have appeared in the order," he and his associates would certainly combat them whenever they were encountered.[42]

Here as elsewhere Ubertino emphasizes that he is not interested in defending every single statement Olivi ever made. While he has no doubt that Olivi's intentions were pious, it is possible that he erred occasionally. Ubertino and his associates follow the author himself in submitting Olivi's works to the pope for correction.[43]

Ubertino was writing in the late spring or early summer of 1311,[44] and by that time three theologians had been given the task of examining the questionable parts of Olivi's works.[45] Ubertino seems to announce the completion of their investigation in late summer, 1311, when he says in another work[46] that of the many charges leveled against Olivi by the community the masters had found only three things to be of notable importance (*ponderis notabilis*). The three things were Olivi's views on the divine nature, the rational soul, and Christ's side wound. Even in these cases the masters considered Olivi's intention to be pure and without the stain of heretical depravity.

The existence of this commission of three seems well documented, even if we are forced to rely on Ubertino's passing comment for word of its conclusions. One is less sure about another commission mentioned by a single document found in a single manuscript.[47] The anonymous author of this document presents the judgment of a seven-man commission at the council entrusted by the pope with the task of examining five articles imputed to Olivi. The decision seems to have been less than unanimous, since the document closes with the comment that "four of the seven masters agree on these things" and proceeds to list the four, one by name and three by title or order.

Two of the articles deal with the divine essence. One states that generation and being generated do not pertain to the divine essence as it is common to the persons in the same way that it does to the subsisting persons, a view which Olivi could certainly endorse. The other deals with Olivi's assertion that the essence

---

[36] *Ibid.*, pp. 400–402.
[37] *Ibid.*, p. 402.
[38] The first work mentioned by Ubertino is II *Sent.*, q. 50 (II, 32), where Olivi does indeed base his argument on the assumption that the wound came after Christ's death. This is apparently a question written before Olivi came upon the alternate hypothesis. So far Ubertino is quite right. Nevertheless Doucet, 1935: p. 432, is correct in saying that Ubertino distorts Olivi's position when he says that in the John commentary Olivi defends the common view and "strongly argues that it should be held." In reality Olivi leaves the matter wide open.
[39] *Ibid.*, pp. 402–405.
[40] *Ibid.*, pp. 407 f.
[41] *Ibid.*, p. 409.

[42] *Ibid.*, pp. 410 f.
[43] *Ibid.*, pp. 412 f.
[44] Ehrle, "Zur Vorgeschichte des Concils von Vienne," p. 375.
[45] See Ubertino da Casale, 1886: pp. 382 and 416; Bonagratia de Bergamo, 1887: p. 36; Raymundus de Fronciacho, 1887: pp. 20 f.
[46] Ubertino da Casale, 1887, *Declaratio*, p. 191.
[47] It is published by Fussenegger, 1957: pp. 155–177.

of the son, insofar as it is of the son, is personally distinguished from the father or the essence of the father. The commission notes that in the context of Olivi's writings such an assertion is safe enough, although it may sound dangerous.

The other three articles deal with the standard issues of the soul, infant baptism, and Christ's side wound. Regarding the first, the commission determines that Olivi is not wrong in believing that, although the soul is the form of the body, it is not such according to its intellective part. As to the second, the commission notes that, if Innocent III lists as an acceptable opinion the view that grace is not given to infants in baptism, Olivi is certainly quite safe in suggesting that they are given grace but not habitual grace.

So far Olivi is four-for-four. Only on the fifth issue does the commission desert him. They characterize as erroneous any view which would consider it less certain to say the side wound was inflicted after death than to say the opposite. The text of Matthew (!) and the writings of the *sancti* are, they say, against such a view.

After listing these articles, the author of the document observes that "the decretal was made according to the relation of these four, and thus it was determined that brother Peter John was catholic and his books were made public throughout the whole world." The decretal in question would seem to be *Fidei catholicae fundamento,* which, as we will see in a moment, is some what less kind to Olivi. The author of this document is obviously an Olivi fan who wishes to put the best possible face on the conciliar actions concerning him. Nevertheless, there seems no obvious reason to doubt that he is conveying conclusions reached by at least some members of a papal commission.

Clement also seems to have solicited the views of individual theologians outside the order. Two such works are extant. One, by Aegidius Romanus,[48] seems to be based partly on Olivi's 1285 reply to the Paris commission, although other things were considered. It passes negative judgment on twenty-four articles, ten of them dealing with the divine nature and six with grace. The remainder cover the standard accusations concerning marriage, the soul as form of the body, *usus pauper,* Christ's side wound, Franciscans who become bishops, and burial of the dead. The other work, by Augustinus Triumphus,[49] condemns twelve articles in even harsher terms. In addition to the predictable issues of the divine essence, soul as form of the body, infant baptism, character, marriage, burial of the dead, Christ's side wound, *usus pauper,* and Franciscan bishops, Augustinus attacks Olivi's views on quantity and the relationship between conservation and creation.

Whatever the various commissions and theologians may have thought, in 1312 Pope Clement V announced his own opinion in two bulls, *Exivi de paradiso* and *Fidei catholicae fundamento.* The first, which deals with the poverty question, is largely irrelevant to Olivi's troubles, since it skirts the theoretical issues debated in his case. One might say that it contradicts Olivi in some respects, but by the same token it contradicts the apologists for the opposite view.[50]

The other bull offers a rather perplexing problem. In the first place, there is at least some difference of opinion regarding the number of articles it censured. While some fourteenth-century documents refer to three articles, Raymond of Fronsac [51] mentions a fourth one while another source from the period speaks of only two.[52] A more serious problem concerns the relationship between the bull and Olivi. Does it condemn Olivi's views or not? Scholarly opinion has been and still is divided.

In the decretal as we have it the pope addresses himself to three important issues.[53] First, he announces that the lance pierced Christ's side after his death. Second, he asserts as Christian dogma that the rational or intellective soul is form of the body and anyone denying this truth is a heretic. Third, he recognizes the variety of opinion among theologians on the effect of infant baptism and determines that "the opinion which says informing grace and the virtues are conferred in baptism is to be chosen as more probable and more consonant with the words of the *sancti* and modern doctors of theology."

An opening passage leading up to the assertion about the side wound dwells upon Christ's divine and human nature. Raymond of Fronsac's purported fourth article is the result of his attempt to wring from this passage a condemnation of Olivi's thoughts on the divine essence. This interpretation seems a bit far-fetched, although it may be that in this initial passage the pope is actually getting a running start at the second issue, the soul, since christological objections were sometimes raised against Olivi's opinion on that matter. In any case, one can hardly isolate the passage as a definitive statement on a separate issue.

What does all this have to do with Olivi? That is a question which has perplexed historians for some time.[54] Several different problems are involved here. First, do the views implicitly or explicitly condemned in this decree actually accord with Olivi's opinions? Second, whatever the answer to the first question may be, did the pope *think* he was dealing with Olivi's views?

---

[48] Published in Amorós, 1934.
[49] *Tractatus contra divinatores et sompniatores,* edition cited in bibliography.
[50] Thus the bull brands as "presumptuous and temerarious" those who, in the battle over whether *usus pauper* is included in the vow, characterize the opposite view as heretical. See *Corpus iuris canonici* 2: p. 1199.
[51] Raymundus de Fronciacho, 1887: pp. 24 f.
[52] This document is quoted by Ehrle, 1885–1888: 4: p. 63.
[53] See *Corpus iuris canonici* 2: p. 1132.
[54] For an overview of the controversy and three of the most recent contributions see Amorós, 1934: pp. 408–420; Partee, 1960: p. 241–253; Schneider, 1973: pp. 215–223 and 247–257.

Third, why is Olivi not mentioned by name? We can take these questions in order.

As we have seen, Olivi once unquestioningly accepted the idea that Christ received the spear wound after his death, but some time before he wrote his commentary on the gospel of John news of a mystical vision led him to investigate whether that gospel could be harmonized with the opposite order of events. He found a way to do so and presented it in the John commentary. Thus the view implicitly condemned in *Fidei catholicae fundamento* is clearly the one stated by Olivi on one occasion. Although he offers it without assertion, he finds it quite intriguing and at least leaves the matter open.

The case of infant baptism is roughly similar. We have seen that Olivi, while avoiding a definite assertion, clearly favors the view which the decree considers less probable. It is a strange sort of decree which orders theologians to choose a position, not because it is right, but because it is "more probable." Nevertheless, the fact remains that the view theologians are ordered to choose is not the one Olivi would have wished.

We are left with the issue of the rational or intellective soul as form of the body. Here the case is quite different. Efrem Bettoni observes that if Olivi had been alive in 1312 "he would have been ready to subscribe to the conciliar definition, convinced that he had never taught the contrary."[55] In fact, Olivi *did* subscribe to the definition on several occasions, since his opponents persisted in reading his position as a denial of precisely this point.[56] The difference between Olivi and his adversaries was real enough, but it lay on an entirely different plain.

The second question is more difficult, since the answer must be coaxed out of a thin and rather ambiguous collection of documents from the period. Once one compensates for the prejudice of those conventuals who wanted to interpret the decretal as a thoroughgoing condemnation of their theological *bête noir* and those spirituals who wanted to believe that Olivi's thought remained untouched by the council, what evidence we have seems to suggest that the pope thought he was dealing with views actually held by Peter John Olivi.[57] After all, he had put a whole series of theologians to work examining Olivi's theology, and these three issues were prominently mentioned throughout the whole process. It would hardly be surprising if Clement thought of the decretal as contradicting views offered by Olivi, particularly since in two out of three cases he would have been right. How sophisticated he was about the third view is, of course, hard to say.

The most perplexing evidence in this regard is furnished by Raymond of Fronsac,[58] who insists that after the council was over Clement was asked who should watch over Olivi's writings. The pope replied something like "that cursed, condemned doctrine" or "that cursed doctrine was condemned." Raymond claims that testimonial letters to this effect are available and cites witnesses, one of whom would have been alive when he wrote. The question is how far one wishes to trust Raymond under such circumstances, and it is hard to arrive at a definite answer.

Of course, even if we assume—as it seems we must—that the pope had Olivi in mind, we might still ask whether he had *only* Olivi in mind. We have seen that others (including Ubertino) shared Olivi's interest in an alternate reading of John 19 and that his view of infant baptism was not unique. The decretal seems to acknowledge the latter point. The fact remains, however, that the views in question were being considered primarily because Olivi was said to hold them.

As for the third question, it is at least possible to argue that the pope was following Ubertino's advice: Correct those aspects of Olivi's thought which are questionable, but protect Olivi's reputation as a pious, catholic Christian. This is what Ubertino says the commission of three did,[59] and this is essentially how a number of Olivi's later followers interpreted the decretal.[60] As far as they were concerned three opinions had been censured, but Olivi's person and the rest of his thought had thereby been declared orthodox.

An alternate hypothesis would be that the decretal did not specifically name Olivi because it did not have to do so. It was, after all, an attempt to define doctrine, not to discipline a man who had been dead for fourteen years. Thus it did what it was supposed to do without naming anyone. Moreover, mention of Olivi would have been not only unnecessary but impolitic, since Clement's goal was to patch together the Franciscan order through a decision both sides could live with. Questionable doctrine, of course, had to be expunged, but any personal judgment on Olivi would have ruffled spiritual feathers and hardened conventual resistence to spiritual demands.

XI. THE CONDEMNATION OF THE REVELATION COMMENTARY

Clement V had intervened in the spiritual-conventual dispute with an eye toward uniting the order. If his efforts were not rewarded with immediate success, he nevertheless kept trying. In the months immediately after the council of Vienne he continued to busy himself with crises in the order, trying to restrain the spirituals from rebellion against their superiors and to coerce the

---

[55] Bettoni, 1959: p. 376.
[56] See, for example, *Letter*, f. 51v and *Responsio* I, p. 128.
[57] The best collection of citations in this regard is furnished in Amorós, 1934: pp. 408–420.

[58] Raymundus de Fronciacho, 1887: pp. 24 ff.
[59] Ubertino da Casale, 1887, *Declaratio*, p. 191.
[60] Amorós, 1934: p. 418.

superiors into a more positive attitude toward the spirituals.[1] In July, 1312, he deposed the provincial minister and fifteen father guardians in Provence, replacing them with leaders who would be more conciliatory toward the spirituals.

If Clement was to succeed he needed the aid of a cooperative minister general, and he got one when Alexander of Alexandria was elected in the spring of 1313. Although hardly a spiritual himself, Alexander soon demonstrated his flexibility by assigning them the convents of Narbonne, Béziers, and Carcassonne. The way was being prepared for a new accommodation in southern France.

Unfortunately the experiment was of short duration. Clement V died in April, 1314, and Alexander died in October of the same year. The moderate, conciliatory pope and general were gone, to be succeeded for the moment by a power vacuum soon filled by aggressive leaders on both sides. The French spirituals were placed under oppressive superiors, a situation remedied by the spirituals themselves when they seized the convents of Béziers and Narbonne. Their actions served to escalate hostilities elsewhere, and by the time a new pope and minister general could take charge the situation had deteriorated badly.[2]

Moreover, the new pope and minister general were notably different from the ones they replaced. In the spring of 1316 the general chapter at Naples chose Michael of Cesena as its leader and he soon launched an offensive against the spirituals, particularly demanding that they demonstrate allegiance to their superiors and observe uniformity with the rest of the order in their clothing, abandoning the short and squalid habits which marked them out from their conventual brothers. The issue of clothing was not a new one. Decades earlier the provincial of Ancona had campaigned against rigorists who "wore cloaks that came up to their buttocks."[3] After 1316, however, this question would stand alongside the possession of wine cellars and granaries as one of the *cause celèbres* dividing the order.

In the summer of 1316 Michael was blessed with a pope who would support him against the spirituals. John XXII was elected in August, installed in September, and immediately bombarded with pleas for aid from both wings of the order. John soon began an investigation which convinced him that the spirituals must be brought to heel.[4] In the spring of 1317 defiant spirituals were hailed into the papal court, cursorily examined, and detained or imprisoned.[5] In the fall of that year the bull *Quorumdam exigit* called the zealots back to the fold. The bull explained that, while *Exivi de paradiso* had called for *vilitas* in clothing, it had given the superiors the task of determining what constituted *vilitas*. Again, while *Exivi de paradiso* had disapproved of granaries and wine cellars, it had left superiors with the option of using them when the occasion demanded. John's message to the spirituals is encapsulated in a single line: "Poverty is great, but unity is greater; obedience is the greatest good if it is preserved intact."[6]

Historians traditionally regard *Quorumdam exigit* as a revelation of John's legalistic mentality. Manselli notes that John ignored the issues of poverty and the rule, concentrating instead on disciplinary or juridical questions. The bull, Manselli says, displayed John's characteristic psychology, which was that of a jurist without any sensitivity to the religious values prized by the spirituals.[7] While there is a great deal of truth in such a characterization, Lambert is probably also correct in arguing that John was motivated by genuine concern over the apocalyptic views of the spirituals.[8] He saw the spirituals' rebellion against their superiors as part and parcel of a heretical eschatological perspective.

Lambert's suggestion is supported by two bulls which John fired off in December, 1317, and January, 1318, *Sancta Romana* and *Gloriosam ecclesiam*. The second, aimed primarily at some Italian spirituals, is most interesting for our purposes, since it deals with these spirituals not simply as a factious clique but as a heretical sect. They are charged with distinguishing between a carnal church led by the pope and other prelates and a spiritual church to which real authority has now passed. They, of course, are the spiritual church, the only ones who truly observe the gospel of Christ. The priests of the carnal church are now devoid of sacerdotal power. The Italian spirituals are also accused of refusing to swear oaths; of claiming that sacraments are worthless if performed by a priest stained with mortal sin; and of unspecified errors concerning marriage, the coming of Antichrist, and the end of the age.[9]

Meanwhile Michael of Cesena had capitalized on his papal support and moved decisively against the spirituals in southern France. In October, 1317, he confronted the spirituals who had been collected by John XXII with two questions: Would they comply with the demands of *Quorumdam exigit* and did they believe that the pope had the power to demand what he had demanded in the bull?[10] Twenty-four said no and were turned over to the inquisitor of Provence, Michael the

---

[1] For what follows see Lambert, 1961: ch. 9.

[2] See Manselli, 1959: ch. 5.

[3] *Chronica XXIV generalium*, p. 263.

[4] For the following see Lambert, 1961: ch. 10 and Manselli, 1959: ch. 5.

[5] Angelo Clareno, 1886: pp. 144 ff., may be exaggerating a bit in his narrative of the event, but he was in a position to know what went on and can be given guarded credence at this point.

[6] Sbaralea and Eubel, 1759–1904: **5**: p. 130b. I use the translation in Lambert, 1961: p. 214.

[7] Manselli, 1959: pp. 130 and 137.

[8] Lambert, 1972: pp. 123–143.

[9] Sbaralea and Eubel, 1759–1904: **5**: pp. 137–142.

[10] Raymundus de Fronciacho, 1887: p. 30.

Monk, whose earlier treatment of the spirituals had led Clement V to reproach him and remove him from office.[11]

Michael the Monk was successful in gaining affirmative answers from twenty of the group, leaving five unconvinced. In the meantime, he solicited a wide range of opinion on whether their stance toward the pope was heretical. He was told that it was. Of the remaining five brothers, one finally recanted and was sentenced to perpetual imprisonment, while the others, obstinate to the end, were burned in the market place at Marseilles on May 7, 1318.

The fires at Marseilles signalled the end of an era in which conventuals and spirituals could cross swords as two more or less legitimate factions within a single order. One faction had now emerged victorious and the other could either knuckle under, get out, or be persecuted. Getting out was, of course, no mean feat for the average friar, but a few leaders with important patrons managed to accomplish it. By the end of 1317, Ubertino of Casale had become a Benedictine and Angelo Clareno a Celestinian. The old war horses of the spiritual cause were quietly leaving the field.

Other friars might lack the opportunity for an official transfer, but they could at least vote with their feet. Some of those who had avoided Michael the Monk by abjuring their errors now regretted their weakness, fled from their convents, and became fugitives protected by pious laymen. A letter from Michael to the inquisitor of Tuscany warns of these escapees and suggests that when they are apprehended the authorities should get the names of those who had aided them.[12] The inquisition was beginning to follow a trail which would lead beyond the order to a devout laity.

Thus the pope, the minister general, and the inquisition had acted against the spirituals, but they had not thereby eliminated the problem. The opposition had become a resistance movement, complete with an underground railroad. The church had given it four martyrs and would soon give it three more when, in October, 1319, the first lay supporters were burned. Others would follow.

These Franciscans and laymen had good reason to fear the inquisition, but they were shocked by the spectacle of a rich and powerful church directing its forces against poor, pious spirituals. The established church was acting in ungodly fashion and had to be defied. Moreover, many were equipped with an eschatology which made sense of what they saw. That eschatology was derived in large part from the writings of Peter John Olivi. As they watched the events unroll, they saw Olivi's apocalyptic scenario incarnated before their eyes. The church of Rome was turning into the whore of Babylon. In persecuting evangelical poverty, John XXII was revealing himself as the mystical Antichrist. As Manselli observes, it is no accident that a compendium of Olivi's Revelation commentary appeared in the vulgar tongue shortly after the four spirituals were burned at Marseilles.[13]

And there was more to come. So far John's intervention had been welcomed by the conventuals. From 1321 on they would be less grateful for his attention, for in that year his interest began to focus on their own notion of Franciscan poverty. According to a medieval source, the occasion for this shift was an inquisitorial process at Narbonne in which John of Beaune, a Dominican inquisitor, derived from a lay supporter of the spirituals a series of assertions including the idea that Christ and his disciples possessed nothing individually or in common.[14] As was the custom, John sought advice on the suspect theses from a number of local experts. In the process he discovered that a *lector* in the local Franciscan convent, Berengar Talon by name, thought the proposition about Christ's poverty to be sound doctrine supported by *Exiit qui seminat*. John accused him of heresy and demanded an abjuration, whereupon Berengar appealed to Rome. John XXII responded by circulating the disputed thesis among cardinals and theologians in order to get their views.

The story is a good one and there is no strong reason to reject it. Nevertheless, some recent scholars have pointed out that the truth of the matter may be more complex and John may have been prepared to react vigorously to the issue because the question of Christ's poverty had already risen in the process directed at Olivi's Revelation commentary.[15] At any rate, his decision on the matter traumatized the Franciscan order.[16] His first definite move was the writing of the bull *Quia nonnunquam* in March, 1322. In it the pope lifted the ban placed on discussion of the rule by *Exiit qui seminat*.

The order, understandably alarmed by the idea that John could revise the decretal on which they based their own self-understanding, considered the matter at length when they assembled at Perugia for their general chapter meeting. The result was a letter to John asking him to restore the ban and, more important, an encyclical letter arguing that *Exiit qui seminat* had been incorporated into canon law and therefore could not be changed. The encyclical, produced in a long, unexpurgated edition for scholars and a short, pithy version for general consumption, was designed to present the Franciscan case not only to John but to Christianity at large.

John, who was not habitually gentle in the face of defiance, soon countered with the bull *Ad conditorem*. In it he reaffirmed his right to change his predecessors'

---

[11] Manselli, 1959: p. 151.
[12] *Ibid.*, p. 158.
[13] *Ibid.*, p. 191.
[14] For this event see Lambert, 1961: pp. 223 f. and Manselli, 1959: pp. 209 ff.
[15] See Lambert, 1961: p. 223; Koch, 1933: pp. 308 ff.
[16] For the following see Lambert, 1961: pp. 224–242.

edicts and proceeded to prove his point by changing still another aspect of *Exiit qui seminat*. Nicholas III had protected Franciscan poverty by acknowledging that the things they used really belonged to the papacy. John now announced that they did not. Thus with a stroke of the pen the Franciscans' relation to the books they read, the houses they occupied, and the food they consumed ceased to be one of *nudus usus* and began to look uncomfortably like *dominium*.

Thus the Franciscans' conception of their own poverty had been badly shaken. Their view of Christ's poverty was soon dealt with just as severely. In November, 1323, John issued the bull *Cum inter nonnullos*, which condemned as heretical the propositions that Christ and his disciples owned nothing either in private or in common and that they had no right of use, sale, donation, or exchange in regard to those things which scripture says they had.

The precise relation of this bull to *Exiit qui seminat* is somewhat ambiguous, since John did not speak in terms of *dominium* or *proprietas*. Nevertheless, the bull clearly challenged the Franciscan interpretation of *Exiit qui seminat* and of Christ's poverty. Thus the pope who had helped Michael of Cesena to crush the spirituals now denied the self-understanding shared by spirituals and conventuals alike.

The conventual reaction was slow to develop, but it burst into open rebellion in 1328 when Michael of Cesena, William of Ockham, and others fled the papal court and jointed John's enemy, the emperor Lewis the Bavarian. Among the spirituals and their lay supporters, the revolution had long since begun. John's actions in 1323 could only intensify their feeling that he was the Antichrist, or at least a heretic bent on resisting the new age of evangelical perfection.

One wonders how Olivi himself would have reacted. We have seen how much importance he attributed to the absolute poverty of Christ and his disciples, and how he described Franciscan poverty as a restoration of the apostolic situation. We have seen his emphasis on *Exiit qui seminat* as a guarantee of the Franciscan way. We have seen his fear that this guarantee would be challenged by a future pope who would attack the *ecclesia spiritualis* on behalf of the *ecclesia carnalis*. Given these factors, Olivi's response to the events of 1323 might seem predictable. Bettoni observes that, if Olivi had been alive in 1312, he would have subscribed willingly to Clement's decision on the soul as form of the body. Granting that such is the case, one might be tempted to guess that, if he had lived on until 1323, he would have seen little alternative except to man the barricades. Nevertheless, the human drama is too complex to encourage such speculation. If (as we shall see later in this chapter) at least some of Olivi's admirers could make their peace with John XXII, perhaps Olivi himself would have done so.

Olivi was not forgotten while all this was going on. His doctrine was still an issue, but by this time attention had focused upon a single work, his Revelation commentary. We have seen that interest in Olivi's apocalyptic thought was not entirely absent from earlier disputes, but that the lion's share of attention had been lavished upon other matters. After Vienne, the focus shifted noticeably.

The reason for this new interest is not hard to see. The continued activity against the spirituals had produced a flowering of apocalyptic thought. The resultant eschatological perspective had in turn strengthened the spirituals' will to resist authority. As the spirituals and their lay supporters read Olivi's Revelation commentary in the light of current events, they saw his apocalyptic fantasies turning into realized eschatology before their eyes. Such was certainly the case when John XXII attacked first the spirituals and then Franciscan poverty itself, but it was already happening earlier in some circles, as we have seen from the complaints of the conventuals at Vienne and from John's remarks in *Gloriosam ecclesiam*.

Thus it is understandable that John should have accompanied his campaign against the spirituals with an investigation of Olivi's Revelation commentary. The affair began when John entrusted the matter to the Dominican cardinal Nicholas of Prato.[17] He drew up a list of dubious propositions and turned them over for comment first to a single theologian and then to a commission of eight. This process was underway by the time the four spirituals were sentenced at Marseilles in May, 1318. Michael the Monk remarks in his sentence that the errors held by the accused were derived from the Revelation commentary and some *opuscula* by Olivi, works which have been committed to certain cardinals and masters for examination. While this case is pending, he says, no one should revere Olivi as a saint or holy man.[18]

Fortunately the report of the eight-man commission has survived and we are thus able to see how they reacted to Olivi's Revelation commentary.[19] Their most common objection is to Olivi's comments regarding the carnal church, which they identify with "the Roman Church" or "the Catholic Church." Of the sixty articles censured by the commission, twenty-two of them bear directly upon this problem. The second most common objection is to Olivi's statements regarding the preeminence of the sixth and seventh periods of church history over preceding times. Fifteen articles on this matter are criticized because they imply that the sixth and seventh periods will witness knowledge and virtue superior to that of the apostles, while eight more are attacked because they suggest that these periods

---

[17] For the following see especially Pásztor, 1958: pp. 376 ff.

[18] Quoted in Pásztor, 1958: p. 368.

[19] This document, which we shall call the *Littera magistrorum*, is published in *Stephani Baluze Miscellaneorum*. See Koch, 1933: p. 306 for comment on the reliability of Baluze's edition.

are related to the preceding five as the church was related to the synagogue.

It is not hard to recognize that the commission and Olivi represent two drastically different views of the church and its history. At the center of the commission's view (and at the center of history in the commission's view) stands the Roman Catholic Church, created by Christ and perduring in roughly the same form throughout the ages. The commission focuses on what we would call today "the institutional church."

Because this church was established by Christ and immediately blossomed under the apostles, being given at that tender age all that was necessary for its functioning and appropriate for Christians on this earth, the commission rejects Olivi's expectation that the church will receive greater wisdom or virtue in the final period.[20] In reply to Olivi's suggestion that there will be a third age appropriated to the holy spirit, the commission primly announces that Christ's promise concerning the coming of the holy spirit was fulfilled at Pentecost.[21]

Because the church as the commission envisages it does not change in any essential way, the commission rejects the idea of a decline in the fifth period leading to a situation in which church leaders combat the evangelical life and rule.[22] When the church was entrusted with leadership it was given the power and guidance necessary to perform that task, and it is unthinkable that it should fail. The commission's refusal to imagine any real change in the church leads inevitably to its rejection of a condemnation of the carnal church in the sixth period and a transfer of power to a new sort of leadership.[23] "In the entire church there is a single primacy residing within the Roman church. Beginning with Peter it has continued without interruption or transference until now and will always continue in his legitimate successors until the consummation of this world."[24]

If the commission will not accept Olivi's progressive view of church history, it is only natural that it will not accept his view of the role played by Francis and his order within that history. For the commission the Franciscans are not essentially different from other orders in piety, knowledge, or historical mission. Their rule is no more sacrosanct than that of the Benedictines. The commission emphasizes (again *contra* Olivi) that the Roman church has the power to abrogate any rule it has approved including that of St. Francis, but in the same breath it notes the practical impossibility of ever destroying such a good and holy rule. It does, however, condemn the false understanding of that rule held by Olivi and his sect.[25]

The commission feels that Olivi's tendency to rank Francis just behind Christ and his mother is a slur against the apostles and other holy men, while the legend about his future resurrection is "a fantastic fiction" which Olivi might better have left unrecorded.[26] They indignantly reject the notions that pontifical authority will be transferred to an evangelical order at some future date [27] and that the Franciscan rule is the same as the evangelical life observed by Christ and is therefore immutable by the pope.[28] The latter, to be sure, gives Olivi's censors some trouble, since his identification of the rule with Christ's life is affirmed by *Exiit qui seminat*. They resolve the dilemma by deciding that such an identification must have a good and bad sense, with Olivi of course choosing the bad one. Other speculations about the order are dismissed as "temerarious and fantastic divination."[29] Olivi's theories about the conversion of the Moslems, Jews, and pagans strike the commission as dangerous apocalyptic moonshine without any scriptural or rational authority.[30]

So far we have been comparing the commission with Olivi as the commission sees him. Is it the real Olivi, however? Like most good questions, this one does not allow any simple negative or affirmative answer. Certainly there are some distortions. The carnal church is not simply identifiable with the Roman Catholic Church in Olivi's writings. It is not, in fact, identifiable with any institution but represents instead the totality of anti-Christian forces operating in the guise of the true church yet actually dedicated to radically different goals.

Again, the commission rather oversimplifies Olivi's progressive view of church history. This fact is seen, for example, in their perversion of his attitude toward the apostles. Although Olivi certainly posits a preeminence of the sixth and seventh periods over the first five, it does not thereby follow that he considers the apostles inferior in every important respect to members of the Franciscan order. As we have seen, he considers this problem elsewhere and is careful to avoid any such implication, preferring to see in the apostles a fulfillment of evangelical perfection occurring at the beginning of church history and only to be rivaled in the sixth and seventh periods. The commission often ignores the extent to which the progress of the third general age is not innovation but renovation, a restoration of the apostolic life. Of course, even when they do recognize the element of restoration they cannot accept it in the form offered, as is evident from their anxiety regarding Olivi's identification of the Franciscan rule with Christ and the apostles.

---

[20] *Littera magistrorum*, art. 5, 40, 60.
[21] *Ibid.*, art. 13.
[22] *Ibid.*, art. 23, 26, 38.
[23] *Ibid.*, art. 10, 12, 18, 19.
[24] *Ibid.*, art. 18.
[25] *Ibid.*, art. 24.
[26] *Ibid.*, art. 28, 38.
[27] *Ibid.*, art. 47.
[28] *Ibid.*, art. 22.
[29] *Ibid.*, art. 27, 31. Similar expressions are used throughout the work to describe Olivi's predictions regarding the sixth and seventh periods of the church. See art. 35, 36, 52, 59.
[30] *Ibid.*, art. 12, 38.

The commission distorts Olivi partly because it reads him in the light of the spirituals as encountered in 1319. Their tendency in this regard is beautifully illustrated in a passage demonstrating that Olivi's fulminations against the carnal church are actually aimed at the Roman Catholic Church.[31] Olivi says, the commission notes, that the evangelical life will be defended by its professors and condemned by the carnal church. Since those of his sect pertinaciously defend an interpretation of the rule condemned by the church while the majority of the Franciscan order accept the interpretation approved by the church, it follows that when Olivi speaks about the carnal church he actually means the Catholic Church. Such an argument, suggesting as it does that Olivi not only agreed with the spirituals of 1319 but wrote with their case in mind, offers a rather depressing insight into the degree of historical perspective maintained by the commission.

Having said so much, one must still grant the extent to which the commission read Olivi correctly. In contrast to their essentially static view of church history he offers a dynamic vision which posits real change. Moreover, this change is hardly peripheral. Institutions may remain, but they will be transformed so radically that they might just as well be new. While Olivi remains unable to conceive of a church without hierarchy, he envisages a dramatically different type of hierarchy in the third general age, one in which superiors will be such not merely through juridical power but through that real authority which flows from inner excellence. Ecclesiastical splendor will be replaced by evangelical poverty. Learning will be transmogrified from the bookish practices of the second age into the *intelligentia spiritualis* of the third. These are important changes and the commission, having perceived them as such, rejected them.

The commission was also at least partly correct about the negative side of Olivi's prophecies. Although they misunderstood Olivi's *ecclesia carnalis* and perhaps gave insufficient weight to his prediction that the great persecution would come under a schismatically elected pseudopope rather than a genuine pope, they were right in understanding Olivi to say that the forces of evil would capture the highest offices in the church and that evangelical perfection would be combated by an array of prelates and scholars commanded from Rome. It was simply unthinkable to the commission that Christ would ever allow his church to fall into such horrible disrepair.

Note that, while the commission's reservations are intimately connected with what we have called the progressive aspects of Olivi's view, they are not entirely limited to that sphere. Certainly the commission criticizes Olivi because it understands him to posit a preeminence of the sixth and seventh periods over the first five and a preeminence of the Franciscans over the apostles. Certainly, as we have noted, the commission often ignores the elements of renovation (as opposed to pure innovation) in the events of the sixth period of church history. Nevertheless, even when they acknowledge the element of renovation they cannot accept it in the form offered. This fact is evident from their anxiety regarding Olivi's identification of the Franciscan rule with Christ. Whether the events of the sixth period were conceived as innovation or renovation, novelty or return to the apostolic pattern, they were in any case unacceptable if they implied a radical alteration of church life as it had existed for the last few centuries.

These facts are worth stressing if only because so many people have been tempted to ignore them and imply that Olivi's censure was the result of a terrible misunderstanding. About a year before the commission reached its decision Ubertino of Casale was being grilled at Avignon about Olivi's orthodoxy. Confronted with a group of suspect articles, Ubertino was asked whether Olivi taught them in his Revelation commentary. He answered that the assertions indeed belonged to Olivi, but that their meaning could be appreciated only by reading them in their original context rather than treating them as *nudos articulos*.[32] A number of historians have followed Ubertino's lead in suggesting that Olivi's meaning was distorted by ripping passages out of context.

In reality the commission did nothing of the sort. The preface to their report explains that Bishop Nicholas sent them not only the questionable articles but the entire Revelation commentary and asked them both whether the articles were erroneous and whether they were actually contained in the commentary.[33] The commission members were able to read them in context and seem to have done so at least accurately enough to detect a real difference between Olivi and themselves. It seems safe to conclude that, even if the commission had been entirely correct in interpreting Olivi, it still would have rejected him.

The commission was not the only group examining Olivi in 1319. During the same year the general chapter meeting of the Franciscan order was held, significantly enough, at Marseilles. At the gathering a series of errors culled from Olivi's writings was examined and condemned. All brothers harboring or using his works were excommunicated. The censure was approved by a commission of twelve masters and bachelors of theology.[34]

Thus Olivi's writings were again placed beyond the pale. His cult had already suffered a serious setback the preceding year. We have seen that Olivi's tomb was a pilgrimage site. Despite the opposition of the

---

[31] *Ibid.*, art. 29. For analogous passages see art. 30, 34, 35.
[32] See Pásztor, 1958: pp. 374 f.
[33] *Littera magistrorum*, pp. 213 f.
[34] Amorós, 1931: p. 509. See Pásztor, 1958: pp. 376–379.

conventuals, the Olivi cult grew in the first decade of the fourteenth century. Just prior to the council of Vienne we find the citizens of Narbonne protesting to the pope that Olivi's books were unjustly condemned and asking that a *reverentia specialis* be allowed his body.[35] The cult emerged unscathed from the council, although it was still opposed by the leadership of the order. A provincial statute of 1313 warned the brothers of Provence against illicit veneration of an uncanonized dead man;[36] yet it was in 1313 that Angelo Clareno wrote describing the crowds at Olivi's tomb, saying they equaled those at the Portiuncula.

The clearest indication of precisely what went on at Narbonne is provided by an anonymous treatise of 1316 defending the spirituals of Narbonne and Béziers. In answer to charges concerning the Olivi cult, the author replies that brothers do not refer to Olivi as "St. Peter" (*sanctum Petrum*), although they can and do call him a holy man (*sanctum virum*) without violating the sacred canons. Nor do they show him the reverence due to canonized saints. Solemn prayers and offices are not recited in his honor as is the custom with canonized saints, nor is his name inserted in the calendar. Instead, on the day of his death or at some other time, the people come to his tomb, God is praised and glorified, a solemn mass is said for the virgin mother, and the evidences of miracles wrought through him during the preceding year are displayed. The writer notes that such practices, far from being illegitimate, constituted a normal part of the processes leading to the canonization of Francis, Dominic, Anthony of Padua, and Louis of Toulouse. Moreover, the pilgrims to Olivi's tomb include not only simple laymen and Franciscans but cardinals, bishops, and other leaders of the church.[37]

The cult continued unabated until 1318, when the order moved resolutely to crush it. Some time during that year Olivi's body was removed from its tomb at Narbonne. The body was spirited away—so expertly that we still do not know what they did with it—and the tomb was destroyed.[38]

After this flurry of activity in 1318 and 1319 one might have expected the pope to strike rapidly against Olivi's Revelation commentary; yet little happened for some time. No official action was taken before September, 1322, when John XXII announced that he was reserving final judgment on the matter for himself, and activity after that date seems to have been conducted at a very leisurely pace. John extracted four articles from the Revelation commentary and submitted them to at least two (probably at least three) scholars for an opinion.[39]

The first of these articles is a passage in which Olivi argues that the pontificate as first given to Peter involved the fullness of apostolic perfection but was later justly commuted to a condition allowing temporal possessions. The second article deals with the wonders of the third age. Olivi says all knowledge of the incarnate word will be known not only by simple *intelligentia* but by taste and touch (*gustativa et palpativa experientia*), for Christ promised that when the spirit of truth came it would teach us all truth.

The third article involves the question of predestination. The pope inquires whether it is correct to say that the number of the elect is predetermined in such a way that if one falls through sin another must be substituted.

The fourth article deals with St. Francis. John asks whether it is proper to say that Francis is revealer of the evangelical life to be propagated in the sixth and seventh periods and its greatest observer after Christ and his mother.

As one might have expected, these articles were not well received by the judges. In the case of the first one, both scholars whose opinions have survived objected to the idea that temporal possessions were only given to the papacy from the time of Constantine on. Here, in effect, the judges were objecting to the very thing concerning which John was coming to grips with: the Franciscan order, the absolute poverty of Christ and his apostles. One scholar also objected to the other part of the statement, noting the implication that in the sixth period of the church apostolic succession will pass "to certain spirituals who will have no temporal possessions." It was, of course, this aspect of the matter which elevated it from a theological question to an existential concern for John, since some spirituals were already saying that the heralded time was at hand.

The second article presented the same problem it had already offered to the commission of eight.[40] The judges simply would not accept the notion of a future state in which spiritual gifts would surpass those of the apostles. One of them identified it is as a recrudescence of the heresy introduced in the preceding century by Gerard of Borgo San Donino. Moreover, this articles bore some relation to what would become one of John XXII's pet theological concerns, the beatific vision. In fact, the article was attacked by John himself in a sermon probably delivered in 1325 or 1326.[41] In this sermon John argues that Olivi's predictions about human knowledge in the new age would

---

[35] Raymundus de Fronciacho, 1887: p. 13. See also Bonagratia de Bergamo, 1887: p. 36.

[36] Delorme, 1921: p. 430.

[37] MS. Vat. Borgh. 85, f. 102a-b, quoted by Ehrle, 1887: p. 443. The miracles performed through Olivi are attested to in inquisitorial records of the processes against various Beguines.

[38] Angelo Clareno, 1886: pp. 129, 149 and 293; Bernardus Guidonis, 1886: p. 287.

[39] See Pásztor, 1958: pp. 386 ff.; Pásztor, 1970: pp. 82 f.; and Koch, 1933: pp. 310 ff. Pásztor argues convincingly that the three extant opinions are by three different people, whereas Koch assumes that two of them are by the same person.

[40] *Littera magistrorum*, art. 13.

[41] It is published in Pásztor, 1958: pp. 417–424.

make men not *viatores* but *comprehensores* who need no mediator. He then poses an imaginary objection that it is at least theoretically possible for God to be seen in this life. John proceeds to argue at length against this view, and is thus launched on a long voyage which would eventually lead him into dangerous theological waters.

Both extant opinions on the third article attack it for making nonsense of the doctrine of predestination. If a man is elect, then he is infallibly predestined to salvation by God, and the idea of his losing that status is unacceptable.

The sole surviving opinion on the fourth article reacts much as the commission of eight did to Olivi's image of St. Francis. While Francis was a pious man, it is blasphemous to place him before the apostles as Olivi does.

Once the judges' views on the four articles were added to the report by the eight-man commission, John could claim a relatively broad consensus among the scholars he had consulted. Moreover, lest anyone mistake the debate for a purely theoretical affair, the evidence pouring in from the inquisition showed that Olivi's views could be given a frightening application. Finally, just to underline the manifold possibilities of Olivian thought, Louis the Bavarian's Sachsenhausen appellation of April, 1324, closely paraphrased Olivi in the process of attacking John XXII's stance on Franciscan poverty.[42] Posthumously at least, Olivi was becoming a very dangerous man and needed to be dealt with.

The pope did so on February 8, 1326, with a condemnation of the Revelation commentary which went almost completely unheralded by the writers of his day, the only known reference to it being a terse comment by Bernard Gui. Thus, six years after the investigation officially began, it was brought to a close with one more censure against Olivi's thought. It would be nice to know more about the condemnation, but we do not.

It is noteworthy that the process began around four years before John XXII came to grips with the Franciscan order over poverty and ended almost three years after John had disposed of Christ's absolute poverty in *Cum inter nonnullos*. Joseph Koch and others argue that this sequence of events is hardly fortuitous.[43] John wanted the Revelation commentary condemned because he saw the use to which it was being put by the spirituals. By the time the commission of eight had finished its work, he saw that a thoroughgoing censure of the commentary and its message could be carried out only if he could rid himself of the doctrine of Franciscan poverty as accepted by the order as a whole and even apparently by Nicholas III in *Exiit qui seminat*, particularly the notion that the Franciscans, in owning nothing, were restoring the life-style of Christ and the apostles. He attacked both ends of this proposition in 1322 and 1323, dispensing first with the Franciscans' absolute poverty and then with Christ's.

Although there is little evidence showing how the issues were connected in John's mind, in an attenuated form Koch's argument is not only plausible but quite convincing. Exposure to Olivi's views on the shape of church history must have caused John and his advisers to look with new interest at the supposedly orthodox Franciscan self-understanding. The commission of eight is a case in point. In their report they are profoundly uneasy in the presence of Olivi's assertion that the Franciscan rule is the gospel which Christ observed and imposed on his apostles, realizing as they do that at this point they are dealing with more than Olivi's personal eccentricity. They avoid the problem by recourse to an unexplained distinction between a proper (papal) and improper (Olivian) sense of these words. Elsewhere they feel moved to point out that Christ had a purse and the apostles collected money.[44] They are unimpressed by the significance Olivi assigns to St. Francis, preferring to see him as one of many holy men in recent church history. In each of these cases the commission scents an error but is rather tentative about attacking it directly. In each case it is in the presence of a view held not only by Olivi but by the Franciscan community in general. It is not surprising that such considerations should have led John beyond Olivi to the order itself.

At any rate, Olivi had now been censured again, this time twenty-eight years after his death. Enough was enough, however. The condemnation of the Revelation commentary climaxed the last official investigation into Olivi's thought. Olivi himself was by no means forgotten. While John was attacking Franciscan poverty and the Revelation commentary, Olivi's star was in the ascent among those who had broken with the church and particularly among the Beguines in southern France. For renegade Franciscan spirituals and the embattled laymen who harbored them, Olivi's commentary was an inspired prediction of the trials they themselves were enduring. Thus Olivi became a prophet and more than a prophet. He became an eschatological figure prophesied in the book of Revelation.

Olivi is mentioned prominently in the voluminous inquisitorial records dealing with the Beguines. Among the standard questions with which the inquisitors taxed their prisoners (who included, incidentally, Olivi's own niece)[45] there was sure to be one about Olivi's works.

---

[42] See Ehrle, 1887: pp. 540–552.

[43] Koch, 1933: pp. 308 f. The nexus between the two issues is also stressed by Lambert, 1961: pp. 221–223 and *idem*, 1972: pp. 133–135.

[44] *Littera magistrorum*, art. 34.

[45] She helped her mother to shield escaping Franciscans, one of them a member of the family. The record of her hearing is one of several produced by Manselli, 1959: appendix 3. Hers appears on pp. 319–321.

Bernard Gui, in his manual for inquisitors, offers a list of leading questions to ask about Olivi [46] and a generous section predicting how they will be answered.[47] He provides a sobering insight into how far the Olivi cult had progressed by the early 1320's.

The Beguines, Gui says, believe that Olivi's teachings were revealed to him by God, as he himself disclosed. An uncanonized saint, he is the greatest doctor since the apostles and evangelists. His teachings, along with those of St. Paul, must be observed in their entirety by the church and not changed by a single letter. Olivi is, in fact, the angel with a face like the sun in Revelation 10: 1–2, for the truth of Christ and the understanding of the Apocalypse were revealed to him alone among all doctors.[48] If the pope should condemn his writings it would simply mean that the pope was a heretic.

Inquisitorial records support Gui's description. Perhaps the most striking case is that of Prous Boneta, who was examined in 1325.[49] In Prous the mythologizing of Olivi is complete. She has done to Olivi what he and others did to Francis. In fact, although Francis is still present in Prous's confession, Olivi has surpassed him in importance. Francis is Elijah and Olivi is Enoch, both bearing witness to the new age; yet Olivi marks the point at which the new age comes into being. When Christ was born from Mary the holy trinity placed all of its power in the son. This power lasted until the trinity invested all of its power in the holy spirit given to Olivi.[50] God gave Olivi as much grace as he gave to Christ insofar as he was man. Just as God ruled the church through the two fleshly bodies of Christ and his mother, he now rules it through the two spiritual bodies of Olivi and Prous herself.[51]

Prous pays a good deal of attention to Olivi's *scriptura*. Perhaps her use of the singular means that she is thinking of the Revelation commentary. At any rate, this *scriptura* was produced through divine dictation by the power of the holy spirit and he who wishes to be saved must believe in what is written there (just as he must believe in Prous's own words). The *scriptura* was attacked by the powers of evil, notably John XXII and Thomas Aquinas. Aquinas played Cain to Olivi's Abel, spiritually slaying his brother by assaulting the *scriptura*.[52] John played the same role and that of Caiaphas as well, slaying Christ.[53] He also functioned as Herod, with the executed Beguines cast as the holy innocents. The result was a profound alteration in the economy of salvation. From the time Olivi's *scriptura* was condemned, the sacrament of the altar has lost its power and will never regain it again.[54]

As long as Olivi was the object of such adulation, it is understandable that his works should have been regarded with suspicion; yet there is no reason to conclude that he was read only by Beguines and renegade Franciscans in the 1330's and immediately thereafter. Many of his admirers remained in the order, and concerted action against them would have been difficult in the chaotic years following Michael of Cesena's defiance of John XXII. The continued utilization of Olivi's writings is shown by a curious document which originated in Persia and eventually came to rest in the Vatican archives.[55]

On March 20, 1334, two cardinals at Avignon were given a document aimed at certain Franciscans living in Tauris. It seems that the Dominicans in Persia had taken an interest in the opinions held by these Franciscans, and had collected some materials on them through the authority of the bishop of Tauris, who was also a Dominican. These materials had been brought to Avignon by Rainerius of Vercelli, O.P.

The document is divided into three parts, the first being a sworn statement by Rainerius himself in which he narrates all the heterodox Franciscan views which have come to his attention. The second part contains the sworn testimony of several Italian merchants living in Tauris. The third is a selection of private correspondence between three friars of Tauris and two confreres residing in the monastery of St. Thadeus, near Maku in greater Armenia.

The statements by Rainerius and the merchants contain a series of assertions purportedly made by seven Franciscans at Tauris. Most of these comments reflect the climate of opinion following John XXII's action on Franciscan poverty in the 1320's. One is not reminded explicitly of Olivi. Most of the "dangerous" comments recorded therein are assertions that Christ and the apostles were without possessions or that John XXII was heretical in determining otherwise. The errant Franciscans are also cited as affirming that John held a heretical view of the beatific vision; that he contradicted earlier popes on the issues of Franciscan poverty; and that Thomas Aquinas was a heretic on the issue of Christ's poverty.

There are approximately nineteen instances of the various types of assertion listed in the preceding para-

---

[46] Bernardus Guidonis, 1886: pp. 280 ff.

[47] *Ibid.*, pp. 272 f. See also pp. 265 and 270.

[48] Identification of Olivi with the angel of Rev. 10: 1 f. is amply documented by other sources from the period 1318–1325. See Manselli, 1959: pp. 166 and 182 f. for examples. We have seen that Olivi was identified with an angel of the Apocalypse even before the council of Vienne. See Raymundus de Fronciacho and Bonagratia de Bergamo, 1886: p. 371, where it is not clear whether the angel of Rev. 10: 1 is meant.

[49] Her confession is edited by May, 1955: pp. 3–30.

[50] *Ibid.*, pp. 18 f.

[51] *Ibid.*, p. 22.

[52] *Ibid.*, p. 24.

[53] *Ibid.*, pp. 12, 14.

[54] *Ibid.*, pp. 12, 15.

[55] This document is published in Golubovich, 1906–1927: 3: pp. 442–450. See also pp. 436–442 for introductory remarks by Golubovich. I am grateful to E. R. Daniel for calling my attention to this source.

graph. In addition, there are three comments which challenge ecclesiastical authority. One Franciscan is reported to have said that he would not believe John if he determined against the Franciscan rule. Another is said to have announced that because of his heretical views on poverty John had lost his power and should no longer be obeyed. Still another is recorded as saying that a certain bishop appointed by John was in fact no true bishop, since he had been created by a heretic.

Three other comments have an apocalyptic ring. In one, John is identified with the beast of the Apocalypse. In another, a Franciscan claims that "because the Latins did not wish to hear the truth, the friars minor wished to preach and speak to the Saracens." Finally, one brother is said to have announced that the order would be divided into three parts, of which only one, the part which went to the east, would be saved.

It is hard to view these statements as distinctively Olivian, although some are more so than others. It would, of course, be nothing short of astounding to find that Olivi identified John XXII with either of the two beasts mentioned in Revelation 13; yet in his exegesis of Revelation 13:11, having described the beast ascending from earth as the mass of pseudoprophets within Christianity, he displays some enthusiasm for the theory that their leader (or, in apocalyptic terms, the head of the beast) will be a pseudopope, and much of what he says about the beast's activities could easily be applied to John XXII and the poverty question. As to the statement concerning the Franciscan mission to the Saracens, one is of reminded of Olivi's contention that in the coming days of tribulation the Christian gospel will be heard more readily among the Greeks, Saracens, and Jews than among the Latins, or his belief that the Greeks will be illumined by spiritual men who will come to them from the Latin world at a time when the malicious jealousy of many Latins compels them to go. The third statement, which projects a threefold division of the order and limits salvation to a single part, is not really consistent with Olivi's thought.[56]

So far Olivi's connection with the difficulties in Tauris seems to be a rather tenuous one. The situation changes radically, however, when we come to the third part of the document presented by Rainerius to the cardinals. One wonders what sort of espionage activity the Dominicans practiced in order to obtain these personal letters. Reprehensible as it might have been, historians may be tempted to thank them for it.

In one letter, a friar at the monastery of St. Thadeus announces that William Saurati has begun to lecture on the gospel of Matthew "and completely follows Peter John." In another, the writer, presumably William himself, states that he is now lecturing on Matthew and requests the commentary on the Apocalypse, presumably Olivi's. Two other letters, this time from brothers at Tauris, seek William's advice. One is by a partisan of Michael of Cesena, who complains that William's letter answering their questions on the current leadership crisis was not satisfactory. The writer, George of Adria, apologizes for speaking irreverently, but says he did so "because I see great danger and do not fully understand your views." At one point in the letter he appeals to William's reputation as an Olivi scholar. "You know better than I," he says, "that among those who followed the doctrine of Peter John there were many who had a correct understanding of his doctrine and many who had a distorted one."

The other letter to William is by a genuinely troubled soul who has difficulty reading the apocalyptic timetable and seeks William's expert advice. Is the Antichrist supposed to be from the tribe of Dan? Is he to be a Christian? A pope? A lord in temporal matters, spiritual matters, or both? Is he to come in our time? What errors will he preach? Will all believe him? Will he go to Jerusalem? The writer, John of Florence, confides that he has wondered whether Peter of Corbaro, the Franciscan whom Lewis of Bavaria installed as antipope in 1328, might be the Antichrist, with Lewis himself functioning as the beast. Among the many matters which concern him John cites the fact that, although according to Olivi the conversion of schismatics and Saracens by the Franciscans should begin that year, the Dominicans seem to be doing better at it for the moment.

These letters show that, prohibitions and condemnations notwithstanding, Olivi was still read and admired within the Franciscan order. Moreover, by this time various interpretations of the provençal thinker had evolved and were being used to buttress different stands in the current dispute. Thus it is impossible to identify Olivi's supporters with a single "radical" or "spiritual" group in the 1330's.

William Saurati is a good example of the dangers inherent in linking Olivian apocalyptic with the radical wing of the order. According to the *Chronicle of the Twenty-four Generals*[57] he was one of the friars from Aquitaine sent to Armenia in 1332 by the minister general, Gerald Odonis, at the request of the uniate archbishop Zacharias. Fluent in Armenian, William preached, lectured, baptized, and translated with great effect during his stay in the east.

In other words, a devotee of Olivian apocalyptic was sent to Armenia by a minister general who had been elected in 1329 because he was a pliant man who would cooperate with John XXII and who had, in fact, been cooperating with him ever since.[58] Far from consider-

---

[56] Olivi identified the beast of Rev. 13:11 with a pseudopope in *Apoc.*, ff. 90vb-91ra and 93ra. His comments on the move from Latins to Saracens and Greeks are found in *Apoc.*, f. 73va and *Jn.*, f. 32vb.

[57] *Chronica XXIV generalium*, p. 506. See also Golubovich, 1906–1927: 3.

[58] See Moorman, 1968: pp. 321–328.

ing this posture an affront to God, William apparently remained loyal to Gerald at least as late as 1333, when the surviving letters were written. At the same time, he seems to have retained at least the grudging respect of brothers like George of Adria, who leaned toward Michael of Cesena.

The outcome of the Dominican campaign against the erring Franciscans of Tauris is unknown to us, but the *Chronicle of the Twenty-four Generals* may provide a hint.[59] Immediately after telling about the Franciscans who went east in 1332 and 1333, the chronicler, an Aquitainian like William Saurati and Gerald Odonis,[60] describes the fate of a certain saintly Franciscan "in those parts" who, along with eleven like-minded brothers, made such progress in holiness that the twelve were eventually transferred from their convent to various others. It seems that the devil, offended at their noteworthy sanctity, induced certain other Franciscans to suspect them. Although it is impossible to determine the meaning of this report, it is interesting that the document presented in Avignon by Rainerius of Vercelli contains the names of eleven Franciscans, including that of William Saurati.

At any rate, it is clear that Olivi was still being read within the order as late as the 1330's. His reputation during the rest of the Middle Ages has not been studied in any great detail, but the attitude of such respectable Franciscans as Bartholomew of Pisa in the late fourteenth century and Bernardino of Siena in the midfifteenth shows that he was not considered completely beyond the pale.[61] The manuscript evidence has not been examined systematically, but it will certainly show that Olivi's works were well received by a number of Franciscans in the fifteenth century, not all of them observants. Toward the end of the century Sixtus IV, a Franciscan who ruled as pope from 1471 to 1484, legitimized current practice by lifting the ban on Olivi's works. It was imposed again by the Franciscans themselves in 1500,[62] but some of Olivi's writings were printed in Paris and Venice during the first two decades of the sixteenth century. These works, along with a few others published in the eighteenth century on the mistaken assumption that they were written by St. Bonaventure, were the only writings by Olivi to be published until the end of the nineteenth century, when the Jesuit scholar Franz Ehrle wrote the series of essays which began Olivi's modern rehabilitation as an important medieval thinker. The obvious neglect of Olivi's writings during the intervening centuries can be accounted for partly by Olivi's shady reputation, but it is probably also due to the fact that scholarly interest was concentrated on a small number of major medieval theologians and philosophers.[63]

Twentieth-century scholars have begun to correct this deficiency. During the last few decades at least some of Olivi's works have been edited and a series of articles and monographs have clarified certain aspects of his thought.[64] No real consensus has emerged as yet, but the editions and studies have just begun. It remains to be seen whether Olivi's involvement in the information explosion will dispel or deepen the controversy that has surrounded him since the thirteenth century.

XII. SOME FINAL OBSERVATIONS

It is almost impossible to consider Olivi's story without asking two questions about it. First, are his difficulties explicable? Knowing as much as we do about his career and the debates which surrounded him, can we see why he aroused such a furor?

The second question is whether his difficulties were justified. In other words, did he deserve the criticism directed against him? This time the question itself has its difficulties, since it assumes the existence of some transhistorical criterion by which Olivi's views can be measured. Such criteria do exist, and we tend to apply them consciously or unconsciously in cases like the present one; yet they vary wildly among different individuals and there seems little justification for inflicting the author's own perspective on the unsuspecting reader at this point.

One can, of course, rephrase the question in such a way as to make room for a respectable amount of historical relativism. We can ask whether the censured views were so obviously at variance with commonly held beliefs of his time that one might have expected them to be condemned. Once the question is cut down to these proportions, it is little more than a subdivision of the first question.

The reader, having made his way through the first eleven chapters of this study, will at least be in a position to appreciate how complicated such questions can be. In Olivi's case we must try to distinguish between his views as presented by his enemies and his views as he himself understood them. Both must be placed in the context of intellectual developments during the period. This means relating them, not to a static notion of orthodoxy, but to an organic, dynamic, and thus somewhat amorphous body of thought which was changing even while the campaign against Olivi was being waged. Moreover, one must constantly speak of particular issues, not of Olivi's thought in general. Finally, serious attention must be paid to the precise historical situation in which his views were debated.

---

[59] *Chronica XXIV generalium*, p. 507. See also Golubovich, 1906–1927: 3: pp. 451 f.

[60] See Anglade, 1913.

[61] See Bartholomaeus, 1906/1912: pp. 340 and 540; Pacetti, 1945: pp. 109–130; or Pacetti's comments in his edition of Olivi's *Quaestiones quattuor de domina*, pp. 30*–59*.

[62] Ehrle, 1887: pp. 457 f.

[63] This possibility is suggested by Douie, 1932: p. 265.

[64] For Olivi's fate since Ehrle see Flood's introduction to *Rule Commentary*, pp. 1–23.

It is impossible to weigh Olivi's difficulties correctly unless one places them in the context of such ongoing disputes as the battle over Aristotle at Paris and the battle over poverty within the Franciscan camp. All of this is admittedly a big order. Nevertheless, a few conclusions can be drawn at this point, although modestly and with one eye demurely directed toward future research.

In the areas of philosophy and theology we examined several issues that had remarkable staying power: marriage, baptismal grace, the sacramental character, the divine essence, the predicaments, and the soul as form of the body. In these cases we saw that Olivi was outside the main current of Franciscan thought in his day; yet we also saw that in most areas Olivi's views were not unique. In none of them can one say that Olivi's position offered a clear and indisputable danger to Christian dogma as the medieval church understood it. In some areas, far from attacking traditionally accepted positions, Olivi was himself profoundly conservative inasmuch as he continued to raise old questions and weigh old points of view which were going out of fashion in his own time. Such is certainly the case in his discussions of marriage, infant baptism, and the divine essence. Olivi's conservatism might also be said to have played a role in the disputed areas of his thought insofar as his suspicions regarding Aristotle, "the god of this age," encouraged greater flexibility in the consideration of philosophical questions such as those concerning the predicaments.

Nevertheless, Olivi's conservatism was tempered by a striking originality which allowed him to ring some surprising changes on the old tunes. The full measure of this originality is seen in his thoughts on the soul as form of the body and the sacramentality of marriage/monasticism/virginity. Perhaps he was a bit too original for his own health. It is an attribute not always valued by scholars and administrators.

In the area of Franciscan poverty, as in philosophy and theology, certain aspects of Olivi's thought were attacked with monotonous regularity. As we have seen, these involved *usus pauper,* procurators, burial, and Franciscan bishops. Here again we can affirm that the censured views were hardly Olivi's own individual whims, but were held by a sizable faction within his order. Moreover, it would be hard to brand them as radical. Again the idea of Olivi as a conservative might be said to have some validity. Certainly it would be fair to say that his position on poverty represented an attempt to protect old values from the threat of new institutional realities. Perhaps David Flood is right in suggesting that "Olivi's trouble came from attempts of others to change the institution or from their inclination to let it drift, while he sought to conserve and strengthen it."[1]

---

[1] Introduction to *Rule Commentary,* p. 90.

The various issues mentioned above continued to exercise scholars from the 1280's through the council of Vienne. After the council, attention was increasingly focused upon another area, Olivi's theology of history. Here there can be little question as to why Olivi was attacked. His understanding of the church and its development in time was diametrically opposed to the one held by Pope John XXII and the theologians who surrounded him. It is important to recognize, however, that the offending elements in Olivi's thought were not all original creations. Some of them were common features of Franciscan thought in his time. When Olivi lauded the absolute poverty of Christ and his apostles or eulogized Francis as the *renovator* of that poverty, he was saying things that any Franciscan would have understood and appreciated; yet such sentiments are intimately related to the historical perspective which John's advisers found disturbing. Olivi did go well beyond most of his confreres in elaborating the future role of the order and working out its implications for church government. Thus, while John XXII eventually clashed with the order on the questions of poverty past and present, in Olivi's case the future was also at issue, and understandably so.

Like Olivi's theology of history, his thoughts on Christ's side wound became an important issue rather late. The first evidence of dissatisfaction on this score stems from the fourteenth century. Here again, however, one can understand why Olivi was in for trouble. His alternate reading of John was questionable, and his reason for suggesting it was even more so. It is not surprising that some scholars objected.

It seems safe to conclude from what we have said so far that the various censures directed against Olivi's writings cannot be explained simply by examining his views in the light of what would pass for orthodox thought in his own time. Although it is easy to see why his comments on Christ's side wound invited criticism and why his theology of history must have proved offensive to the pope, purely doctrinal comparisons will offer no obvious reason why the majority of the disputed theses should have been attacked as energetically as they were. The intensity of the assault on Olivi can be appreciated only when it is placed in the context of historical events. In the first place, we must realize that Olivi wrote in a period when theology was developing rapidly and theologians were beginning to become concerned about its direction. Both Olivi and his detractors reflect the predicament of a generation which sought to maintain stability in the midst of change. The boundary between orthodoxy and heterodoxy was quite unclear, yet scholars and ecclesiastics felt particularly called upon to defend that boundary with all the weapons at their disposal. The result is seen in the condemnations of the 1270's and beyond. Thus Olivi was placed in an environment which proved especially conducive to attacks on his philosophy and theology.

We must not forget the other body of thought which was developing rapidly in Olivi's time: Franciscan ideology. We have seen that Olivi began his teaching career at a monent when the order was witnessing serious differences of opinion regarding the theory and practice of poverty. Here again Olivi was caught in an environment which encouraged attacks on his thought. It is obvious that the poverty dispute contributed to assaults on all areas of Olivi's thought, since those who disliked his view of *usus pauper* found it profitable to strike out at any area where his opinions seemed questionable. Nevertheless, there is no reason to portray the poverty dispute as the sole cause of such attacks. It would be more accurate to say that the dispute made Franciscan theologians consider Olivi's purported errors more seriously and at greater length than might otherwise have been the case.

Finally, we must recognize the impact of the challenges to ecclesiastical authority which rocked the church in the early fourteenth century. Granting that the condemnation of the Revelation commentary reflected clearcut ideological differences between Olivi and his censors, it is still questionable whether the condemnation would have taken place if the commentary had not provided inspiration for a grass-roots revolt against ecclesiastical authority, a revolt which developed in the wake of the conventual-spiritual dispute and the tension between John XXII and the order. Here again the attacks on Olivi's thought are fully appreciated only by placing them in their historical context.

Having said so much, however, we must acknowledge that the historical context is largely unknown. We are painting with an extremely broad brush when we speak of the conflict over Aristotle, the spiritual-conventual dispute, and the trouble between John XXII and the Franciscan order. The historical context of Olivi's difficulties would be intelligible to us only if we could gain some knowledge of Olivi's immediate environment. Unfortunately we are largely ignorant of such matters. We know almost nothing about the personalities with whom Olivi had to deal in southern France, just as we know almost nothing about events in that area during Olivi's lifetime.

In fact, embarrassingly little is known about certain important aspects of Olivi himself. Those who loved and detested him in southern France dealt with him, not as a disembodied series of *quaestiones*, but as a man. They reacted to the way he looked, spoke, and acted, all of which is lost to the modern historian. We are not entirely ignorant concerning his personality, since his writings provide some insight in this respect. Nevertheless, we must recognize that a great deal has escaped us. We will never understand that peculiar chemistry which produced veneration in Olivi's followers and resulted in the Olivi cult after his death. We find such things hard enough to grasp when we encounter them in our own time. How can we expect to comprehend them in the case of a man who has now been dead for seven centuries?

BIBLIOGRAPHY OF WORKS CITED

It is important to emphasize that the following is a list of works cited in this book, not an exhaustive bibliography of writings by and about Olivi. The latter sort of bibliography is, indeed, unnecessary, having been supplied by Servus Gieben, "Bibliographia Oliviana (1885–1967)," *Collectanea Franciscana* 38 (1968): pp. 167–195. Moreover, Fr. Gieben plans to bring his bibliography up to date in the near future.

It should also be noted that the following is by no means a selective bibliography. Some of the works cited here would have sought in vain for this author's *imprimatur* if he had been in a position to judge, while other writings not included in this bibliography should be considered required reading for Olivi scholars. The thoughtful and penetrating contributions of Ernst Stadter particularly come to mind in this connection.

In the case of unpublished works, I have streamlined the bibliography by listing only the manuscript cited in the footnotes, although in most cases that manuscript was compared with others. My choice of manuscripts in this regard should not be taken as a critical judgment.

Like others before me, I have had to face the problem of how to list the many primary sources published by Franz Ehrle in *Archiv für Literatur- und Kirchengeschichte des Mittelalters* (Berlin, 1885–1900), cited in this bibliography as *Archiv*. My own solution is to list them by the *incipit* unless some obvious short title can be used.

BY OLIVI

Biblical Commentaries

Lectura super Genesim, MS. Florence, Bibl. Naz. Conv. Sopp. G 1. 671.
Lectura super Isaiam, MS. Padua, Univ. 1540.
Lectura super prophetas minores, MS. Paris, Bibl. Nat. lat. 507.
Lectura super Iob, MS. Florence, Bibl. Laur. Conv. sopp. 240.
Lectura super Ecclesiasten, MS. Rome, Vat. Urb. lat. 480.
Lectura super Mattheum, MS. Oxford, New College 49.
Lectura super Marcum, MS. Rome, Vat. Ottab. lat. 3302.
Lectura super Lucam, MS. Rome, Vat. Ottab. lat. 3302.
Lectura super Ioannem, MS. Florence, Bibl. Laur. Plut. 10 dext. 8.
Lectura super apocalypsim, MS. Rome, Bibl. Ang. 382.

Quaestiones de perfectione evangelica (as numbered in MS. Rome, Vat. lat. 4986)

1. *An contemplatio sit melior ex suo genere quam omnis alia actio.*
2. *An contemplatio principalius sit in intellectu quam voluntate.*
3. *An studere sit opus de genere suo perfectum.*
4. *An aliquod opus vitae activae praeter regimen animarum et praedicationem sit melius ex suo genere quam studium.* Questions 1–4 published in Emmen, Aquilinus and Feliciano Simoncioli. 1963–1964. "La dottrina dell'Olivi sulla contemplazione, la vita attiva e mista." *Studi Francescani* 60: pp. 108–167.
5. *An sit melius aliquid facere ex voto quam sine voto,* in: Emmen, Aquilinus. 1966. "La dottrina dell'Olivi sul valore religioso dei voti." *Studi Francescani* 63: pp. 88–108.
6. *An virginitas sit simpliciter melior matrimonio,* in: Emmen, Aquilinus. 1974. "Verginità e matrimonio nella valutazione dell'Olivi." *Studi Francescani* 64: pp. 11–57.
7. *An votum vitandi suspectum consortium vel colloquium implicetur in consilio evangelico,* MS. Rome, Vat. lat. 4986.
8. *An status altissime paupertatis sit simpliciter melior omni statu divitiarum,* MS. Florence, Bibl. Laur. 448.
9. *An usus pauper includatur in consilio seu in voto paupertatis evangelice, ita quod sit de eius substantia et integritate,* MS. Florence, Bibl. Laur. 448.
10. *An pauperibus evangelicis sit perfectius et convenientius victum suum adquirere per mendicitatis questum aut per manuale opus seu laboritium,* MS. Florence, Bibl. Laur. 448.
11. *An vovere alteri homini obedientiam in omnibus, que non sunt contraria anime et evangelice regule seu perfectioni sit perfectionis evangelicae,* MS. Florence, Bibl. Laur. 448.
12. *An romano pontifici in fide et moribus sit ab omnibus catholicis tanquam regule inerrabili obediendum,* in: Maccarrone, Michele. 1949. "Una questione inedita dell'Olivi sull'infallibilità del Papa." *Rivisita di Storia della Chiesa in Italia* 3: pp. 309–343.
13. *An papa possit renuntiare papatui,* in: Oliger, Livarius. 1918. "Petri Iohannis Olivi de renuntiatione papae Coelestini V quaestio et epistola." *Archivum Franciscanum Historicum* 11: pp. 309–373.
14. *An papa possit in omni voto dispensare et specialiter in votis evangelicis,* MS. Florence, Bibl. Laur. 448.
15. *An vivere de prebendis vel quibuscumque redditibus vel vivere de possessionibus absque vendicatione cuiuscunque dominii vel iuris possit esse licitum pauperibus evangelicis,* MS. Florence, Bibl. Laur. 448.
16. *An professio paupertatis evangelice et apostolice possit licite ad talem modum vivendi reduci, quod amodo sufficienter vivat de possessionibus et redditibus a papa vel mundanis principibus certis procuratoribus commissis,* MS. Rome, Vat. Lat. 4986.
17. *An vovens evangelium vel aliquam regulam simpliciter et absque determinatione teneatur observare omnia, que in eis sunt contenta,* in: Delorme, Ferdinand. 1941. "Fr. P. J. Olivi quaestio de voto regulam aliquam profitentis." *Antonianum* 16: pp. 131–164.

Other

Amplior declaratio quinti articuli, qui est de divina essentia, in: Laberge, Damasus. 1935–1936. "Fr. Petri Ioannis Olivi, O.F.M., tria scripta sui ipsius apologetica annorum 1283 et 1285." *Archivum Franciscanum Historicum* 29: pp. 98–141, 365–395.
Commentarius in quattuor libros sententiarum, MSS. Padova, Univ. 637, 1540 and 2094.
De perlegendis philosophorum libris, in: Delorme, Ferdinand. 1941. "Fr. Petri Joannis Olivi tractatus 'De perlegendis philosophorum libris.'" *Antonianum* 16: pp. 31–44.
De veritate indulgentiae de Portiuncula, in: *Acta ordinis minorum.* 1895. 14: pp. 139–145.
Epistola ad Conradum de Offida, in: Oliger, Livarius. 1918. "Petri Iohannis Olivi de renuntiatione papae Coelestini V quaestio et epistola." *Archivum Franciscanum Historicum* 11: pp. 309–373.
Epistola ad R., in: Petrus Iohannis Olivi. 1509. *Quodlibeta* (Venice), ff. 51v-53r.
Epistola ad regis Sicilie filios, in: *Archiv* 3: pp. 534–540.
Expositio super regulam, in: Flood, David. 1972. *Olivi's Rule Commentary* (Wiesbaden).
Impugnatio XXXVII articulorum, in: Petrus Iohannis Olivi. 1509. *Quodlibeta* (Venice), ff. 42r–49v.

Quaestio de trinitate, in Schmaus, Michael. 1930. *Der Liber Propugnatorius des Thomas Anglicus und die Lehruntreschiede zwischen Thomas von Aquin und Duns Scotus* (Münster i.W.), Teil 2, Band 2: pp. 143–228.

Quaestio quid ponat ius vel dominium, in: Delorme, Ferdinand. 1945. "Question de P. J. Olivi 'Quid ponat ius vel dominium' ou encore 'De signis voluntariis.'" *Antonianum* 20: pp. 309–330.

Quaestiones in secundum librum sententiarum. 1921–1926 (3 v., Quaracchi).

Quaestiones quattuor de domina. 1954 (Quaracchi).

Quod regula fratrum minorum excludit omnem proprietatem, in: *Firmamentum trium ordinum.* 1511 (Paris). 4: ff. 107vb–111rb.

Quodlibeta. 1509 (Venice).

Quoniam contra paupertatem evangelicam, MS. Rome, Vat. lat. 4986.

Responsio P. Ioannis ad aliqua dicta per quosdam magistros Parisienses de suis quaestionibus excerpta, in: Laberge, Damasus. 1935–1936. "Fr. Petri Ioannis Olivi, O.F.M., tria scripta sui ipsius apologetica annorum 1283 et 1285." *Archivum Franciscanum Historicum* 28: pp. 126–130.

Responsio quam fecit P. Ioannis ad litteram magistrorum praesentatam sibi in Avinione, in: Laberge, Damasus. 1935–1936. "Fr. Petri Ioannis Olivi, O.F.M., tria scripta sui ipsius apologetica annorum 1283 et 1285." *Archivum Franciscanum Historicum* 28: pp. 135–155, 374–407.

Tractatus de merito Christi, MSS. Rome, Vat. Borgh. 173 and Vat. Borgh. 54.

Tractatus de sacramentis, MS. Rome, Vat. lat. 4986.

BY OTHERS

Acta capitulorum ordinis praedicatorum, in: *Monumenta ordinis fratrum praedicatorum historica.* 1898 (Rome). 3.

ALBERTUS MAGNUS. 1890–1899. *Opera* (38 v., Paris).

ALVERNY, MARIE-THÉRÈSE D'. 1974. "Un Adversaire de Saint Thomas: Petrus Ioannis Olivi." *St. Thomas Aquinus, 1274–1974* (Toronto), pp. 179–218.

AMORÓS, LEO. 1931. "Series condemnationum et processuum contra doctrinam et sequaces Petri Ioannis Olivi." *Archivum Franciscanum Historicum* 24: pp. 495–512.

—— 1934. "Aegidii Romani impugnatio doctrinae Petri Ioannis Olivi an. 1311-12, nunc primum in lucem edita." *Archivum Franciscanum Historicum* 27: pp. 399–451.

ANGELO CLARENO. 1885. *Epistola excusatoria,* in: *Archiv* 1: pp. 521–533.

—— 1885. *Fratribus universis,* in: *Archiv* 1: pp. 543–544.

—— 1886. *Historia septem tribulationum ordinis minorum,* in: *Archiv* 2: pp. 108–336.

ANGLADE, MARIE-PASCAL. 1913. "Sur la patrie de Fr. Gerard Odonis, M.G." *Archivum Franciscanum Historicum* 6: pp. 392–396.

AUGUSTINUS TRIUMPHUS. 1911. *Tractatus contra divinatores et sompniatores,* in: Scholz, Richard. 1911. *Unbekannte kirchenpolitische Streitschriften aus der Zeit Ludwigs des Bayern* (Rome) 2: pp. 485–490.

BALIĆ, CARLO. 1958. "The Mediaeval Controversy over the Immaculate Conception up to the Death of Scotus." *The Dogma of the Immaculate Conception* (Notre Dame), pp. 161–212.

BARTHOLOMAEUS DE PISA. 1906/1912. *Liber de conformitate Beati Francisci ad vitam domini nostri Jesu Christi,* in: *Analecta Franciscana* 4–5.

BENZ, ERNST. 1964. *Ecclesia Spiritualis* (Stuttgart).

BERNARDUS GUIDONIS. 1886. *Practica inquisitionis heretice pravitatis* (Paris).

BETTINI, ORAZIO. 1958. "Olivi di fronte ad Aristotele." *Studi Francescani* 55: pp. 176–197.

BETTONI, EFREM. 1959. *Le Dottrine filosofiche di Pier di Giovanni Olivi* (Milan).

BIHL, MICHAEL. 1929. "Statuta generalia ordinis edita in capitulis generalibus celebratis Narbonae an. 1260, Assisi an. 1279 atque Parisiis an. 1292." *Archivum Franciscanum Historicum* 34: pp. 13–94, 284–358.

BURKITT, F. C. 1922. "Ubertino da Casale and a Variant Reading." *Journal of Theological Studies* 23: pp. 186–188.

BURR, DAVID. 1971. "The Apocalyptic Element in Olivi's Critique of Aristotle." *Church History* 40: pp. 15–29.

—— 1971. "Petrus Ioannis Olivi and the Philosophers." *Franciscan Studies* 31: pp. 41–71.

—— 1972. "Olivi on Marriage: The Conservative as Prophet." *Journal of Medieval and Renaissance Studies* 2: pp. 183–204.

—— 1972. "Scotus and Transubstantiation." *Mediaeval Studies* 34: pp. 336–360.

—— 1974. "Quantity and Eucharistic Presence: The Debate from Olivi through Ockham." *Collectanea Franciscana* 44: pp. 5–44.

—— 1975. "Olivi and Baptismal Grace." *Franziskanische Studien* 57: pp. 1–24.

BONAGRATIA DE BERGAMO. 1887. *Nuper controversia,* in: *Archiv* 3: pp. 36–41.

BONVENTURA. 1882–1902. *Opera* (11 v., Quaracchi).

CALLEBAUT, ANDREAS. 1929. "Acta capituli generalis Mediolani celebrati an. 1285." *Archivum Franciscanum Historicum* 22: p. 273–291.

Chartularium universitatis parisiensis. 1889 (Paris).

Chronica XXIV generalium. 1897 (Quaracchi).

Corpus iuris canonici. 1959 (Graz).

CROWLEY, THEODORE. 1950. *Roger Bacon* (Louvain).

DANIEL, E. RANDOLPH. 1968. "A Re-examination of the Origins of Franciscan Joachitism." *Speculum* 43: pp. 671–676.

—— 1969. "Apocalyptic Conversion: The Joachite Alternative to the Crusades." *Traditio* 25: pp. 127–154.

—— 1975. *The Franciscan Concept of Mission in the High Middle Ages* (Lexington, Kentucky).

DELORME, FERDINAND. 1921. "Constitutiones provinciae Provinciae saec. XIII–XIV." *Archivum Franciscanum Historicum* 14: pp. 415–434.

—— 1945. "Notice et extraits d'un manuscrit franciscain." *Collectanea Franciscana* 15: pp. 5–91.

DENIFLE, HEINRICH. 1885. "Das Evangelium aeternum und die Commission zu Anagni." *Archiv* 1: pp. 49–142.

DENIFLE, HEINRICH, and FRANZ EHRLE. 1885–1900. *Archiv für Literatur- und Kirchengeschichte des Mittelalters* (7 v., Graz).

DMITREWSKI, M. 1924–1925. "Fr. Bernard Délicieux, O.F.M., sa lutte contre l'inquisition de Carcassonne et d'Albi, son procès 1297–1319." *Archivum Franciscanum Historicum* 17: pp. 183–214, 313–333, 457–488; 18: pp. 3–32.

DOUCET, VICTORINUS. 1933. "P. J. Olivi et l'Immaculée Conception." *Archivum Franciscanum Historicum* 26: pp. 560–563.

—— 1935. "De operibus manuscriptis Fr. Petri Ioannis Olivi in bibliotheca Universitatis Patavinae asservatis." *Archivum Franciscanum Historicum* 28: pp. 426–441.

DOUIE, DECIMA. 1932. *The Nature and the Effect of the Heresy of the Fraticelli* (Manchester).

DURANDUS DE S. PORCIANO. 1571. *In Petri Lombardi sententias theologicas commentariorum libri IIII* (Venice).

EASTON, STEWART. 1952. *Roger Bacon and his Search for a Universal Science* (Oxford).

EHRLE, FRANZ. 1885–1888. "Die Spiritualen, ihr Verhältniss zum Franciscanerorden und zu den Fraticellen." *Archiv* 1: pp. 509–569; 2: pp. 106–164; 3: pp. 553–623; 4: pp. 1–200.

—— 1886. "Zur Vorgeschichte des Concils von Vienne." *Archiv* 2: pp. 353–416.

—— 1887. "Petrus Johannis Olivi, sein Leben und seine Schriften." *Archiv* **3**: pp. 409–552.
EMMEN, AQUILINUS. 1962. "Doctrina Petri Ioannis Olivi de baptismo parvulorum effectibus." *Antonianum* **37**: pp. 350–392.
—— 1967. "Virginità e matrimonio nella valutazione dell'Olivi." *Studi Francescani* **64**: pp. 11–57.
EMMEN, AQUILINUS, and FELICIANO SIMONCIOLI. 1963. "La dottrina dell'Olivi sulla contemplazione, la vita attiva e mista." *Studi Francescani* **60**: pp. 382–445; **61**: pp. 108–167.
FELDER, H. 1904. *Geschichte des wissenshaftlichen Studien im Franziskanerorden bis um Mitte des 13. Jahrhunderts* (Freiburg i. Br.).
FUSSENEGGER, GEROLDUS. 1933. "Definitiones capituli generalis Argentinae (1282)." *Archivum Franciscanum Historicum* **26**: pp. 127–140.
—— 1957. "Relatio commissionis in concilio Viennensi institutae ad decretalem "Exivi de paradiso' praeparandum." *Archivum Franciscanum Historicum* **50**: pp. 155–177.
GOLUBOVICH, GIROLAMO. 1906–27. *Biblioteca bio-bibliografica della terra sancta e dell'oriente francescano* (5 v., Quaracchi).
GRATIEN DE PARIS. 1913. "Une lettre inédite de Pierre de Jean Olivi." *Études Franciscaines* **29**: pp. 414–422.
—— 1928. *Histoire de la fondation et de l'evolution de l'ordre des frères mineurs au XIIIe siècle* (Paris).
GUILLELMUS DE OCKHAM. 1494–1496. *Opera Plurima* (4 v., Lyon).
HADRIANUS A KRIZOVLJAN. 1957. "Controversia doctrinalis inter magistros franciscanos et Sigerum de Brabant." *Collectanea Franciscana* **27**: pp. 121–165.
—— 1961. "Primordia scholae franciscanae et thomismus." *Collectanea Franciscana* **31**: pp. 133–175.
HEYNCK, VALENS. 1956. "Zur Datierung der Sentenzenkommentare des Petrus Johannis Olivi und des Petrus de Trabibus." *Franziskanische Studien* **38**: pp. 371–398.
—— 1964. "Zur Datierung einiger Schriften des Petrus Johannis Olivi." *Franziskanische Studien* **46**: pp. 355–364.
HEYSSE, ALBANUS. 1918. "Descriptio codicis bibliothecae Laurentianae Florentinae, S. Crucis, plut. 31 sin. cod. 3." *Archivum Franciscanum Historicum* **11**: pp. 251–269.
HOCEDEZ, E. 1932. "Le Condemnation de Gilles de Rome." *Recherches de Théologie Ancienne et Médiévale* **4**: pp. 34–58.
IOACHIM DA FIORE. 1527. *Expositio in apocalypsim* (Venice).
IOHANNES DUNS SCOTUS. 1598. *In quartum librum sententiarum perutiles quaestiones* (Venice).
JARRAUX, LOUIS. 1933. "Pierre Jean Olivi, sa vie, sa doctrine." *Études Franciscaines* **45**: pp. 129–153, 277–298, 513–529.
KOCH, JOSEPH. 1927. *Durandus de S. Porciano* (Münster i. W.).
—— 1930. "Philosophische und theologische Irrtumslisten von 1270 1329." *Mélanges Mandonnet* (Paris), pp. 309–329.
—— 1930. "Die Verurteilung Olivis auf dem Konzil von Vienne und ihre Vorgeschichte." *Scholastik* **5**: pp. 489–522.
—— 1933. "Der Prozess gegen die Postille Olivis zur Apokalypse." *Recherches de Théologie Ancienne et Médiévale* **5**: pp. 302–315.
LAMBERT, MALCOLM. 1961. *Franciscan Poverty* (London).
—— 1972. "The Franciscan Crisis under John XXII." *Franciscan Studies* **32**: pp. 123–143.
LEFF, GORDON. 1967. *Heresy in the Later Middle Ages* (2 v., Manchester).
—— 1968. *Paris and Oxford Universities in the Thirteenth and Fourteenth Centuries* (New York).
Littera magistrorum, in: Baluze, Stephan. 1678. *Stephani Baluze Miscellaneorum* (Paris), pp. 213–267.
Littera septem sigillarum, in: Fussenegger, Geroldus. 1954. "'Littera septem sigillorum' contra doctrinam Petri Ioannis Olivi edita." *Archivum Franciscanum Historicum* **47**: pp. 45–53.
LITTLE, A. G., P. MANDONNET and P. SABATIER. 1903. *Opuscules de critique historique* (Paris).
LUTHER, MARTIN. 1883– . *Werke* (67 v., Weimar).
—— 1912–1921. *Tischreden* (6 v., Weimar).
MCGINN, BERNARD. 1971. "The Abbot and the Doctors." *Church History* **40**: pp. 30–47.
MAIER, ANNALIESE. 1951. "Per la storia del processo contro l'Olivi." *Rivista di Storia della Chiesa in Italia* **5**: pp. 326–339.
—— 1955. *Metaphysische Hintergründe der Spätscholastischen Naturphilosophie* (Rome).
—— 1964/67. *Ausgehendes Mittelalter* (2 v., Rome).
MANSELLI, RAOUL. 1955. *La "Lectura super Apocalypsim" di Pietro di Giovanni Olivi* (Rome).
—— 1959. *Spirituali e Beghini in Provenza* (Rome).
—— 1972. "Une grande figure Serignanaise: Pierre de Jean Olivi." *Études Franciscaines* **12**: pp. 69–83.
MAY, WILLIAM. 1955. "The Confession of Prous Boneta, Heretic and Heresiarch." *Essays in Medieval Life and Thought* (New York), pp. 3–30.
MOORMAN, JOHN. 1968. *History of the Franciscan Order* (Oxford).
NICHOLAUS EYMERIC. *Tractatus de conceptione B. Virginis,* MS. Rome, Vat. lat. 10497.
OLIGER, LIVARIUS. 1918. "Petri Iohannis Olivi de renuntiatione papae Coelestini V quaestio et epistola." *Archivum Franciscanum Historicum* **11**: pp. 309–373.
PACETTI, DIONYSIUS. 1945. "Gli scritti di San Bernardino da Siena." *S. Bernardino da Siena* (Milan), pp. 109–130.
PARTEE, CARTER. 1960. "Peter John Olivi: Historical and Doctrinal Study." *Franciscan Studies,* **20**: pp. 215–260.
PÁSZTOR, EDITH. 1958. "Le Polemiche sulla 'Lectura super Apocalipsim' di Pietro di Giovanni Olivi fino alla sua condanna." *Bullettino dell'Istituto Storico Italiano per il Medio Evo e Archivio Muratoriano* **70**: pp. 365–424.
—— 1970. "Giovanni XXII e il Gioachimismo di Pietro di Giovanni Olivi." *Bullettino dell'Istituto Storico Italiano per il Medio Evo e Archivio Muratoriano* **82**: pp. 81–111.
PETRUS DE PALUDE. 1493. *In quartum sententiarum* (Venice).
PETRUS LOMBARDUS. 1916. *Libri IV sententiarum* (Quaracchi).
Quod doctrina Petri Ioannis fuit iuste damnata, in: DELORME, FERDINAND. 1945. "Notice et extraits d'un manuscrit franciscain." *Collectanea Franciscana* **15**: pp. 5–91.
RATZINGER, JOSEPH. 1959. *Die Geschichtstheologie des heiligen Bonaventura* (Munich).
RAYMUNDUS DE FRONCIACHO. 1887. *Sol ortus,* in: *Archiv* **3**: pp. 7–32.
RAYMUNDUS DE FRONCIACHO and BONAGRATIA DE BERGAMO. 1886. *In nomine domini,* in: *Archiv* **2**: pp. 365–374.
RAYMUNDUS DE FRONCIACHO and BONAGRATIA DE BERGAMO. 1887. *Infrascripta dant,* in: *Archiv* **3**: pp. 141–160.
REEVES, MARJORIE. 1969. *The influence of Prophecy in the Later Middle Ages* (Oxford).
REEVES, MARJORIE, and BEATRICE HIRSCH-REICH. 1972. *The Figurae of Joachim of Fiore* (Oxford).
RICHARDUS DE MEDIAVILLA. 1591. *Quodlibeta* (Brescia).
SALIMBENE. 1966. *Chronica* (Bari).
SBARALEA, J. H. 1908–1936. *Supplementum ad scriptores trium ordinum S. Francisci* (3 v., Rome).
SBARALEA, J. H., and C. EUBEL. 1759–1904. *Bullarium Franciscanum* (7 v., Rome).
SCHMAUS, MICHAEL. 1930. *Der Liber Propugnatorius des Thomas Anglicus und die Lehrunterschiede zwischen Thomas von Aquin und Duns Scotus* (Münster i. W.).
SCHNEIDER, THEODOR. 1973. *Die Einheit des Menschen* (Münster).

SOUTHERN, R. W. 1972. "Aspects of the European Tradition of Historical Writing: 3. History as Prophecy." *Transactions of the Royal Historical Society* **22**: pp. 159–180.

STANISLAO DA CAMPAGNOLA. 1971. *L'Angelo del sesto sigillo e l' "alter Christus"* (Rome).

STEENBERGHEN, FERNAND VAN. 1970. *Aristotle in the West* (Louvain).

THOMAS AQUINAS. 1936. *Tractatus de unitate intellectus* (Rome).

—— 1964–1966. *Summa theologiae* (60 v., New York).

THOMAS, ANTOINE. 1913. "Le vraie nom du frere mineur Petrus Johannis Olivi." *Annales du Midi* **25**: pp. 68–69.

TIERNEY, BRIAN. 1972. *Origins of Papal Infallibility* (Leiden).

TOCCO, FELICE. 1909. *Studi Francescani* (Naples).

UBERTINO DA CASALE. 1886. *Sanctitati apostolicae,* in: *Archiv* **2**: pp. 377–416.

—— 1887. *Declaratio,* in: *Archiv* **3**: pp. 162–195.

—— 1887. *Sanctitas vestra,* in: *Archiv* **3**: pp. 51–89.

—— 1961. *Arbor vitae crucifixae Jesu* (Torino).

WADDING, LUKE. 1931–1951. *Annales minorum* (30 v., Quaracchi).

INDEX

Ad conditorem, 82–83
Ad fructus uberes, 7
Aegidius Romanus, 9, 77, 79
Albert the Great, 37
Albigensian crusade, 33
Alexander of Alexandria, 81
Amici spirituales, 66
Angel as a separate species, 30
Angelo Clareno, 7, 22(fn.), 35–36, 40, 42, 67–68, 73–74, 81(fn.), 82
Antichrist, 10, 13, 21–24, 30–31, 72–73, 81–83, 89
Apocalyptic thought, 9–10, 17–24, 30–35, 39, 66, 70–78, 81–90
Apologia of 1285, 42–44, 46, 50–51, 53–54, 61–62, 65, 67, 79
Aristotle, 8, 13, 21, 25, 27–31, 43, 53–54, 56, 59–60, 62, 91–92
Arius, 18, 30–31
Arlotto of Prato, 8, 38, 41–42, 67
Arnold Galhardi, 38
Arnold of Roquefeuil, 38, 67
Assisi, 9, 11, 15
Augustine of Hippo, 18, 27
Augustinian order, 9
Augustinus Triumphus, 79
Authority and obedience, 21–24, 33, 39, 42–43, 52, 64, 69–78, 81–92
Averroes, 8, 28, 30, 43, 59
Avicenna, 8

Baptism, 46–50, 65, 75, 77, 79–80, 91
Bartholomew of Pisa, 6, 90
Beguines, 72–74, 82, 86–88
Berengar Talon, 82
Bernard Délicieux, 76
Bernard Gui, 5, 73, 87–88
Bernardino of Siena, 90
Bettini, Orazio, 28
Bettoni, Efrem, 31, 53–54, 60–61, 80, 83
Béziers, 5, 33, 81, 86
Bible, interpretation of, 9–10, 13–14, 17–24, 25, 30–35, 72–73, 88–90
Bishops, Franciscan, 62–65, 75, 77, 79, 91
Bonagratia of Bergamo, 38, 75–77
Bonagratia of St. John in Persiceto, 8, 14, 37–42, 78
Bonaventure, 6–7, 10, 14–15, 17, 20(fn.), 28–31, 57, 62, 66, 77, 90
Boniface VIII, 69, 74, 77
Books, in relation to Franciscan poverty, 16, 32
Brother Ar., 38–40, 54–55, 59–61, 66
Burial, 65, 75, 78–79, 90

Carcassonne, 81
Carnal church, 20–24, 33, 35, 81, 83–85
Cathari, 18, 21, 30, 33
Celestine V, 23–24, 69–70, 72–73
Censures and condemnations of Olivi, 14, 35–66, 74, 79–80, 83–87
Character, sacramental, 46–50, 75, 77, 91
Christ, and eucharistic presence, 56–61; and Francis, 19–22, 84, 86–87, 91; and Franciscan poverty, 10, 12, 14, 16, 20–23, 33, 62, 64, 71, 81, 83–87, 91; and the third age, 17–23, 84–86; as a pattern for suffering, 22, 32, 39, 88
Chronicle of the Twenty-four Generals, 41–42, 67–69, 89–90

Clement V, 75, 79–82
Clothing, Franciscan, 62, 70–71, 81
Commission of eight (1318–1319), 83–85
Commission of seven (1283), 41–44, 50, 61–62, 65–66, 69, 75. See also *Letter of the Seven Seals* and *Rotulus* of 1283
Commission of seven (1311), 78–79
Commission of three (1311), 78
Commission of twelve (1319), 85
Conrad of Offida, 20, 66, 69–71
Constantine, 64, 86
Contemplation, 19, 22, 24–25, 34–35, 76
Cult at Narbonne, 73–75, 83, 85–86
Cum inter nonnullos, 83, 87
Cyprian, 64

Daniel, E. Randolph, 3, 38(fn.), 88(fn.)
Death of Olivi, 5, 72–73
Divine Essence, 50–52, 75–79, 91
Dominican order, 7, 8, 9, 14, 88–89
Doucet, Victorin, 36–37, 78(fn.)
Douie, Decima, 3, 90(fn.)
Droco, 41
Durandus of St. Porciano, 9, 46, 49

Education of Olivi, 5–6, 31–32
Ehrle, Franz, 31, 37–38, 40, 70, 90
Eternity of the world, 28–29
Eucharist, 56–61
Exiit qui seminat, 7, 11, 14, 24, 66, 69–71, 82–84, 87
Exivi de paradiso, 79, 81
Exultantes in domino, 66

Fidei catholicae fundamento, 79–80
Flood, David, 3, 17(fn.), 91
Florence, 9, 36, 67–68
Francis of Assisi, 6, 10, 12, 19–23, 30–35, 40, 70–71, 76, 84–88, 91

George of Adria, 89–90
Gerald Odonis, 89
Gerard of Borgo San Donino, 10, 20, 86
Gerard of Prato, 41
Giles of Bensa (Baysi), 41
Gloriosam ecclesiam, 81
Grace, 46–50, 75, 77, 79, 91
Gratien de Paris, 37–38
Gregory IX, 66
Gregory X, 7

Henry of Ghent, 60
Heynck, Valens, 6, 11(fn.), 47(fn.), 49(fn.)
Heysse, Albanus, 5(fn.), 67(fn.), 73
History, periodization of, 17–18, 20–24, 30–35, 64, 83–85, 88, 91
Holy spirit, age of, 18–24, 33–35, 83–84, 86, 88
Hugh of Digne, 7, 10, 62

Immaculate conception, 35–36
Innocent III, 46–47, 50–52, 77, 79
Islam, 21–23, 28, 30, 34, 43, 48, 84, 89

Jansen, Bernard, 53
Jarraux, Louis, 36
Jerome, Saint, 18, 62
Jerome of Ascoli, 6–7, 35–37, 46–47
Jerome of Catalonia, 74

Joachim of Fiore, 9–10, 17, 19, 24, 35, 50–52, 73
John XXII, 65, 81–83, 86–89, 91–92
John of Beaune, 82
John Duns Scotus, 50, 60, 61
John of Florence, 89
John of Murrovalle, 41, 67, 69, 72, 74–75
John of Parma, 7, 10, 66
John Pecham, 8, 14, 62, 77
John of Wales, 41
Judaism, 18, 21–23, 34, 39, 84, 89
Justification, 48

Koch, Joseph, 37–42, 82(fn.), 87

Lambert, Malcolm, 6(fn.), 7, 40(fn.), 74(fn.), 81, 87(fn.)
Leo, Brother, 20, 70
Letter of the Seven Seals, 41–45, 47, 50–55, 61–62, 65–66, 77
Letter to Conrad of Offida, 69–72
Letter to R., 32, 37–41, 44, 46–47, 49, 52, 54, 61, 66, 76
Letter to the sons of Charles II, 32, 72
Lewis the Bavarian, 83, 87, 89
Lewis, Warren, 3, 72(fn.)
Luther, Martin, 73
Lyons, Council of, 7

Manselli, Raoul, 17, 18(fn.), 19, 31, 34, 72(fn.), 74(fn.), 81
Marriage, 36–37, 44–46, 75, 77, 81, 91
Marseilles, 76, 82–83, 85
Martin IV, 7, 11, 67, 73
Matthew of Aquasparta, 67
Matthew of Bouzigues, 76
Michael of Cesena, 81, 83, 88
Michael the Monk, 81–83
Milan, Chapter of, 66–67
Missions, 22–23, 34, 39, 68, 84
Money, 14, 65–66, 70–72, 87
Montpellier, 6, 36, 67–69, 78

Narbonne, 5–6, 8, 15, 72–75, 81, 85–86
Nicholas III, 7, 15, 24, 62, 66, 76, 77, 83, 87
Nicholas IV, 36, 68–69. See also Jerome of Ascoli
Nicholas of Prato, 83, 85
Nicolas Eymeric, 36
Nimes, 44
Nuntius, 66

Oliger, Livarius, 70
Ordinem vestrum, 66
Origen, 18, 30–31

Papacy, 21–24, 64, 69–75, 78, 82–89
Paris, 5–6, 8–9, 20–21, 25, 28, 32–33, 37–39, 41–42, 51, 67–69, 73, 75, 78, 90
Perugia, Chapter of, 82
Peter of Corbaro, 89
Peter Lombard, 6, 46–47, 50–52, 77
Peter of Palude, 46
Petrus de Trabibus, 68
Philosophy, Olivi's attitude toward, 25–35, 43
Pistoia, 9
Plato, 27, 31
Poverty and evangelical perfection, 11–12

Poverty controversy, before Olivi, 6–7, 18, 20–21, 33; during Olivi's lifetime, 6–7, 14–17, 20–24, 31, 38–40, 61–72; after Olivi's death, 74, 83, 87–92
Predestination, 86–87
Predicaments, 52–61, 91
Procurators, 65–66, 70–71, 90
Prous Boneta, 88

Quantity, 54–61, 79
Quanto studiosus, 66
Quia nonnunquam, 82
Quo elongati, 66, 70–71
Quorumdam exigit, 81

Rainerius of Vercelli, 88, 90
Raymond of Fronsac, 38–40, 67–69, 75–77, 79–80
Raymond of Gaufredi, 37, 67–69, 72
Richard of Mediavilla, 41, 54, 61, 67
Robert Kilwardby, 8–9
Roger Bacon, 8–9
Rome, 11, 22–23, 89
Rotulus of 1283, 41–44, 50, 55, 61–62, 65

Saint Thadeus, monastery of, 88
Salimbene, 10
Sancta Romana, 81
Schneider, Theodor, 53–54
Siger of Brabant, 8, 53
Simon of Lens, 41
Sixtus IV, 90
Smalley, Beryl, 3
Soul as form of the body, 52–54, 75, 77–80, 91
Spiritual Franciscans, 6–7, 36, 67–72, 74–83, 87–90
Stadter, Ernst, 93
Steenberghen, Fernand van, 8
Stephen Tempier, 8, 57
Strassburg, 9, 39, 40–41
Study, role of, 25, 31–35

Tauris, 88–89

Teaching career of Olivi, 6, 11, 31–32, 35–44, 67–68
Thomas Aquinas, 8–9, 14, 28–30, 50, 53–54, 57–60, 88
Tierney, Brian, 23–24, 72
Time and aeviternity, 29–30
Tocco, Felice, 67

Ubertino of Casale, 40, 67–69, 72–80, 82, 85
Ubertus Guidi, 9
Usus pauper, 14–17, 20, 32, 38–40, 61–65, 67–70, 75, 77–79, 91–92

Vienne, Council of, 50, 54, 68–69, 75–80, 86, 91
Vow of poverty, 12, 15–16, 61–65, 75, 77, 79

William de Mare, 9, 16
William of Ockham, 50, 83
William Saurati, 89–90
Wound in Christ's side, 75–80, 91

MEMOIRS
OF THE
AMERICAN PHILOSOPHICAL SOCIETY

The Life of Arthur Young, 1741–1820. JOHN G. GAZLEY.
Vol. 97. xviii, 727 pp., 23 figs., 1973. $10.00.

Medical Men at the Siege of Boston, April, 1775–April, 1776: Problems of the Massachusetts and Continental Armies. PHILIP CASH.
Vol. 98. xiv, 185 pp., 11 figs., 1973. Paper. $3.00.

Crucial American Elections. ARTHUR S. LINK et al.
Vol. 99. x, 77 pp., 1973. $3.00.

John Beckley: Zealous Partisan in a Nation Divided. EDMUND BERKELEY and DOROTHY SMITH BERKELEY.
Vol. 100. xvi, 312 pp., 6 figs., 1973. $6.00.

Peter Tudebode: Historia de Hierosolymitano Itinere. JOHN HUGH HILL and LAURITA L. HILL.
Vol. 101. xii, 137 pp., 2 maps, 1974. $5.00.

Benjamin Franklin's Philadelphia Printing: A Descriptive Bibliography. C. WILLIAM MILLER.
Vol. 102. xc, 583 pp., illus., 1974. $40.00.

The Anschluss Movement in Austria and Germany, 1918–1919, and the Paris Peace Conference. ALFRED D. LOW.
Vol. 103. xiv, 495 pp., 4 figs., 4 maps, 1974. Paper. $8.00.

Studies in Pre-Vesalian Anatomy: Biography, Translations, Documents. L. R. LIND.
Vol. 104. xiv, 344 pp., 54 figs., 1975. $18.00.

A Kind of Power: The Shakespeare–Dickens Analogy. ALFRED B. HARBAGE. Jayne Lectures for 1974.
Vol. 105. x, 78 pp., 1975. $4.00.

A Venetian Family and Its Fortune, 1500–1900: The Donà and the Conservation of Their Wealth. JAMES C. DAVIS.
Vol. 106. xvi, 189 pp., 18 figs., 1975. $6.50.

Academica: Plato, Philip of Opus, and the Pseudo-Platonic Epinomis. LEONARDO TARÁN.
Vol. 107. viii, 417 pp., 1975. $20.00.

The Roman Catholic Church and the Creation of the Modern Irish State, 1878–1886. EMMET LARKIN.
Vol. 108. xiv, 412 pp., 2 figs., 1 map, 1975. Paper. $7.50.

Science and the Ante-Bellum American College. STANLEY M. GURALNICK.
Vol. 109. xlv, 227 pp., 1975. Paper. $5.00.

Hilary Abner Herbert: A Southerner Returns to the Union. HUGH B. HAMMETT.
Vol. 110. xvi, 264 pp., 20 figs., 1976. Paper. $5.00.

Census of the Exact Sciences in Sanskrit. Series A, Volume 3. DAVID PINGREE.
Vol. 111. vi, 208 pp., 1976. Paper. $15.00.

Cyriacus of Ancona's Journeys in the Propontis and the Northern Aegean, 1444–1445. EDWARD W. BODNAR, S.J., and CHARLES MITCHELL.
Vol. 112. viii, 90 pp., 24 figs., 1976. Paper. $6.00.

TRANSACTIONS
OF THE
AMERICAN PHILOSOPHICAL SOCIETY

Mappae Clavicula: A Little Key to the World of Medieval Techniques. CYRIL STANLEY SMITH and JOHN G. HAWTHORNE.
Vol. 64, pt. 4, 128 pp., 1 fig. (color), 40 pls., 1974. $7.00.

Benjamin Rush: Philosopher of the Revolution. DONALD J. D'ELIA.
Vol. 64, pt. 5, 113 pp., 1974. $5.00.

Ritual Structure and Language Structure of the Todas. MURRAY B. EMENEAU.
Vol. 64, pt. 6, 103 pp., 1974. $6.00.

Gears from the Greeks: The Antikythera Mechanism—A Calendar Computer from ca. 80 B.C. DEREK DE SOLLA PRICE.
Vol. 64, pt. 7, 70 pp., 45 figs., 1974. $5.00.

The Imperial Library in Southern Sung China, 1127–1279: A Study of the Organization and Operation of the Scholarly Agencies of the Central Government. JOHN H. WINKELMAN.
Vol. 64, pt. 8, 61 pp., 8 figs., 1974. $5.00.

The Czechoslovak Heresy and Schism: The Emergence of a National Czechoslovak Church. LUDVIK NEMEC.
Vol. 65, pt. 1, 78 pp., 1975. $6.00.

Distractions of Peace During War: The Lloyd George Government's Reactions to Woodrow Wilson, December, 1916–November, 1918. STERLING J. KERNEK.
Vol. 65, pt. 2, 117 pp., 1975. $6.00.

Classification and Development of North American Indian Cultures: A Statistical Analysis of the Driver-Massey Sample. HAROLD E. DRIVER and JAMES L. COFFIN.
Vol. 65, pt. 3, 120 pp., 12 figs., 5 maps, 1975. $7.00.

The Flight of Birds. CRAWFORD H. GREENEWALT.
Vol. 65, pt. 4, 67 pp., 41 figs., 1 pl., 1975. $7.00.

A Guide to Francis Galton's English Men of Science. VICTOR L. HILTS.
Vol. 65, pt. 5, 85 pp., 6 figs., 1975. $5.00.

Justice in Medieval Russia: Muscovite Judgment Charters (Pravye Gramoty) of the Fifteenth and Sixteenth Centuries. ANN M. KLEIMOLA.
Vol. 65, pt. 6, 93 pp., 1975. $5.00.

The Sculpture of Taras. JOSEPH COLEMAN CARTER.
Vol. 65, pt. 7, 196 pp., 72 pls., 2 maps, 1975. $18.00.

The Franciscans in South Germany, 1400–1530: Reform and Revolution. PAUL L. NYHUS.
Vol. 65, pt. 8, 47 pp., 1975. $3.00.

The German Center Party, 1890–1906. JOHN K. ZEENDER.
Vol. 66, pt. 1, 125 pp., 2 figs., 1976. $7.50.

Perugia, 1260–1340: Conflict and Change in a Medieval Italian Urban Society. SARAH RUBIN BLANSHEI.
Vol. 66, pt. 2, 128 pp., 2 maps, 1976. $8.50.

Crystals and Compounds: Molecular Structure and Composition in Nineteenth-century French Science. SEYMOUR H. MAUSKOPF.
Vol. 66, pt. 3, 82 pp., 4 figs., 1976. $4.50.

The Bourgeois Democrats of Weimar Germany. ROBERT A. POIS.
Vol. 66, pt. 4, 117 pp., 1976. $6.00.